Inclusion and Exclusion Through Youth Sport
Edited by Symeon Dagkas and Kathleen Armour

Sport Education
International perspectives
Edited by Peter Hastie

Cooperative Learning in Physical Education
An international perspective
Edited by Ben Dyson and Ashley Casey

Equity and Difference in Physical Education, Youth Sport and Health
A narrative approach
Edited by Fiona Dowling, Hayley Fitzgerald and Anne Flintoff

Game Sense
Pedagogy for performance, participation and enjoyment
Richard Light

Ethics in Youth Sport
Policy and pedagogical applications
Stephen Harvey and Richard Light

Assessment in Physical Education
A sociocultural perspective
Peter Hay and Dawn Penney

Complexity Thinking in Physical Education
Reframing curriculum, pedagogy and research
Edited by Alan Ovens, Tim Hopper and Joy Butler

Pedagogies, Physical Culture, and Visual Methods
Edited by Laura Azzarito and David Kirk

Contemporary Developments in Games Teaching
Edited by Richard Light, John Quay, Stephen Harvey and Amanda Mooney

Sport, Fun and Enjoyment
An embodied approach
Ian Wellard

The Philosophy of Physical Education
A new perspective
Steven A. Stolz

The Philosophy of Physical Education

The discipline area of physical education has historically struggled for legitimacy, sometimes being seen as a non-serious pursuit in educational terms compared to other subjects within the school curriculum. This book represents the first attempt in nearly thirty years to offer a coherent philosophical defence and conceptualisation of physical education and sport as subjects of educational value, and to provide a philosophically sound justification for their inclusion in the curriculum.

The book argues that rather than relegating the body to "un-thinking" learning, a person's essential being is not confined to their rationality but involves an embodied dimension. It traces the changing conceptions of the body, in philosophy and theology, that have influenced our understanding of physical education and sport, and investigates the important role that embodiment and movement play in learning about, through and in physical education. Physical education is defended as a vital and necessary part of education because the whole person goes to school, not just the mind, but the thinking, feeling and acting facets of a person. It is argued that physical education has the potential to provide a multitude of experiences and opportunities for students to become aware of their embodiment, explore alternative modes of awareness and to develop insights into and new modes of being not available elsewhere in the curriculum, and to influence moral character through the support of a moral community that is committed to that practice.

Representing a sophisticated and spirited defence of the educational significance and philosophical value of physical education and sport, this book will be fascinating reading for any advanced student or researcher with an interest in physical education, the philosophy of sport or the philosophy of education.

Steven A. Stolz, PhD is a lecturer in education at La Trobe University, Australia.

Routledge Studies in Physical Education and Youth Sport
Series Editor: David Kirk
University of Bedfordshire, UK

The *Routledge Studies in Physical Education and Youth Sport* series is a forum for the discussion of the latest and most important ideas and issues in physical education, sport and active leisure for young people across school, club and recreational settings. The series presents the work of the best well-established and emerging scholars from around the world, offering a truly international perspective on policy and practice. It aims to enhance our understanding of key challenges, to inform academic debate, and to have a high impact on both policy and practice, and is thus an essential resource for all serious students of physical education and youth sport.

Also available in this series

Children, Obesity and Exercise
A practical approach to prevention, treatment and management of childhood and adolescent obesity
Edited by Andrew P. Hills, Neil A. King and Nuala M. Byrne

Disability and Youth Sport
Edited by Hayley Fitzgerald

Rethinking Gender and Youth Sport
Edited by Ian Wellard

Pedagogy and Human Movement
Richard Tinning

Positive Youth Development Through Sport
Edited by Nicholas Holt

Young People's Voices in PE and Youth Sport
Edited by Mary O'Sullivan and Ann Macphail

Physical Literacy
Throughout the lifecourse
Edited by Margaret Whitehead

Physical Education Futures
David Kirk

Young People, Physical Activity and the Everyday
Living physical activity
Edited by Jan Wright and Doune Macdonald

Muslim Women and Sport
Edited by Tansin Benn, Gertrud Pfister and Haifaa Jawad

The Philosophy of Physical Education

A new perspective

Steven A. Stolz

Routledge
Taylor & Francis Group

LONDON AND NEW YORK

First published 2014
by Routledge
2 Park Square, Milton Park, Abingdon, Oxon OX14 4RN

and by Routledge
711 Third Avenue, New York, NY 10017

Routledge is an imprint of the Taylor & Francis Group, an informa business

British Library Cataloguing-in-Publication Data
A catalogue record for this book is available from the British Library

Library of Congress Cataloging-in-Publication Data
Stolz, Steven A.
The philosophy of physical education : a new perspective / Steven A. Stolz.
    pages cm – (Routledge studies in physical education and youth sport)
    Includes bibliographical references and index.
    1. Physical education and training–Philosophy. I. Title.
    GV342.S73 2014
    613.7–dc23   2014004463

ISBN: 978-1-138-79228-9 (hbk)
ISBN: 978-1-315-76225-8 (ebk)

Typeset in Times New Roman
by Wearset Ltd, Boldon, Tyne and Wear

To Samantha, Rebecca, Jessica and Amy.

Without your patience, care, encouragement and love none of this would be possible.

The theory of the body schema is, implicitly, a theory of perception. We have relearned to feel our body; we have found underneath the objective and detached knowledge of the body that other knowledge which we have of it in virtue of its always being with us and of the fact that we are our body. In the same way we shall need to reawaken our experience of the world as it appears to us in so far as we are in the world through our body, and in so far as we perceive the world with our body. But by thus remaking contact with the body and with the world, we shall also rediscover ourself, since, perceiving as we do with our body, the body is a natural self and, as it were, the subject of perception.

(Merleau-Ponty, 1945/1962, p. 239)

Contents

Figures

Foreword

Jānis (John) T. Ozoliņš

Physical education and sport have not enjoyed a place of esteem within the curriculum in recent times, especially when compared to more cerebral pursuits such as science, mathematics and literature. They have been an afterthought, a diversion from the serious business of intellectual development. Grudgingly, school systems have admitted that there is something to be said for having a sound mind in a sound body, but only because a mind needs to be clear and sharp. Intellectual labours will lack acuity if the body is ill or is tired and stressed and so the benefits of physical education and sport are extolled not for their own sakes, but for the development of the mind. Though Aristotle himself was no dualist and did not hold that the body was unimportant, at the top of his hierarchy of being we find those creatures (human beings) who have a rational nature. Indeed, human beings are identified by Boethius as being "substances with a rational nature". What this suggests is that what is essential about human beings is their rationality and this is exercised by their minds. Corporeality is not unique to us, whereas the rational mind, capable of reflecting on and constructing theories from the sense perceptions it receives, is our crowning glory, distinguishing us from lesser creatures. In Western philosophy, influenced by Descartes, the body largely disappears from view as a proper subject of attention of intellectual thought.

It is not surprising, then, that education, which is directed towards the growth of human beings in the acquisition of skills and capacities, has concentrated on the development of the intellectual and cognitive side of human beings. Sports, moreover, often thought interchangeable with physical education, are games and these are leisure activities, far removed from the serious business of education. Physical education and sport have at best an ambiguous place in the curriculum. This book argues powerfully against two things, first, the view that physical education and sport have only a marginal and contested place in the curriculum and, second, against a dualist conception of human beings which splits their mental side from their physical side. It draws on Merleau-Ponty, arguing against a separation of mind and body and proposing that intellectual activity can only occur because human beings are embodied.

This is an important book because it contains an almost encyclopaedic coverage of the various conceptions of physical education, sport and games that abound in the literature, as well as forensic attention to the justificatory arguments that have been offered for the inclusion of physical education and sports in the curriculum. It does not deny that there is merit in some of these justificatory arguments, but does not gloss over their weaknesses. It shows a command of the key debates about the place of physical education and forges its own justification for physical education and sport in the curriculum, basing it on a holistic conception of human beings as being body *and* mind. Simply put, to be a human being is to be bodily and to be in the world is to be corporeally in it. This is not to reduce the mind to the body, since neither is it true that human beings are bodies only. This is clearly argued, for example, in the discussion of Ryle's account of knowing how and knowing that, since there is a sense in which the body knows and so can be educated.

There is much in this book that will repay a careful reading. It traces the historically shifting conceptions of physical education, its connections to sport and to the various justifications offered for its inclusion over time. It shows very sharply how in education the body has become estranged from the mind and argues vigorously and passionately for their re-unification. On this view, physical education and sport in the curriculum are not justified because they lead to health or because they instil moral virtue or because they are useful divertissements, though it is not denied that they can do all these things. They are justified because education of the body is intimately connected with education of the mind and vice versa. It is time that physical education and sport were brought in from the cold and given an equal place alongside numeracy and literacy in the education of human beings. This book provides significant and plausible argument why we should do so.

Jānis (John) T. Ozoliņš FHERDSA, FPESA, MACE

Foreign Member, Latvian Academy of Sciences,

Professor of Philosophy, *Australian Catholic University*

Preface

> Consider, for example, the activities that we call "games". I mean board-games, card-games, ball-games, athletic games, and so on. What is common to them all? – Don't say: "They *must* have something in common, or they would not be called 'games'" – but *look and see* whether there is anything common to all. – For if you look at them, you won't see something that is common to *all*, but similarities, affinities, and a whole series of them at that. To repeat: don't think, but look! – Look, for example, at board-games, with their various affinities. Now pass to card-games; here you find many correspondences with the first group, but many common features drop out, and others appear. When we pass next to ball-games, much that is common is retained, but much is lost. – Are they all "*entertaining*"? Compare chess with noughts and crosses. Or is there always winning and losing, or competition between players? Think of patience. In ball-games, there is winning and losing; but when a child throws his ball at the wall and catches it again, this feature has disappeared. Look at the parts played by skill and luck, and at differences between skill in chess and skill in tennis. Think now of singing and dancing games; here we have the element of entertainment, but how many other characteristic features have disappeared! And we can go through the many, many other groups of games in the same way, can we see how similarities crop up and disappear.
>
> (Wittgenstein, 1953/2009, p. 36ᵉ; §66)

Consider the following thought experiment. If I was an "outsider" looking into everything about physical education for the first time: What would I see? As Wittgenstein would say, "...don't think, but look!" No doubt, I would see a diverse array of activities ranging from informal play to formal play which involve rules and skills that we normally call sport. I might see the teaching and learning of psychomotor skills so that students can play certain games and/or sports that are part of the curriculum. Likewise, I might see the teaching of clearly demarcated bodies of knowledge within the curriculum that have a clear scientific underpinning in order to fulfil distinctly educational purposes of certification. I might hear its practitioners talk about teaching "theoretical" and "practical" lessons depending on how and where this content was to be taught; for instance, inside or outside the normal classroom in places like gymnasiums, specifically demarcated fields or courts. Is there anything "common to all" these things I may see so I can provide an explanation or description to other "outsiders" and/or "insiders" about what physical education is? Maybe, I could argue that a fairly common feature of physical education is the place where it is traditionally practised, that being in educational institutions like primary and secondary schools. Likewise, another commonality in physical education is the use of games and sports as a medium to teach an array of alleged and aspirational educational aims ranging from the psychomotor, the socio-moral, the cognitive and the affective. But the problem is, as soon as I visit school X, and then school Y, certain "characteristic features" that may have had direct or indirect affinities surrounding physical education in school X have now "disappeared" in school Y, in part due to how physical education is practised within these educational institutions. Furthermore, I may have visited school X ten to twenty years prior to school Y, in which case, the differences between how physical education was practised in school X and school Y would have been quite noticeable. Conversely, maybe there are no noticeable differences between how physical education was practised in school X and school Y due to significant commonalities, such as the use of games and sports taught with an educational intent. Either way, this thought experiment raises a number of rather awkward philosophical questions, such as: What is physical education? Can there be an objective or universal essence of physical education? What does it mean to know what physical education is? What sort of activities should physical education promote? What is the educational purpose of physical education? Can physical education fulfil all (psychomotor, socio-moral, cognitive and affective) of these alleged educational aims? Are the practices of physical education any different today, say, from ten, twenty, thirty or more years ago? What sorts of knowledge should be promoted by schools and educational institutions? Is the pursuit of knowledge a suitable goal for schools and educational institutions?

Some years ago it occurred to me that definitions or explanations surrounding the nature of physical education could not account for the diverse array of practices found within educational institutions. Indeed, Wittgenstein (1953/2009, p. 25e; §46) makes it clear that whenever we engage in "language-games" it is not a question of an "either that it *is* or that it *is not*" because it is "impossible to give an explanatory account of any primary element". In one sense, the reason why engaging in "language-games" is a futile activity is in part due to the multifarious way we use language, and in another sense we are attempting to describe something that does not have a fixed meaning or is *a priori* knowable. Wittgenstein therefore insists that we should look for the meaning of concepts through their use, not by trying to define terms or concepts according to necessary and sufficient conditions which can be ascertained by what or how it describes.

In fact it seems *de rigueur* in the literature to argue that physical education is in crisis because there is no general consensus within the profession due to rival and competing traditions of physical education surrounding its nature and status within education, and consequently is in need of reform.[1] One of the driving influences and justifications of the "physical-education-in-crisis" discourse is based on the notion that due to the considerable disparity that exists between how physical education is practised within educational institutions has led to the perception of a field that is a house divided amongst itself due to competing and rival traditions *about* physical education. But conflict between, and within traditions is not a new phenomenon, because traditions experience from time to time what MacIntyre (1977, 1988, 1990, 2007) refers to as "epistemological crises", and when these become serious, and when devotees of these same traditions recognise a crisis, progress is possible through the construction of a new narrative. Furthermore, when traditions are in good working order, continuous conflict *about* its particular point and purpose is a normal part of what it means to be a tradition of practices. This is further reinforced by MacIntyre (2007, p. 222) who states:

> ...when an institution – a university, say, or a farm, or a hospital – is the bearer of a tradition of practice or practices, its common life will be partly, but in a centrally important way, constituted by a continuous argument as to what a university is and ought to be or what good farming is or what good medicine is. Traditions, when vital, embody continuities of conflict.

Here we can start to see that physical education is part of a historical tradition that is dynamic and forever evolving in its pursuit to understand what physical is and ought to be, or what good physical education is, leaves it open to contestability due to its incompleteness. However, it is important to emphasise that this is not a straightforward process because it requires the initiation of individuals into the practices of that tradition to constantly interpret and reinterpret what it means to become a practitioner in the tradition. Consequently, this book emerged from extended reflection on the inadequacies of my own first-hand experience and practice as a physical education practitioner, and from a growing dissatisfaction with the conceptions of physical education that exist in academic discourse.

What follows is what I see as a need in the contemporary literature for an updated work from a distinctly philosophical point of view that attempts to take account of recent developments in the field for the possible benefit of a professional or wider readership. In response to this goal, this book has three broad aims. First, I briefly revisit some of the philosophical arguments in the literature that argue against the inclusion of sport and physical education[2] within educational institutions as a means to contextualise my critical discussion, highlight the strengths and weaknesses of different influential traditions in physical education and, most importantly, provide what I see as new and alternative conceptions of sport and physical education that are cogent and defendable from an educational point of view. In fact, problems such as this one to a great extent are the *raison d'être* of educational philosophy and theory. Second, I have considered it important to critically engage in this work from a distinctly philosophical perspective under the influence of what is often referred to as educational philosophy and theory. Third, where possible I have furnished the reader with some understanding of the significant influence of past and present philosophers, such as Plato, Aristotle, Descartes, Aquinas, Wittgenstein,

Merleau-Ponty, Ryle, Peters, Hirst, Dearden, Arnold, Meier, Polanyi, Dreyfus, Carr, Winch, MacIntyre and Ozolins.

This book consists of six chapters. As far as possible each chapter develops and builds upon the arguments of the preceding chapters in what is meant to be a continuous narrative. It is important to note that this book is concerned with developing arguments towards what is ultimately to be generally coherent and cogent justifications of sport and physical education within educational institutions. If for some reason my arguments are deemed to be incoherent, then it goes without saying that the onus falls on the reader or critic to outline in detail why and in what respects this may be the case.

My intent in this book is to argue that sport and physical education plays a crucial role within the curriculum and hence needs to be a necessary part of educational institutions as much as any other subject area. If we are serious about an integrated view of the human person, then physical education is a necessary part of a well-balanced education. A central and reoccurring theme throughout my book is that we become aware of our embodiment through a family of physical activities in physical education that rebalances the disproportionate emphasis on the development of the mind and restores to education a balance that has been previously missing. Anyone disposed to regard the body lightly needs to recognise that the primacy of perception elucidates that the basis of our cognition is through bodily experience. This claim is a powerful one because it reasserts that human beings are not dualistic entities consisting of a mind and a body. More importantly, it emphasises how human beings actively interact with their environment to make sense of the world, not from some passive contemplative perspective outside the world, but through being a part of the world. Greater recognition, then, needs to be given to the role embodiment and corporeal movement plays in student learning, particularly since our engagement with the world is not just limited to the cognitive domain and a large part of our interest in the world is emotional, practical, aesthetic, imaginative, and so on. Consequently, I will argue that embodiment in education should be taken seriously because movement experiences in and through physical education can provide opportunities that are humanising and provide authentic opportunities to concretely reinforce the point that a person's essential being is more than just his or her rationality; he or she is a being-in-the-world.

As mentioned earlier, in order to provide a coherent apology[3] for sport and physical education I will critically discuss what I consider to be the main philosophical arguments contravening their alleged educational value or significance as a means to construct a cogent philosophical apology for sport and physical education. As I will argue throughout this book, and especially in Chapters 1 and 2, if sport and physical education are to be given a legitimate place within education it needs to challenge prejudicial attitudes toward the body first, before attempting to develop sophisticated philosophical justifications their inclusion within educational institutions. A natural starting point is R. S. Peters' (1966) earlier work on educational activities and their justification within the curriculum. He criticises physical activities as lacking a wide-ranging cognitive content because they are merely a matter of "knack". This account privileges intellectual activities as superior due to their cognitive content, whereas physical activities which are inherent features of physical education programmes are only part of the school curriculum because they serve purposes other than educational ones, such as maintaining students' health through fitness. Although this work was published some time ago, his views were consistent with those adopted by some policy makers or institutional leaders of such programmes, particularly in theory laden educational institutions where the academic mind reigns supreme and strives for promotion at the expense of other modes of inquiry. The effect of this has been to relegate the body to "unthinking" learning, not to mention failing to acknowledge that a person's essential being is not just confined to his or her rationality, but involves an embodied dimension. Certainly, this view by no means denies the importance of intellectual education but seeks to restore a balance in education that recognises the important role embodiment and corporeal movement plays in learning, in, by and through physical education.

Part of the reason why practical pursuits within the curriculum like sport and physical education are often undervalued is due to the concept of practical knowledge being misunderstood, plus a general unwillingness to count any non-theoretical knowing as important. This is understandable taking into consideration that the concept of practical knowledge or "knowing how" is located in an area of constant philosophical dispute of an epistemological kind. Compounding the issue further is the epistemological implication that the physical or "doing" is somehow set apart from cognitive development and is anti-intellectual. In Chapter 3, I argue that part of the reason why such assumptions continue to exist is the powerful influence of the "intellectualist legend" that permeates educational thinking. For instance, generally speaking, "knowing that" is commonly associated with intellectual operations and conceptions of cognition, whereas, to the layperson, "knowing how" is considered to be devoid of any cognition, and performance is just a matter of conditioning or habit. Such a view is problematic in the sense that intelligence as understood in "knowing that" is not equivalent to "knowing how". In order to challenge this dualistic conception of mind and body I draw on Polanyi's work on knowing by tacit inference to emphasise that coming to know cannot occur without an embodied existence. The claim Polanyi makes that all knowledge is grounded in tacit knowing is a powerful one, because it reasserts – as does the phenomenologist, Merleau-Ponty – that human beings come to know and understand through a process of internal integration that cannot be verbally articulated. I argue that we need to reconsider our understanding of human knowledge because we possess a practical knowledge of our bodies that is personally meaningful and can be cultivated in physical education over a period of time. Since physical education predominantly deals with practical knowledge, Ryle's conceptual account of intelligence concepts or epithets is particularly apt to accommodate descriptions and evaluations of performance which are applicable to practical pursuits within the curriculum. First, Ryle's account dispels the absurdity of the intellectualist doctrine that tries to treat actions or "know how" as the same as intellectual (cognitive) operations.

Second, when intelligence epithets are applied to someone we ascribe an ability to do something, not what they may know in terms of intellectual operations of cognition. The relevance for physical education is significant because we can judge the quality of single actions and skills and compare one person's skills with those of another, or evaluate whether the skills of a person have improved or worsened. Although Ryle does not specifically discuss how every action that requires "know how" can be evaluated, his views are consistent enough to gain a deeper appreciation of evaluative concepts that apply both to actions and "know how" that have serious implications for judging performance in physical education. Sorting out the conceptual confusion that surrounds our thinking about embodied understanding in its various ways of knowing in physical education represents only one part of my apologia. I argue, however, that in order to promote change in, by and through physical education we not only need to make students' personal experiences meaningful, but also educationally meaningful. To do this we need to locate the body as the focal point in the production of the lived experience, and also recognise the role corporeal movement and embodiment plays in learning, in, by and through physical education.

In Chapter 4, I outline how in physical education the conscious decision by the profession to promote and utilise play, games and sport as a mechanism for transmitting educational ends brought with it unforeseen problems. Although this brought about a kind of theoretical legitimacy for physical education that was greatly desired, it presented new problems, like the conceptual confusion surrounding the interrelationship of play, games and sport (the so-called "tricky triad") in physical education. In a way, this confusion has been the source of many problems in physical education because there has been a general tendency to view physical education as sport (or games), physical education as play or any other combination. I argue that it is a conceptual mistake to view each in isolation because it decontextualises the multifarious nature of movement activities found in physical education, but most importantly, it neglects to highlight the educative intent which neither play nor sport in isolation can provide. I argue that contemporary Western culture has failed to acknowledge an appropriate philosophical foundation for the phenomenon of play because we have misunderstood its nature and at the same time failed to recognise that each form of play in essence is a human activity which has transcendental possibilities derived from the experience of play that are not possible elsewhere. I argue that within the context of the hermeneutic–phenomenological framework physical education attempts to make the subjective and interpersonal process meaningful. This is why physical education should be treated as a necessary and vital part of education, because physical education activities offer opportunities to explore alternative modes of awareness and to develop insights into and new modes of being and possibilities perhaps not readily available elsewhere in the curriculum.

In Chapter 5, I revisit the claim that playing certain games and sports can provide opportunities to develop moral character and hence qualify for inclusion within the curriculum based on its moral education potential. Historically there has been strong educational support for the role of competitive games and sports in the physical education curriculum. Even though the games playing ethic that originated in the public schools of Britain in the nineteenth century was considered to be antiquated and in decline by the early twentieth century, its resilience as an educational ideology had not diminished, but had been recast as a new version of physical education. Part of the reason why this occurred was due to the profession being quick to capitalise on sports' universal popularity and the similarities competition has with some of the most basic themes of life, such as success and failure, good and bad behaviour and so on. But most importantly, during a time when physical education was attempting to align itself with broader educational aims it was easy to reconstruct a version of physical education that had been around almost a century by the mid-1950s. Understandably, when combined with the popularity of sport within Western culture and the symbolic value attached to it, it is not surprising that this became one of the central philosophical features of physical education from the mid-twentieth century onwards. Although in Chapter 5 I argue that the cultivation of character can be encouraged in physical education and provide an arena for practising moral behaviour that is supported by a moral community with a commitment to that practice, I caution that it is misleading to imply or expect the inculcation of certain qualities to directly accompany the practice of certain competitive games and sports in physical education. I emphasise that this possibility is not unique to sport and we should not overstate its role, but in saying this, games and sport in physical education provide opportunities for practising habitual modes of conduct. Since school communities are moral habitats in which young people spend considerable time it seems reasonable to argue that sport and physical education are also moral habitats to which young people belong and can also influence moral character.

In the final Chapter 6, I discuss how physical education is located within a historical tradition that is dynamic and constantly changing due to ongoing and continuous debates surrounding its particular point and purpose. Indeed, I argue that the rhetoric within the physical education literature has contributed somewhat to the view that the various traditions of physical education are in continual conflict with each other because of the logical incompatibility of some traditions; this incompatibility also invokes concerns of incommensurability. Understandably, this has led to the situation where incommensurable traditions of physical education experience their own internal conflicts and tensions to the point where they are either destroyed, divide into two or more warring traditions, become extinct or emerge in response to circumstances and progress the tradition. The dilemma is that when two or more rival and apparently incommensurable traditions confront each other two central problems emerge: (1) How do we decide between rival or competing accounts when there is no neutral standpoint? and (2) By what standards are these rival or competing accounts to be evaluated? In order to make sense of the rival and competing traditions found within physical education I use MacIntyre's seminal work to understand why and how these conflicts can be rationally resolved in some cases by arguing for a new tradition of physical education which I refer to as embodied learning.

In conclusion, I think Jesse Williams (1951) was right when he pointed out that physical experience in its broadest expression is one way of reconnecting individuals with the senses and restores a balance in education that has been previously missing. Indeed, we should not lose sight of the important role embodiment and corporeal movement play in student learning. This is why physical education should be a necessary part of the curriculum because the whole person goes to school, not just the mind, but the thinking, feeling and acting facets of a person. Furthermore, what I find particularly attractive about physical education is its potential to provide a multitude of experiences in different environments that can open up new opportunities for students to explore alternative modes of awareness and to develop insights into and new modes of being and possibilities perhaps not readily available elsewhere in the curriculum. In essence this is the advantage physical education has over other curriculum subjects. Consequently, my hope is that this book will make a highly original contribution to knowledge in the fields of the philosophy of sport and physical education, and will be a crucial text for physical educators, academics, policy makers and anyone interested in justifying sport and physical education within the curriculum or their activity from a philosophical point of view – not to mention contribute to bringing it out of the shadows, and into, if not pride of place in the curriculum, at least a respected one.

Steven A. Stolz
Faculty of Education
La Trobe University
February 2014

Notes

1 Some scholars have argued that the "physical-education-in-crisis" discourse has been counterproductive to changing the practices of physical education because it has led to an intensification of intellectually grounded knowledge *about* physical education. This in turn has legitimised those seeking reform as experts with authority *about* physical education. See for example Thorpe's (2003) article in *Sport, Education and Society*.
2 My use of the term "sport and physical education" is deliberate. See Chapter 1, section 2 and Chapter 1, endnote 14 for more detail surrounding why I have done this.
3 See Chapter 1, endnote 2 for an explanation of why I intentionally use the term "apology".

Acknowledgements

It is sometimes hard to know quite where to begin when acknowledging those who have assisted me in bringing this book to publication. In saying this, it would be remiss of me not to mention the following people (in no particular order of priority): first, my parents, Frederick and Lois who instilled in me a sense of hard work and perseverance as an important attribute for achieving anything in life; second, both my wife, Samantha, and children, Rebecca, Jessica and Amy, who have had to endure many inconveniences over the years because of my single-mindedness to work on this project; third, Jānis (John) T. Ozoliņš for his unwavering belief in me and this project – you have personified what it is to be a mentor, colleague and friend – and fourth, my former and current colleagues and students. Over the years I have benefited greatly as a result of first-hand experience, observation from on-site school visits, discussions with teachers from a diverse array of curriculum backgrounds, a general comment unknowingly stimulating interest that has led me to explore conceptual possibilities, unnoticed alternatives, test assumptions, and so on. Lastly, I would like to record my thanks to both David Kirk as the editor of this series and to John Quay with whom I share a similar passion for educational philosophy and theory that has resulted in many intellectually stimulating conversations. In a sense, you have all contributed in some way to this book, either directly or indirectly on many different levels.

I would like to thank the editors of *Educational Philosophy and Theory* (Michael Peters) and *European Physical Education Review* (Ken Green) for permission to reuse material published in their journals. Some of this material appears in Chapters 3 and Chapter 6. Likewise, I would also like to the thank the *Journal of the Philosophy of Sport* for giving me permission to reproduce Figure 4.1 as it appears in this book, which originated in K. V. Meier's 1988 article, "Triad trickery: Playing with sport and games".

A similar expression of general, but profound gratefulness is also due to Routledge and for all those involved in the publication process, such as professional editor Steve Turrington for his copyediting services and to the anonymous reviewers who have provided feedback to improve this book.

Of course, I am obliged to say at this juncture, as all authors are, that I am fully responsible for the ideas that appear within the book and, consequently, for any errors and infelicities in the text.

1   On justifications of sport and physical education

Are there good reasons for the inclusion of sport and physical education within educational institutions?

In this chapter, I aim to briefly revisit and explore some of the philosophical arguments that persistently beset that group of educational activities that we generally associate with the conceptual term "physical education".[1] I begin by identifying and critically discussing what I consider to be serious and convincing arguments against the inclusion of sport and physical education within educational institutions as a means to construct an apology[2] and a coherent conceptualisation of sport and physical education. Therefore, my task at hand requires a philosophical justification to the perennial question: Are there any good reasons for the inclusion of sport and physical education in educational institutions? The conclusion, towards which I argue, is that the reasons why these arguments are so prominent and pervasive is the product of, first, misleading philosophical–educational views that are ambivalent towards play, traditional justifications that are flawed, and educational discourses that encourage and favour theory over practice, mental skills over physical skills, extrinsic over intrinsic values, and high culture over low culture as a result of dualism's elevation of the mind over the body; and, second, a failure in part by philosophers of education and physical educationalists to elucidate rational educational justifications and conceptions of sport and physical education that are cogent and defendable.

There are legitimate reasons why the physical education profession,[3] its practitioners and academics ought to be concerned with, and strive for a more secure professional status. Historically, the discipline area has struggled for legitimacy at most, if not all, educational levels due to the damaging claims made by critics who argue that physical education is a trivial pursuit and thereby non-serious compared to other forms of knowledge and understandings that are considered to be educationally worthwhile. It is clear to me that there appears to be a general consensus within the relevant literature that physical education is suffering from a crisis of legitimisation within education, particularly in relation to its nature and status.[4] The reasons why this has occurred are multifaceted and complex, however, the physical education profession and its practitioners have to accept most if not all of the blame for not counteracting such serious claims with coherent reasons. Consequently, a lack of credible promotion has severely impeded the discussion of the educational aims, ideas, values and so on that sport and physical education contributes, to the point where its mere survival within the curriculum is at stake. Kretchmar (1990, p. 97) reinforces this viewpoint further by arguing that physical educationalists lack sufficient passion for their profession, because:

> ... we do not care enough. When we do care it is not with a deeply rooted, reasoned, consistent, durable, reliable passion.... In the absence of deep commitments, I sense that there is a real cause for worry about the expected lifespan of the profession.

Meakin (1983) – writing from a period when physical education scholars were beginning to develop sophisticated justifications for the inclusion of physical education as a school subject within the curriculum – quite rightly raises an interesting point that if a subject's inclusion cannot be justified, it implies one of three things: (1) the subject is harmful to either students or society; (2) even if it does neither students nor society any harm, it does them no good; or (3) even if it does students or society good, it does so to a less significant extent than other curriculum areas (pp. 10–19). Therefore, the question of whether physical education can be justified as part of the curriculum is essentially a moral issue, particularly if the continuation of the subject is perceived to have no educational value or worth. As I see it, part of the problem why the physical education profession has lacked credibility and legitimacy within most educational institutions is in part due to an inability to produce a reasoned account of its practices. Indeed, this will involve a critical review of its practices, which to some in the profession may be quite confrontational, but if those in the profession are serious they need to be able to critically review the premises in which their practices are based. These may be concealed, but unless these premises are revealed and identified there is the risk that they may continue to control and influence physical education practice without their reasoned consent. My point here is that most practical applications will be made from a philosophical position. Whether this can be expressed clearly will not be made clear to the apologist or even to the most ardent critic unless its philosophical justifications are articulated in such a way that they are coherent and accessible to all. Therefore, the reasons why we need justifications for sport and physical education are threefold: first, because it is a simple matter of necessity at the moment; second, those within the profession need to be able to offer cogent justifications as to why sport and physical education should be included within educational institutions; and, third, to identify what the profession is (or ought to be) so those within the profession can defend and further themselves unashamedly.

If those in the profession are serious, they cannot escape the task at hand, which is of an unavoidably philosophical nature. Consequently, I intend to offer an apology for sport and physical education by outlining philosophical justifications for the vexed problem of its educational value or significance. Some supportive philosophical positions are as follows: the importance of play in assisting deep learning; subjective (extrinsic and intrinsic) value; reconceptualising knowledge, reason and education; and integration of the whole body, borrowing heavily from the classical Greek ideals of balance and harmony as a means to avoid the tendency of contemporary education to view agents as dualistic entities (mind and body) and bring into focus the sometimes ignored and forgotten dimension of our corporeal embodiment in education. Furthermore, I intend to illuminate how the experience of movement gives meaning to our existence and constitutes what it means to be a human being. However, before I go on to outline the traditional justifications of physical education some work needs to be done to provide an account of the preliminary philosophical considerations in order to contextualise what follows.

Preliminary philosophical considerations: ambivalence towards play, antiphysicalism, the problem of pleasurable activities and transcendental indifference

The educational value of play has a long history in Western education. Plato (2007, pp. 269–270; 536e–537a) in the *Republic* in his discussion of the education of the philosopher makes the point that anything learnt under duress and without freedom is pointless as it "never sticks", but if the lesson takes the form of play, the learner will learn more. Ideas about play in education have been extensively influenced by psychology, sociology, philosophy and education. Since play was considered to be a naturally instinctive process and engaged in by young people, the desire to connect with this experience and the natural capacities of the learner led to the introduction of play as an educational process. As a result, the acceptance of play, games and sport[5] as a pedagogical method of achieving educational goals significantly transformed physical education, particularly in the twentieth century. According to Mechikoff (2010), the development, acceptance and promotion of play, games and sport as methods for imparting educational ideas is important as it reflected a profound change in philosophical focus due to the growing interest in the phenomenon of play as an educational mechanism of value (see his Chapter 10).

The philosophical position of the body relative to epistemological considerations and the nature of human existence becomes an important issue.[6] This type of discussion might seem irrelevant to an understanding of play theory in physical education; however, our concept of human nature will have a direct bearing on how we think human beings should behave and be educated and, more specifically in this case, how we think someone should be educated physically. According to Fairs (1968), the intellectual orientation of Western thought regarding physical education and the body emerges from two opposing views about physical education that have been significantly influenced by classical Greek culture. Each view of physical education is the end product of a specific sociocultural perspective and its dominant philosophical and anthropological theory of humankind. The first view of physical education is based on the concept of a harmonised and integrated balance of mind and body as the only pathway to the development of all a person's faculties and potentialities. Fairs (1968) goes on to add that this "naturalistic" viewpoint is commonly attributed to the Periclean Greeks because they epitomised and exemplified the practical expression of this ideal. For instance, Plato (2007) makes it clear in the *Republic* that physical education is a balanced concept taking two forms – physical and intellectual (gymnastics for the body and music for the soul) – that evolved from the application of the "whole man" philosophy of education (pp. 101–110; 403d–412a).[7] In pursuit of this ideal, humankind had to resist the temptation to develop any particular part of the body at the expense of the whole, as this would distort both balance and harmony. In the second concept of physical education, we start to see a diametrically opposed position of the "whole man" idea because the focus shifts to a distinctly one-sided viewpoint in which a person's physical nature is denied and the world of sense is rejected in favour of the self-created world of pure reason. As a result the body is relegated to a low status and the mind elevated to a high status. Fairs (1968) comments that this "antinaturalistic" (or "antiphysicalism") one-sided concept of humankind found its expression in Platonic anthropology and its fundamental doctrine that the body was a source of evil and corruption which keeps us from wisdom and acquiring knowledge. Due to Plato's ambivalence towards the body and the paradoxical way in which he would sponsor two distinctly different philosophical concepts of the body: one being idealism, which emphasises an ascetic and strict puritanical view of the body (see Plato, 1961a, *Phaedo*, pp. 47–50; 66a–67e), while the other, realism, promoted humankind's physical nature and approved the expression of one's natural instincts through the guidance of reason (see Plato, 1961b, *Republic*, pp. 672–687; 431a–444e). Unfortunately, it would appear that in order to improve the intellectual and academic standing of physical education within the curriculum, physical educationalists have been selective in choosing whatever suited them, particularly in relation to Plato's realist position of the body; consequently, it would appear that idealism has come to be associated with the Platonic tradition and its noticeable influence on Western culture, especially in education. The history of education is characterised by a range of culturally dominant positions on reality and conceptions of human nature that have arisen to a position of dominance before being dissolved and replaced by another. In a sense, physical education would appear to be in a constant state of flux due to the dominant fluctuating cultural mentality that exists at any given period of time, to the point where the history of physical education is a representation of Western culture's understanding and interpretation of the dominant position surrounding the body. Fairs (1968, pp. 18–19) confirms the foregoing conclusion when he writes:

> … during the past three thousand years only three centuries have been characterised by a cultural mentality which charged education with the responsibility of the harmonious development of the mind and body, whereas for twenty-seven centuries education has served the needs of *homo asceticus* and his degradation of the body or *homo sensualis* and his idolatry of the body.

According to Reid (1996b), the central Platonic–Cartesian tradition of Western philosophy draws a sharp distinction between the mind (or intellect) and body, which has been historically problematic for physical education. For instance, from a Cartesian perspective, knowledge and understanding stem from the operation of pure reason as intellectual states or activities, and when combined with Platonic idealism the goal of education necessitates the subordination of the physical appetites of the body due to the view that it not only keeps us from wisdom and acquiring knowledge, but is a source of all evil and corruption. Such a view is essentially rational because it places enormous emphasis upon propositional forms of knowledge at the expense of other forms of knowledge. Consequently, given such assumptions, the very nature and meaning of physical education seems problematic because the term "physical" seems to indirectly refer to the body, its nature and functioning, whereas the term "education" typically implies the mind and its development (Reid, 1996b). This influence is significant for physical education because it would appear to be based on dubious philosophical foundations and also the inability to reconcile the dualism of the mind and body that underlies Western culture and its philosophies of education. Reid (1996b) argues that this problem has understandably become a preoccupation for physical educationalists due to the paradoxical nature it seemingly rests upon. This is further compounded by the subject's concern with accepting the "doctrine of the educational primacy of theoretical over practical knowledge", together with the assertion that physical activities can be systematically changed in order to meet certain theoretical knowledge requirements and thereby enable physical education to satisfy the "epistemological dimension" of the official view of education (Reid, 1996b, p. 13). Certainly I think we can learn much from and at the same time gain some traction from ancient Greek culture, which managed to give physical education an intellectual respectability because it avoided the tendency to view human beings as dualistic entities (mind and body), a view which so often characterises modern education; and, unfortunately for physical education, the acceptance of the "whole man" concept, either in theory or practice, has been one of the rarities in the history of Western culture.[8] This is reinforced further by Van Dalen and Bennett (1971, p. 47) when they articulate skilfully the Athenian ideals of complete harmony and beauty by stating:

> The Greeks gave physical education a respectability that it has never since achieved. They accorded the body equal dignity with the mind. They associated sport with philosophy, music, literature, painting, and particularly with sculpture. They gave to all future civilisations important aesthetic ideals: the ideals of harmonized balance of mind and body, of body symmetry, and of bodily beauty in repose and in action.

Therefore, it is my claim that if the body is considered to be integrated with the mind in a psychosomatic relationship, the body will have value and be esteemed, and, consequently, physical education will be in harmony with intellectual education in the fullest sense of a person's capacities and potentialities. It will be crucial to my argument to resolve the mind–body relationship by providing a resultant view of the body with a legitimate body focus in education so a subject like physical education, which primarily deals with a special form of corporeal discourse, will achieve the recognition it desires. I will return to this argument again at the end of this chapter in more detail.

Historically, antiphysicalism has been a repressive and perpetual undercurrent in the development of physical education. To fully comprehend the cultural repression of the body and physical education in Western culture, I think, it is necessary to understand how the development of the intellectualistic tradition and religious asceticism has been influential in shaping powerful prejudicial views of the body and physical education in education. The basis of this development can be attributed to Plato's dualistic anthropological position of personhood composed of an immortal soul (bearer of a person's rational faculties) that temporally inhabits an evil body. The method whereby the soul can be released from its bodily corruption and the evil material world was through asceticism and the rejection of the body. Likewise, when Plato claims that a person's rational faculty can be cultivated by separating and elevating the higher rational soul from its lower irrational part, we have the inspiration and the justification of the intellectual tradition in education. According to Fairs (1968), the depreciation of the body and the low status of physical education in Western culture would appear to have been further compounded when asceticism and intellectualism evolved in such a way as to complement and supplement one another in their common degradation of the body and their systematic effort to form human beings into an "ascetic animal". As a result this has had a considerable influence on the history and course of human thought, particularly in European religious traditions. For instance, it was long accepted by the Reformed churches that the body was considered as something unclean and inferior that represented the animal part of human beings, which needed to be controlled, managed and disciplined. Consequently the denial and rejection of bodily-type pleasures such as play, games and sport is just an extension of the attitudes towards the things of the body that can be linked to Calvinistic Puritanism and are deeply rooted in Platonic thought. Basic to this puritanical mentality was a view that the body was the cause of our sinful nature and as a result the mind suffers from this contact. The Puritan work ethic (also commonly known as the Protestant work ethic) came to be promoted in various forms by intertwining moralistic aims of education that instilled the traits of piety and honesty in the minds of children, whilst at the same time emphasising the characteristics of the Protestant work ethic such as respecting hard work, material frugality, shunning idleness and frivolity, to the point where some adherents explicitly discarded the nature and purposes of play, games and sport in education as, first, a massive waste of time that needed to be redeemed; and, second, as a kind of bondage to gross bodily appetites that needed to be escaped from in order to achieve wisdom. For the person in whom the Protestant work ethic is firmly established it is difficult, if not impossible to change such a mindset, particularly in communities where human and material resources are scarce, because the main focus becomes the bare preservation of life and, understandably, play, games and sport seem to be frivolous in comparison. Such views changed significantly in the nineteenth century and Old World priorities rapidly changed to the point where Protestants viewed sport as a mere instrument that developed and built character, and that, as part of the curriculum, cultivated desirable social and moral values of courage, honesty, cooperation and so on. I do not think it is an exaggeration to say that to the Puritans it was work which also fulfilled the subsidiary role of exercise that accorded some seriousness to play, but if anything it is recreation that gives work its seriousness and a means to enjoy recreation or at least leisure activities.

The influence of play theory in physical education has historically been received with considerable ambivalence, particularly in isolation. For instance, Aristotle in the *Nicomachean Ethics* observed that to "… spend effort and toil for the sake of amusement seems silly and unduly childish; but on the other hand the maxim of Anacharsis, 'Play to work harder', seems to be right …" (2004, p. 269; 1176b30–35). In this view, play, games and sport are a form of pleasure, which we need because we cannot work continuously. Therefore, we seek pleasure not as an end, but desire it because the activities of play are significantly different from our ordinary life. The notion of hedonism and the values commonly attached to our capacity for pleasure, enjoyment or satisfaction derived from differing kinds of experiences and in particular those associated with play may conflict with other types of values considered to be educationally worthwhile. Misunderstandings surrounding the distinction between play and seriousness seem to threaten the status of physical education because the language of physical education uses the terms "play", "games", "sport" and so on, which seem to reflect a concern primarily with pleasure, leisure, recreation and hedonistic values in general and which as a result also constitute a problem to those who are taken with what they deem to be the seriousness of education (Reid, 1996b). Furthermore, the attempt by physical educationalists to continually attempt to justify the hedonistic values of enjoyment, fun and so on as the prime objectives of physical education has been counterproductive, misguided and destructive, as the promotion of pleasure in isolation is not normally regarded as of educational value. It is to be expected that any subject that bases its inclusion within the curriculum primarily on these grounds is liable to be excluded, or at best relegated to peripheral or extracurricular activity, rather than form part of the educational mainstream. Whilst it may not be unusual to gain pleasure from being engaged in a subject, which is indeed a goal of most teachers' practice across the curriculum, to place an emphasis on pleasure rather than on engagement or even mastery in physical education reveals a misunderstanding of the connection pleasure has with an experience of a particular nature, and most importantly reveals a failure to identify the unique educational features that physical education has to offer. According to Whitehead (1990), physical educationalists have been reluctant to abandon the hedonistic justification even though it does a disservice to their case; what they are really trying to articulate about physical activity is basically the pleasure derived from the successful liaison between motile embodiment and the concrete features of the world. She goes on to add that pleasure can indeed be derived from this embodied experience; however, the real value of physical education does not lie in this pleasure but lies in the development of a specific mode of "relating to the world" (Whitehead, 1990, p. 7). Space does not permit me here to fully survey Whitehead's existentialist and phenomenological viewpoints of the body and its stake in education. I will return to this argument again at the end of this chapter because I wish to continue my critique on the problems of pleasure in education.

Even though pleasure is an important component of the good life, what gives rise to the idea that pleasure may on occasion be detrimental rather than beneficial is the view that it may conflict with values considered to be more important, such as preparing young people in the technical and vocational functions of work. It could be argued that work is instrumentally an economic process, for which education plays an important part in preparing young people for the adult world of work; however, it is the "work-ethic" ideals that underpin work – like skill, discipline, conscientiousness, industry, service and so on – that represent in themselves a set of values that are powerfully influential and significant in education. The problem for physical education, as Reid (1997) outlines, is that there is something deeply paradoxical about championing physical education's alleged economic value as a potential vocation when physical education is commonly associated with play, and play is fundamentally understood as pleasure; consequently, these features seem at odds or even contradictory to most of the work-ethic values presented above. Therefore, the hedonistic characteristics of games and sports, which play a fundamental part in school physical education programmes, are victims of the hedonistic fallacy in which play is a free activity standing outside of "ordinary" life as being "non-serious" (see, for example, Huizinga, 1949, p. 13). Consequently, it follows that playing games (which shares features with play) is also non-serious and a frivolous pursuit because players pursue and desire its hedonistic pleasures such as fun, fantasy, physical challenge and so on at the expense of pursuits deemed to be worthwhile and perceived to be of educational value. The fact that there are many people who make a comfortable living from playing sport and hence take these activities seriously seems contingent upon an accidental fact that does not eradicate the conceptual argument that the activities found in physical education are essentially nonserious activities. Physical education activities are considered to be subordinate to other ends and only considered to be serious if the ends are serious – insofar as they promote, for instance, health, which is accepted as serious – but play, games and sport unjustified against such serious purpose is just trivial. Although we commonly associate and acknowledge a class of things that are serious just because they are intrinsically worthwhile, there appears to be an assertion that playing games cannot be among these things. It is as though the very structure of games renders them non-serious, which is conveyed by the adage "X is just a game", as though there was something inherently trivial about games that makes them unimportant to other ends. According to Dewey (1916/1966), much of the ambivalence that surrounds play has to do with the psychological confusion that exists between play and work due to the economic distinction. The defining characteristic of play is freedom that does not specifically intend to produce any results, whereas work is serious in the sense that it brings greater attention to the specific labour involved in achieving an economic end. He goes on to add that play is psychologically selected for its own sake, in contrast with work which offers little to engage the emotions and the imagination due to its instrumentalist focus on the end product.

The idea of play as an educational process is taken up by Dearden (1968), who does not deny that play is a "non-serious" activity in the sense that it has no ethical value; however, it is chosen because it is free from the demands of the serious business of ordinary life and consequently it does have positive educational merit because play enhances our life and thereby gives it value (see Chapter 5: Play as an educational process). He goes on to add that play is "self-contained" in the sense that it is set apart from serious duties like the work and projects that make up the purposes of our ordinary life and this is essentially why we play, because we are immediately released from these duties momentarily. Even though we pursue play because of these non-serious qualities there are some play activities that have a functional aspect. For instance, we don't play a game in order to become fit. Rather, we play because of the self-contained elements of the game that we are attracted to, such as the pleasure of exercising some skill which may only be available in play, the physical sensation and experience of executing some skill, and so we can realise in ourselves capabilities not realisable fully in our ordinary lives. To some this may be a sophisticated way of drawing our attention to what is brought about by play; however, a cursory observation of young people playing would suggest that there is a great deal unintentionally being picked up and thereby play does have a possible learning function, particularly for children (Dearden, 1968). Dearden (1968) argues that the traditional educational arguments towards play may appear at first glance to be logically flawless and seem to be preoccupied with its utilitarian and economic properties, but they were also involved in an "error which can be made explicit" (Dearden, 1968, p. 103). For instance, the argument goes that play is non-serious, education is serious, therefore education cannot be play. However, what has been ignored is that play can have a serious function, and therefore an educational function. Play is meant to be non-serious or it would not be referred to as play and would not have a clear equivalent in ordinary life. For example, there is nothing in ordinary life which resembles cricket or Australian Rules football. A good cover drive in cricket is simply useless in any other human pursuit and this is exactly why people play games. Ordinary life does not provide enough opportunities at all for such pursuits. Furthermore, game playing allows its participants to explore in safety and learn from their experiences without the consequences of real life. The notion of "play" in the early growth of a child is educationally significant due to the impact it can have upon expanding a child's life space. Playing sport is just another form of play, which can be invaluable to a young person as it can give them the freedom in which they are allowed to be children, to try out a quasi-adult identity, to be in control of the environment where adult power and presence is limited or not present at all, and where the everyday externals of the "normal" environment in which adult power operates are forgotten or at least suspended. The use of games in childhood development cannot be underestimated, particularly as a transitional mechanism for the education of the young.

The idea that pleasure is a bad thing needs to be challenged. Aristotle argued that pleasure is closely linked to human nature and particularly important for the forming of a virtuous character (Aristotle, *Nicomachean Ethics*, 2004, pp. 254–260; 1171a–1174a10). Pleasure is a powerful influence upon virtue and the happy life, because agents freely choose what is pleasant and avoid what is painful. Pleasure is a good, because every rational person seeks it and is attracted to it, and therefore it is assumed that what is most desirable is best. For example, no-one asks why someone is enjoying themselves, because it is assumed that pleasure is desirable in itself. This is why people are drawn to games and sport. Hurka (2007) develops this idea further by emphasising that if a player is attracted to a game for this property, this is a good because the player pursues and takes pleasure in it. Therefore, when you play a game for its own sake because you enjoy rising to challenges presented by a worthy opponent through competition, not just in winning, you do something that is good and do it from a motive that connects directly to its good-making properties. For many people, physical education is considered to be a serious activity that is more than just a fun activity or an optional recreational pursuit. Given the right conditions physical education is educationally beneficial, because it can play a significant role in expressing and exemplifying our values. Some of these experiences are invaluable, ranging, for instance, from learning how to compete with friends, to playing with people one does not like, to persevering during hardships and so on.

Most of the misunderstandings surrounding the nature of physical education and its activities stem predominantly from prejudiced attitudes toward practical knowledge and its educational value, on a narrow and question-begging view of culturally and educationally "worth-while" activities. The use of the term "worth-while activities" owes much to R. S. Peters' (1966) work on educational activities and their justification within the curriculum (see Chapter V: Worth-while activities). He argues that activities classed as pleasurable are notoriously difficult to distinguish and provides four reasons why such a task would be unhelpful. The first problem has to do with claiming that an activity should be engaged in for the sake of pleasure, or because of the pleasure it gives, which will vary from person to person and hence is notoriously subjective. The second problem has to do with the diverse range of activities that could be considered pleasurable and pursued for what they are, which upon closer inspection may be immoral, such as intentionally telling lies. Third, it would be impossible to fully describe in detail pleasurable activities without specifically distinguishing the activity in question. Fourth, the emotional states of pleasure and pain that follow actions may be inseparable from the complexities in which they occur. These arguments outline Peters' position on the type of activities that belong to a general class we call "pleasures" and as a result those activities that do not meet this criteria cannot be "worth-while activities". Therefore, pursuing worthwhile activities is good as long as they connect with a class of activities that are intrinsically desirable and judged to be worthwhile. It is from here that I now turn to a review of Peters' reasons why certain educational activities ought to be "indulged" in to a considerable extent compared with other activities. Peters (1966) develops his ideas of what he considers to be educationally "worth-while activities" by posing a series of questions, "What ought I to do?", followed closely by the question "Why do this rather than that?", to which he methodically responds with his own justifications (Chapter V, sections 3 and 4 from pp. 151–166).

Peter's response to the first question is heavily influenced by the "doctrine of function" and what he considers to be the "good for man", which he goes on to add is to develop those faculties that separate us from other species; so activities which involve or develop the use of reason are worthwhile as they can therefore be instrumental to or lead to other things that are good. Consequently, a person's use of reason and its development features prominently throughout and underpins Peters' "transcendental" argument because it is assumed that activities that appeal to a person's reason are good or intrinsically worthwhile. In his response to the second question, Peters (1966) goes on to set down some of these transcendental activities by arguing that "science, history, literary appreciation, and poetry are 'serious' in that they illuminate other areas of life and contribute much to the quality of living" due to their cognitive content, which makes them distinctly different from games, which have a fabricated end, appear to be set aside from the ordinary aspects of life, and are limited to particular times and places (Peters, 1966, p. 159). Furthermore, he adds that "skills" found in practical activities, such as riding a bicycle, swimming and golf, lack a wide-ranging cognitive content and are largely a matter of "knowing how" (or "knack") rather than of "knowing that" as a species of understanding. According to this account rational activities are superior to games due to their cognitive content, whereas physical education activities are devalued as a mere instrument commensurate with serious ends.[9] For instance, to Peters, physical education is only important because "without a fit body a man's attempt to answer the question, 'Why do this rather than that?' might be sluggish or slovenly" and the act of "physical exercise" is worthwhile in itself because its by-product of a healthy body is considered to be serious (Peters, 1966, p. 163). This only provides a limited justification for engaging in physical exercise, as it does not provide the grounds for superseding theoretical activities based on the argument that rational beings will always find theoretical activities intrinsically worthwhile in themselves and not take the same view of physical activities primarily due to their trivial nature. Consequently, Peters' (1966) conceptual account of education implies the initiation into worthwhile activities must involve knowledge and understanding in some kind of cognitive perspective, which in this case effectively rejects and excludes physical education activities (see Chapters I, II and V).[10]

The question then becomes whether there are any good reasons why a range of physical education activities ought to be regarded as educationally worthwhile compared to non-physical education activities. Peters gives us his clearest insight into what he considers to be the determining factor in the value of curriculum activities when he responds to the self-imposed question, "Why do this rather than that?". His justification is that it is contingent upon the person making the assertion that the activity is worthwhile and consequently it would be irrational to go on asking why one valued this rather than that, because to ask "why" would not be a serious question, since the worthwhile activity already helps them (or anyone else). According to Wilson (1967), to ask whether a particular activity is worthwhile is subjective because what a person considers to be worthwhile and what will help the individual in their pursuit of it can only be resolved empirically and is contingent upon the discriminable characteristics of the agent and of course the activity at a particular time and place. In addition there are many grounds on which some experiences or activities could be rejected on some occasions. He goes on to give the analogous example: if we stop a child from having the experience of climbing a twenty-foot wall (which might well be a worthwhile activity), we may claim to have saved him from potential injury but we have failed to educate him in any sense of why his life was protected and consequently missed the opportunity of his education later on. Wilson (1967, p. 15) adopts the position advocated by Dewey (1938/1963) in *Experience and Education* that education should promote "continued growth" or "education as growing", and argues that it is not the subject per se that is educative but the quality of the experience that is important because there "is no subject that is in and of itself ... such that inherent educational value can be attributed to it". Therefore, the key to this argument is that it is not the activities or the things which certain curriculum areas ask young people to do which makes them educational, but in this case what makes them educational or intrinsically valuable is the experience being more or less conducive to "continued growth" in the long term. This is reinforced further when Wilson (1967, p. 15) states: "certainly there must be 'judgements about ends', but there need be no absolute end to 'ends' ..." because education is concerned with the promotion of continued growth, "not growth towards a full stop". Furthermore, to help someone to discover, engage in and determine what things may be worthwhile for them is the task of education and consequently, "it cannot be done at all if one assumes before one even starts that some things are always worthwhile for everybody, some ends fixed, some wants unchangeable" (Wilson, 1967, p. 16).

As a child grows there will be a diversity of different wants at different times. For instance, he or she may be interested in drawing manga cartoon characters, next time in abstract painting, then by chance he or she comes to appreciate the theatre and begins to study the craft of acting. Now he or she is all for art in its various expressions; however, next he or she moves at a tangent from art altogether and starts to play chess and cricket. On the face of it this may appear to be a succession of random wants of a young person going from one activity to the next without any concern over what the extrinsic ends may be. Certainly, it is clear that Peters' view of education constructs what he considers to be classically orthodox wants and worthwhile activities, but from a young person's point of view these may also appear to be a matter of random wants too, not at all constructed from what a young person wants. Obviously, he or she will need to be as patient with our wants as educators as we are with his or hers, but my concern has to do with insisting on imposing certain predefined activities upon children, like "poetry" in a certain place or time, which could potentially destroy all educability in that direction in the future. This is why engagement is important in educational activities, as there is more likelihood of the experience being more or less conducive to continued growth in the long term rather than some arbitrary constructed extrinsic end that is value loaded and narrowly focused.

According to Whitehead (1990), it is not acceptable for Peters and Hirst to say that the nature and purposes of education need to be the development of theoretical knowledge and understanding framed in a cognitive perspective, because our humanity is not confined to rationality but can be experienced as a being-in-this-world. She goes on to add that to neglect our embodied dimension is to deny our essential nature and the very foundation of our diverse existence in the world, not to mention to highlight prejudicial views of the body. She raises a valid point that Peters' claims about educationally worthwhile activities, even though they have been variously expressed, basically centre on the following notions: first, an activity is seen as worthwhile if there are opportunities to practice "with more or less skill, sensitivity, and understanding" (Peters, 1973, p. 248); second, that it has the capacity to challenge an individual with "unending opportunities for skill and discrimination" (Peters, 1966, p. 157); third, that its participants show respect to the internal standards of the activity; and, lastly, the activity is pursued purely for its own "sake" for the satisfaction it gives the individual (Peters, 1966, 160). Even though these criteria are normally used to justify involvement in activities such as science, philosophy or history there is no reason that physical education activities which focus on exploring and extending a particular mode of "operative liaison" like team games can also satisfy these same criteria (Whitehead, 1990, pp. 11–12). For instance, cricket can be pursued for its own sake, giving its participants the satisfaction in testing their "skill, sensitivity and understanding" by offering "unending challenges", which in turn can "illuminate" the standards and conventions of its practices, which can all be achieved with an effective liaison with their surroundings. The movement-based experiences pursued in physical education are indeed worthwhile activities, which is evident from the number of participants who are engaged in various forms of physical activities like sport and recreational pursuits in Australia[11] and in many other cultures around the world. Consequently, participation is an important part of the lives of many people, which extends beyond the simple use of our embodiment for utilitarian ends or instrumental ends such as good health and fitness. There is real desire to connect with our fundamental nature and engage in the capacities of our embodiment. Whitehead (1990, p. 12) makes the strong point that because embodiment is "something of a mystery in its subtle, yet pervasive role in existence, that the intellectualist finds it difficult to come to terms with". Furthermore, since physical education is a practical subject in the curriculum it is often unvalued primarily because the concept of practical knowledge is not sufficiently understood. According to Carr (1981a), the main differences between theoretical and practical knowledge is the former's concern with the discovery of truths that can be supported by reason and confirmed by experience, whereas the latter is concerned with the execution of purposes in action, conducted in a rational manner and confirmed by a reasonable degree of success. He goes on to add that knowing how is not to be understood in terms of a kind of theoretical reasoning that is associated with practical actions; nor should it, because practical reasoning differs from its theoretical counterpart in many ways. It is a mistake to analyse practical knowledge in reference to theoretical forms of knowledge since it is a function of practical rather theoretical reasoning. Consequently, physical education does have educational value because its significance does not lie simply in the pursuit of propositional knowledge but in practical reasoning, which can be identified as a type of reasoning in its own right and which, like theoretical reasoning, has its own logical standards. I will return to this argument again in succeeding chapters because a brief survey of some of the traditional goods promoted by sport and physical education are needed to determine whether these justifications will augment or diminish my defence. However, before I discuss what I consider to be some of the influential traditions in physical education, something needs to be said about my intentional running together of the terms "sport and physical education" in certain places in this book, so possible confusion can be avoided.

Sport, physical education and Wittgenstein on family resemblances: are we playing language-games?

There has been a general tendency to view sport and physical education as synonymous, or physical education as just sport (or games), as play or any other combination. The problem is that this is a conceptual mistake because it fails to take into consideration many of the significant differences that exist between sport and physical education, particularly within an educational context.[12] Physical education encompasses much more than sport since it includes not just sport, but a family of physical activities that can range from informal to more formalised forms of play, such as games that involve rules and skills that we commonly call sport (Ozolins and Stolz, 2013).[13] Indeed, much has been written to highlight the differences between sport and physical education (see for example Chapel, 2000; Mountakis, 2001; Chapel and Whitehead, 2013). The rationale for this literature aims to bring about greater lucidity to what some see as a detrimental problem in physical education that has never been resolved. Certainly, Chapel (2000) and Chapel and Whitehead (2013) argue that much confusion exists surrounding the nature of physical education because misunderstandings often arise on account of people being confused about the place of sport in physical education. Furthermore, there is a strong undercurrent of attempting to define physical education in order to bring about conceptual clarity as a means of providing cogent justifications for the place of sport and physical education within the curriculum. The problem is that any attempt to define something, particularly notoriously difficult concepts like education, sport, justice, love and so on, is fraught with danger because we are discussing something that is not fixed. Wittgenstein (1953/2009) outlines this very problem in *Philosophical Investigations* when he discusses the multifaceted way in which we use language. His discussion of those things we call "games" is particularly useful in this case because it highlights how we place artificial boundaries around concepts in order to explain what something is. But this tends to lead to misunderstandings and confusion because the "concept of a game is a concept with blurred edges" and cannot be regulated by rigid rules as in the case of mathematics (Wittgenstein, 1953/2009, pp. 37ᵉ–38ᵉ, §§68–71). However, in saying all of this, Wittgenstein was right to argue that we do not need strict boundaries or definitions to come an understanding of what a game is in terms of making the concept usable because we learn things through "characteristic experiences", through "... 'playing a game of chess', 'solving a chess problem', and the like" (Wittgenstein, 1953/2009, pp. 19ᵉ–21ᵉ, §§32–35). Consequently, my combining of the terms "sport" and "physical education" throughout this book is intentionally not fixed because these terms are part of a "complicated network of similarities overlapping and criss-crossing" which I shall say form a "family resemblance" (Wittgenstein, 1953/2009, p. 36ᵉ, §§66–67).[14]

Rather than getting caught-up in counter-productive language-games concerning *what is* or *isn't* educational sport and physical education, as if the essence of each is somehow hidden from us, I think much more can be gained from discussing the way that sport and physical education are used within an educational context. Furthermore, by emphasising what is broadly common between each – such as embodiment and corporeal action or movement – we can start to see that it is not the means that demarcates one activity from the other, but more the *telos* of the activity. For instance, the *telos* of a knife can have various ends that can range between two extremes: a surgeon's saving lives and murdering someone. In this case, the means are the same in both – the knife – but the ends different. By extension, the same applies to sport and physical education within an educational context. Embodiment and corporeal action or movement are both the same means, but sport and physical education can have different ends depending on how the means are used. Consequently, when physical education uses sport, the intention is to bring about educational ends; whereas sport in physical education can serve a diverse array of ends that may or may not be educational in scope.

Traditionally, the dominance of sport, particularly team games in physical education, has strong historical roots in both public and grammar schools originating in the middle of the nineteenth century and in state schools during the twentieth century in Britain, which in turn influenced other educational systems around the world in most English-speaking countries like Australia.[15] However, over time the narrative of physical education has undergone significant historical transformation due to rival and competing traditions of physical education vying to be the dominant set of practices and mode of understanding their importance and worth. In fact, the narrative of physical education needs to be understood against the background of the wider social context. This wider social context consists of sets of practices which serve to explain and describe what physical education is, and these practices, in turn are situated within a tradition. Thus, we can start to see that physical education resides firmly within a historical tradition that is dynamic and forever evolving in its pursuit to understand the tradition that is physical education.

However, this is not a straightforward or easy process because it requires the individual who enters into the tradition to interpret and reinterpret what it means to become a practitioner in the tradition. And it is this concept of "traditions" which owes much to MacIntyre's work, to which I will now turn as a means to make sense of the diverse array of practices found within physical education.

Influential traditions in physical education: traditions are not static, but dynamic

My use of the term "tradition" borrows heavily from MacIntyre's (1988, 1990, 2007) conceptual understanding of traditions of rationality and communities of practice. What MacIntyre means by tradition is dependent upon the wider social context in which sets of practices sustain traditions within communities. In MacIntyre's (2007, p. 222) words, a tradition "... is an historically extended, socially embodied argument, and an argument precisely in part about the goods which constitute that tradition". It is important to emphasise that to MacIntyre (2007, p. 222), traditions are not static, but dynamic, because historically traditions change, develop over time, some "decay, disintegrate and disappear", and some emerge in response to the circumstances.[16] This is why views surrounding the meaning and values of physical education are as old as ancient Greek culture and as diverse as environmental habitats. Hence, why I believe it is worth examining the diverse array of traditions in physical education to determine if there are any commonalities of practice which may serve to elucidate what physical education is. As a result, I present what I consider to be some of the influential traditions of physical education (see Figure 1.1). These being: physical education as health prevention and promotion, physical education as character development and moral education, physical education as art and beauty, physical education as a mechanism for finding meaning through movement, physical education as sport education, physical education as preparation for leisure, and physical education as academic study. I discuss each briefly in turn.

Health tradition: physical education as health prevention and promotion

Physical education is inextricably connected with "health" in contemporary school curricula to the point where it is clearly identifiable in the formal subject title.[17] In this kind of relationship, physical education is viewed as instrumental to good health. The traditional understandings of health, sometimes referred to as health-related exercise in physical education (dynamic conception of health: fitness for activities) share a homeostatic kind of approach in which sport and physical education activities are considered to be instrumental to the maintenance of a healthy organism, so we can adapt to the normal requirements of the life situation (Almond, 1983; Harris, 2005, 2009; Harris and Cale, 1998; Kirk, 1992b; Kirk and Colquhoun, 1989; Tinning, 2010; Wachter, 1985). Some scholars (Evans, 2003; Kirk, 1992b, 1994b, 1999; Kirk and Colquhoun, 1989;

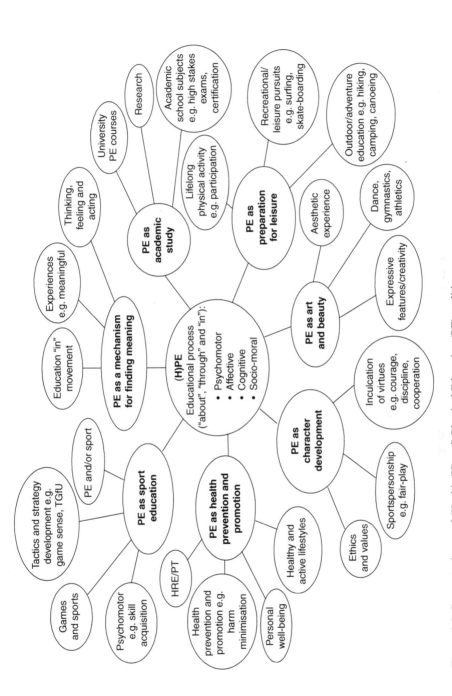

Figure 1.1 Conceptual map of (Health (H) and) Physical Education (PE) traditions.

McNamee, 1988; Tinning and Glasby, 2002; Wachter, 1985), however, have argued that the instrumental view of health in contemporary culture has been superseded by a representational one (representational conception of health: the athletic body), in which the pursuit of fitness has become more than a mere biological necessity: it has now become a social symbol of prestige and social status in which good health is symbolised by the "athletic body".

The origins of current contemporary health justifications can be attributed to the rise of modern science, because it established the idea and provided empirical-scientific data to demonstrate the causal connection between physical inactivity and morbidity rates, and that an increase in physical activity levels can improve public health (Ainsworth, 2005; Evans, 2003; Tinning, 2010). Combine these trends with the fact or fiction of a global obesity epidemic (Gard and Kirk, 2007; Gard and Wright, 2005; Kirk, 2006a) and all give force to the arguments for increased physical education in school and its role as the "new public health" (Tinning, 2010; Tinning and Glasby, 2002). In the emergence of the health tradition within the physical education profession, it has come to be accepted (albeit taken for granted) that it will fulfil a kind of preventative role. Why it is unquestionably accepted is primarily due to the overwhelming scientific evidence that physical activity can have positive health benefits. Additionally, the health crisis that has gained momentum in the media surrounding the prevalence of hypokinetic risks associated with inactivity, such as obesity and other kinds of conditions, in some ways has provided a legitimate justification for incorporating a health-based approach in physical education curricula as a means toward health prevention and to improve public health. The idea is that such an approach taken with young people in schools may positively influence and affect lifetime involvement in health-related exercise and therefore negate any future burden on the already struggling public health system. Whether this approach is a secure foundation on which to build a justification for physical education is questionable, because improved health seems to become the primary end toward which everything else matters at the expense of the means. The physical education-as-health justification becomes instrumentally open-ended and inaccessible to most people, since Western cultureal ideas about health are indistinguishable from the symbolic image of the sporting body, which are based on extreme ideals that are virtually unattainable. Loland (2006) makes the point that contemporary justifications of health provide knowledge of efficient means to reach other ends, but with no clear idea of the goal these means are supposed to serve; consequently it renders the health justification ethically irresponsible at the same time. He goes on to add that health as a justification for physical education is not totally irrelevant, but physical education could act as a counterbalance against the dominant discourses of the medicalisation of modern life and the pursuit of the unattainable body.

Games ethic tradition: physical education as character development and moral education

The cult of athleticism was influential in the British public school system during the second half of the nineteenth century. According to Mangan (1975), the educational ideology was based on the widely held conviction that participation within physical exercise (particularly team games) was an instrument for moral and character training. He goes on to add that this belief was manifest in the form of compulsory physical activity through games as a means of inculcating valuable instrumental and expressive goals such as physical and moral courage, loyalty, cooperation and the ability to both command and obey. At the same time the notions of the "dutiful Christian" and "muscular Christian" came to be associated with athleticism because the value system of games became a vehicle and reflection of the ideals of Christian excellence, and took on new significance when it became linked with an imperialist rationale that advocated for educational institutions to prepare "manly" self-confident, "hardy soldiers", administrators and missionaries who were capable of enduring the physical and psychological rigors of duty in the ever-expanding empire.

It would be purely fanciful to assume that every student played games for their moral attributes; nevertheless, the declared ideological position and widespread acceptance of athleticism as an educational ethos allowed and justified the determined focus on games ideology and the discussion about games above all else (Mangan, 1975). Athleticism as a moralistic ideology came to be increasingly questioned in the early years of the twentieth century due to changing educational priorities and the ascent of both intellectualism and vocational preparation, and by the second half of this century a new ideology of individualism had emerged which excluded service, physical courage, loyalty and so on. However, from the 1950s, games and traditional team sports experienced a rapid increase in popularity to the point where they took up the largest part of school physical education programmes and were considered by some practitioners to be the core of physical education. According to Kirk (1992a), the invention of the games-based approach in physical education can be attributed to the large number of male teachers in the post-war era who were influenced by the alleged benefits associated with team games in public schools and were keen to replicate this approach into the new secondary schools. The shift away from physical training to more of a concern with physical education can be attributed to the belief that competitive team sports and the range of physical activities inherent within its practice provided a positive means of developing moral virtues, and as part of the curriculum contribute significantly to moral education. It is my claim that the traditional games ideology has been, and still is, one of the most powerful influences in contemporary physical education programmes revolving around the predictably homogenised form of team sports, games and skill-based pedagogy.

Such a position views physical education as an instrument that contributes to moral ends that are external to physical education itself. Much has been written about the educational value of the games ideology and this moralist justification for sport and physical education is no stranger to modern society.[18] However, the claims made by such a position have been brought into question and take three forms. First, if we accept the argument that participating in sport cultivates character, then at the same time it is reasonable to assume that morally undesirable qualities such as gamesmanship, meanness of spirit, a win at any cost attitude, a tendency to violence and so on that occur in competitive sport are also likely to be transferred into an agent's moral life. In this case the competitive side of sport may actually be morally miseducative and do more harm than good. Second, the critical factor seems to depend on the pedagogical methodologies applied in practice rather than on the particular subject matter of physical education. Third, physical education academics who reason from statements of belief to fact (these are only "true" values) to normative ends (this is how physical education ought to be practised) are consequently guilty of the naturalist fallacy. The justification of physical education as an uncritical instrument for moral education is problematic, but there is the possibility of justifying physical education from a communitarian ethic in which moral virtues may develop through historical and sociocultural practices.[19]

Aesthetic tradition: physical education as art and beauty

Physical education includes a diverse array of physical activities that can range from competitive games, gymnastics, athletics and swimming, to dance and so on. However, within this wide range of activities, there exist all sorts of differences according to the practical aims or means in which ends are to be achieved, and consequently some activities are deemed to have more aesthetic merit according to their expressive elements. For instance, games come at one end of a kind of spectrum in which competition is assumed; at the other end there is gymnastics, diving, ice skating or ice dance, in which the "manner" of the activity seems to be the central feature of importance. Sometimes it is the aesthetic character of "form" in games that is emphasised – like grace, economy, speed, style, drama and so on – derived from the experience of the specific movement that is assigned the significant aesthetic value and therefore intrinsically part of its game's purpose. According to Louis Reid (1970), when distinguishing between the nature of the aesthetic and of art, there are many human movements in games or athletics that have great positive aesthetic value, but it is wrong to jump to the conclusion that they are art, any more than the flight of a bird is art. He cautions us that when we are talking about art as distinct from aesthetics we must be firm in insisting that in art an artefact has been purposefully made with an essential idea of producing an object in some aesthetic medium. He continues by arguing that the central concept of the aesthetic is not just expression but embodiment of a unique kind in which the expression that there is in art is altered in its embodiment. Anderson (2002) makes a valid point when he says that human movement is a place where we can express our identity, experience what it means to be embodied beings and make sense of the world around us. He goes on to add that human movement of various kinds is both art and techne because skills allow us to be something like a golfer, sculptor and so on; however, such movement has the capacity to also move beyond skilfulness to become art in the more contemporary sense. This is highlighted when he comments that there is obviously a locus of beauty in movements such as ballet, gymnastics and ice skating or ice dancing, but they are exemplary of the aesthetic possibilities found in all human movement and there are times in sport when athletes cross the border from skilfulness to aesthetic beauty – such as Michael Jordan driving to the basket – and consequently such artistry and creativity constitute another way that movement and sport can bring us home to our humanity. According to Kuntz (1974), on the level of physical action something happens physiologically and psychologically between performer and spectator and, as a result, when it is said that physical education is educationally valued because of the aesthetic qualities of human movement being explored, appreciated, experienced from a kinaesthetic perspective and so on, we can precisely understand what this means. Consequently, any given performance can have qualities of the aesthetic for both the performer and the spectator, whether intended or not, because the aesthetic quality of the movements is contingent upon the response of the performer or spectator. As Kuntz (1974, p. 15) suggests, "sport is a truly human form of art, for it is not just the product of man's abilities which is on display; it is man".

Unfortunately, in considering the relationship of art and the aesthetic to physical education, the influence of the obviously expressive aspects of movement, such as ice skating or ice dancing, artistic gymnastics and so on, that are comparable to dance are considered to have aesthetic value and this has led to a tendency in physical education to distinguish between functional or non-art-type activities and artistically expressive activities. The reason why such a distinction has arisen in physical education has more to do with the difficulty and confusion in distinguishing the obvious aesthetic elements that are found in games and sports that are competitive and, subsequently, it is claimed that any aesthetic element is more a by-product to the uncomplicated main aim of scoring points to win. The view that a connection exists between physical education activities and aesthetic values has a long history dating back to ancient Greece; however, the claims made by such a position have been brought into question and take three forms. The first concern has to do with the subjective nature of appraising activities in aesthetic terms, since they are open-ended for us to appraise and, consequently, whether an activity is aesthetic is merely a subjective notion according to an agent's judgements, which as a result weakens the educational value of these activities in physical education. The second concern is that sport is not art, even though some activities may share a family resemblance at times, like ice skating or ice dancing; however, I do not think we could go as far as to call them art, rather than sport, just because there are artistic elements inherent in the activity. Best (1974, 1978) argues that certain sports would seem to have an intrinsic aesthetic element and are therefore intentionally performed to give aesthetic satisfaction, but this does not justify them as art forms. He goes on to add that it would be difficult to imagine a gymnast who included in her sequence movements that expressed her view of war, love or any such issue, and if she did so it would detract from her own performance, unlike art. The third concern has to do with a general misunderstanding of the value of aesthetic activities on some narrow definition of what it means to be a skilled athletic performer; as a result such attitudes are highlighted by the trend at the moment in physical education programmes to focus predominately on team sports, games and skill-based pedagogy which essentially exclude aesthetic type activities.

Phenomenological tradition: physical education as a mechanism for finding meaning through movement

The justification of physical education as a mechanism for finding meaning in movement and what this means in practice has a more sophisticated theme to it as it deals with existential questions such as: Who am I? What can I do? Who are we? What can I achieve? This justification is linked to what is often called the humanist tradition. The best way to view this approach is to come from the perspective that as humans we search and construct meaning for ourselves to better understand our own lives. The seminal work of Arnold (1979a) illustrates this approach as it views physical education as a sort of experience, in which we explore the possibilities and limitations of our bodies in the curriculum via three conceptual dimensions, "about, through and in". He characterises "about" movement as the theoretical knowledge that can be academically studied, whereas education "through" movement has to do with the justifiable application of a family of physical activities, which are normally found in physical education; finally, education "in" movement brings together the view that movement activities when experienced from the perspective of a moving agent permit the actualisation of the agent in a set of distinctive and bodily-orientated contexts that provides opportunities for the agent to learn about themselves and the world they live (Chapter 6: Education, movement and the curriculum). According to Loland (1992, 2006), the justification of meaning in movement focuses is not so much in the instrumental outcome of the activity rather in the abstract ideas of what these experiences mean in practice.

The problems encountered in such a justification of physical education surround the link between phenomenology and existentialism. For instance: Are these experiences good or bad? Can there be any value assigned to a movement? Are the movement experiences that occur in physical education justifiable in the context of human life? Obviously, there are aspects of physical education such as competitive games in which the end is quite clear, however, the experiential qualities claimed by this account may be more shaped by socialisation rather than "in" the experience of exploring the possibilities and limitations of embodied movement. Even though this account has been criticised for being contextually and sociologically naive there are certain aspects of the humanistic tradition such as the exploration of our humanity that are its redeeming qualities that I will pick up on in my account.

Physical education as sport education tradition: preserving elite sporting success

The use of elite sport as a frame of reference for physical education is not new. For some sections of the media and for some politicians, it seems a short step from advocating for more physical education based on the claims that young people are less active now then at some unspecified time in the past and that the causal link in this decline can be attributed to the quantity of physical education, particularly school sport (Kirk, 2004). For instance, the findings of the Crawford Report (Commonwealth of Australia, 2009) made by an Independent Sport Panel, chaired by David Crawford, recommended "reuniting" and "reinvigorate[ing] sport and physical education in the education system" so we can maintain future sporting success. The language and thematic representation of the Crawford Report clearly represented a heavily biased conceptualisation of physical education pedagogy within a sport education framework. According to Kirk (1994a), the place of games and competitive sport has historically been the driving force behind the creation and development of physical education as a formal learning area in Australia. Kirk and Gorely (2000) go on to add that physical education was, and continues to be, an invention, which has served to legitimise the practice of competitive sport in schools, and which can be understood by the pyramid metaphor most commonly used to conceptualise the place of sport in physical education. There are many differing versions of the pyramid model, but they are all ideologically the same: physical education forms the base of the structure where the majority of young people participate in school and learn the fundamental motor skills that can be applied within an ascending scale of competitive contexts with elite sports competition at the top. Furthermore, the success of such an approach is contingent upon widening the base of the pyramid, thereby increasing the potential for greater elite sporting success. Obviously, there are serious flaws to such a geometrical model; for instance, if students are taught poorly at the base and therefore cannot ascend the pyramid basically renders the group as poor performers. Even if they are taught well, the pyramid model systematically excludes young people at various stages, no matter how good they may be. This leads me to my second point of concern: irrespective of how young students are taught, the pyramid model does not seem to be an educationally sound process or even offer genuine experiences of sport for young people. Ennis (1999) provides compelling evidence that the experiences in and perceptions of physical education in its sports-based form can be a harrowing experience, particularly (though not solely) for girls. My concern is that the label of physical education is being used for nothing more than a rhetorical convenience for justifications for sport education. There already exists enough confusion about what constitutes physical education as opposed to sport education and vice versa, and I would argue that this has more to do with competing discourses (Stolz, 2010). This is further reinforced by Penney and Chandler (2000) when they make the penetrating observation that, while physical educationalists may be in agreement about what the subject "is not", there still appears to be no clear idea of what the core aims of the subject are; consequently this is the source of noticeable tension. Normally we associate sport with an emphasis on competition; as a result its purpose is quite a narrow one compared to the multiplicity of learning objectives commonly pursued by physical education. It is not that I wish to do away with competitive games and sports in school physical education, because there are cases in which participation within competitive sporting activities can have a positive educational value given the right conditions.[20] However, I am, first, concerned with the sport education model failing to take into account other aspects of practice which are equally relevant to physical education. Second, I am cognisant of the fact that an over-emphasis on winning or even the "win at any cost" mentality that is so prevalent in elite sport can have negative educational implications. Rather than frame physical education within a seriously flawed pyramid structure in which the range of physical activities are only limited to the preparation and development of prerequisite skills required for participation in elite sport, we first need to identify the elements in sport that are educationally worthwhile so that quality physical education can be replicated in school.

Physical education as preparation for leisure tradition: we work so we can play

The idea that physical education is primarily concerned with the initiation of young people into the various forms of physical play is known as the "recreational" or "leisure" view, because the development of prerequisite skills considered important in leisure pursuits is emphasised. Therefore, physical education conceived in this way is closely linked with leisure education. According to Scraton (1995), by the mid-1980s, "preparation for leisure" came to be emphasised in the teaching of physical education due to the increased leisure time that was associated with economic changes of the period. During this period there was a significant shift in physical education teaching ideologies away from the traditional games approach that stressed the importance of competition through a limited repertoire of team games to the identification and connection with youth trends with the express purpose of adapting school physical education programmes to young people's changing leisure styles (Roberts, 1996a, 1996b). Subsequently, by providing an alternative form of physical education the intent was to redress the growing body of literature surrounding the negative experiences of young people in physical education and school physical education that is irrelevant or boring for adolescents (Ennis, 1999; Flintof, 2008; Flintoff and Scraton, 2001, 2010; Penney, 2002; Penney and Evans, 1999; Smith and Parr, 2007; Tinning and Fitzclarence, 1992).

Physical education as preparation for leisure is an extension of the idea that the main purpose of education is the preparation of young people for work and/ or leisure; in this sense the representation of leisure is the same as vocational skills. For example, if a student's skills are lacking then they need to be re-skilled in preparation for leisure and thereby trained to be fit for life. However, the problems encountered with such an approach are varied and numerous. For instance, the constant tension between the activities of physical education compared to certain educational activities deemed to be worthwhile is most noticeable in Peters' account of education, which I have already alluded to. Second, the ideological shifts made by physical education teachers to accommodate recent trends may be worthy aims, but educationally questionable. Third, my concern is that this is only a representational ideological shift and to suggest that the traditional games ideology that emphasises competition and a limited range of team games has been weakened in any way is a fallacy.

Academic tradition: physical education as academic study

Physical education is often justified within the curriculum as academic study.[21] This is evident in the growth of examinable physical education (Carroll, 1982, 1998; Green, 2001, 2005) and the widespread acceptance of physical education in educational institutions as an academic subject, particularly in senior schooling and tertiary institutions (Brooker and Macdonald, 1995; Macdonald *et al.*, 1999). According to Reid (1996a, p. 95), if physical education wants to justify its place within the education mainstream and if academic credentials are the means to gain entry into the mainstream, then "... physical education must fulfil this requirement by making increased demands of pupils in terms of mastery of propositional knowledge ...", and so the focus shifts to an explicit form of theoretical knowledge rather than the teaching and learning of physical activities that are considered to be problematic. He goes on to add that this has been evidenced by trends in physical education, such as the growth of examinable physical education, the increase in physical education/sports science degrees and widespread acceptance of the "academicisation" of physical education in contemporary curriculum and assessment polices. Certainly, some traction has been gained by such a justification of striving for academic status, particularly within the senior schooling structures, by attracting students who are seeking credentials to work in the health or tertiary sectors. By doing this, it has resulted in securing the profile of physical education, albeit in a limited capacity in the academic realm. There are considerable advantages in such an approach, particularly in senior schooling systems which require all learning to be assessed and moderated, compared to what some consider to be the problematic and subjective nature of many physical activities that take place in physical education that are difficult to assess. According to Brooker and Macdonald (1995), having bought into the "credentialing cycle", physical education can justify itself as a worthwhile activity on par with other academic subjects on offer primarily because it contributes towards senior certificates that are considered valuable under the rationalists' microscope. The problem with such an approach is that the greater emphasis being placed upon the mastery of the theoretical knowledge component of senior school physical education has in turn inadvertently led to a significant decrease in the amount of time in the physical activity component of the subject. There is no question that this approach has set in motion some devastating consequences for physical education, even though in fairness they may have been unintended at the time and born out of a desire for physical education to both survive as a subject and gain mainstream status. The problem with such an approach is that teaching and learning experiences in physical education have become disproportionately theoretical in nature, to the point where physical education has become disconnected from its central tenet, which is concerned with employing physical means to develop each student's whole being.

I will now turn my attention to an account in direct response to some of the serious criticisms levelled against sport and physical education detailed in earlier points of discussion.

The id² of physical education: cutting through the rhetoric and identifying what we are (or ought to be)

I think it is clear from my review of what I consider to be influential physical education traditions that they vary in specificity, explicitness and scope. According to Paul (1996), physical education has historically experienced what he calls a "grandfather clock syndrome" that has caused the ideas of physical education to swing from one extreme position to another, to the point where the pendulum never stops in exactly the same place nor stays near the middle. He goes on to add that many of the swings have made the field of physical education appear as a paradox, as one that is ever changing and yet returning to what it discarded. Understandably, these pendulum swings and their resultant movements have led to serious philosophical conflicts that leave us as a field of "fractured identities". He cautions us that the history of physical education is much like a popular song where the same chorus is continually played over and over again; and consequently after each swing of the pendulum, there are signs that we may be actually writing our own obituary. One of the main reasons why the physical education profession has been in a constant state of flux has to do with the problems surrounding the place and purposes of physical education within educational institutions and its continual preoccupation with reinventing itself in order to remain current, and thereby accrue status by redefining knowledge as a means of entering the academic mainstream. Kirk (2010) reinforces this viewpoint by arguing that school physical education is a socially and culturally constructed concept in the sense that it is a human invention rather than an occurrence in nature, and when in the school curriculum it is the product of competing discourses vying for dominance in different places and times, to the point where the label of physical education is nothing more than a rhetorical convenience in which anything goes (see Kirk, 2010, Chapter 2: Defining physical education and the possibility of the id²). Central to Kirk's (2010) idea is the concept of the "idea of the idea" (shortened to id² for succinctness), which he borrows from Sheldon Rothblatt's (1997) book, *The Modern University and Its Discontents*, as a means to distinguish "physical educationness" from the vast and diverse array of practices claiming to be physical education. The id² of physical education requires some explanation, as a solid grasp of the concept is important to unleashing the power of Kirk's insights on physical education. Thus the id^2 of physical education is best understood as a mechanism that functions as an organising principle by recognising the essential characteristics of physical education found in institutionalised practices (irrespective of place and time). Kirk (2010) acknowledges that there can be no immutable or transcendental essence[22] of physical education; however, in institutionalised practices family resemblances can be found which can deal with the extreme relativist position in which anything goes in the name of physical education.[23]

The reason why Kirk adopts what he calls a "social epistemological approach" in his characterisation of the essence of physical education is to put an end to the ideological discourses competing for dominance in what he considers to be fundamentally the same versions of knowledge. As Kirk so skilfully explains, the form of school physical education (since the 1950s) primarily deals with a special form of corporeal discourse, which he refers to as "physical culture"; learning that occurs in school physical education can transfer to life beyond the school, which he refers to as "transfer of learning"; what are the purposes of practical activities, particularly in relation to "ability" and how it is to be assessed and judged, which he refers to as "standards of excellence"; and, lastly, how physical education reproduces and expresses the significant values of our sporting cultural heritage, which he refers to as "cultural transmission, reproduction and renewal" (Kirk, 2010, Chapter 6: Four relational issues and the bigger picture). He goes on to add that school physical education, such as the multi-activity programmes influenced by the current dominant discourse of "physical education – as-sport-techniques", may appear to be "forward-looking" in relation to growing cultural relevance and feature the use of games and sport to fulfil these aims; however, upon closer inspection these programmes are nothing more than "backward-looking" and built on archaic notions of sport and pedagogy that have been resistant to reform. This situation as a result has inadvertently led to unintended consequences that have contributed to reinforcing social inequality and injustice and reproduced privilege, in direct contradiction to the explicit and implicit claims made by physical education.

According to Kirk, there are consequently three potential physical education future scenarios if the current dominant discourse of "physical education-as-sport-techniques" cannot be radically reformed and the id^2 of physical education is not properly understood instead of viewed as a rival idea of physical education (Kirk, 2010, Chapter 7: Physical education futures?). The first scenario and the most likely short-term outcome is more of the same. In the second scenario, Kirk passionately advocates for radical reform to secure the long-term future of physical education; however, this may be too confrontional for some who have a vested interest in maintaining the status quo which, when combined with the allure and powerful influence of the dominant discourse of "physical education-as-sport-techniques" approach, may be too difficult to overcome. In the third scenario, while the "more of the same" scenario is likely, Kirk warns us that without radical reform there is the real potential that in the long term physical education may become extinct due to a multitude of factors accumulating and conspiring against it.

There is no question that physical education is inextricably linked to the practical body, and consequently the philosophical position of the body and our concept of human nature will have a direct bearing on how we think human beings should behave and be educated and, particularly in this case, how we think individuals should be educated physically. You would think that a field calling itself physical education (or human movement studies, human kinetics and so on) would have sophisticated discourses about the human body, but the predominant influence in physical education is a reductionist view of the body as machine and restricted almost totally to the atomistic, instrumental and mechanistic approach adopted by sports scientists, who have generally embraced a biomedical engineering model of the human body. According to McKay *et al.* (1990, p. 60), the body is seldom portrayed as a "... pleasurable site for ecstatic, aesthetic, vertiginous, autotelic, sensuous and holistic experiences", but portrayed as a biomechanical object that must be managed, maintained, conditioned and repaired for instrumental reasons such as improving performance or physical appearance. Kirk (2010) reinforces this point further when he argues that there is a tendency for physical education to consider only or mainly the body in nature (biological and mechanical) and to ignore or dismiss totally the body in culture (signifying and symbolising). Therefore, if we are serious about enhancing the status and value of physical education we need to develop an educational justification for physical education that celebrates rather than denigrates its practical body-work focus because its current marginalised status hinges upon the low value accorded to young peoples' embodiment in education.

Challenging prejudicial attitudes toward the body and physical education in education: schools are not just places that educate the mind

The history of physical education is a testament to the perennial influence of Plato and Platonism, which I argue still poses a powerful influence in Western culture, particularly on our understandings of corporeal experience in education. Consequently, when corporeal experience is disparaged and ridiculed it renders physical education to a lower status than intellectual education in a hierarchy of educational values, which Peters' (1966) position clearly outlines in his discussion of "intrinsically worth-while activities" (see Chapters I, II and V). In a way Peters' account of education is guilty of compartmentalising education into the education of the mind and education of the body which are symbolic and representative of contemporary education's tendency to view the person as a dualistic being composed of two separate entities: superior mind and an inferior body. However, it is my thesis that when the body is considered to be integrated with the mind in a psychosomatic relationship and balanced between spiritual, intellectual and physical aspects, such an approach is advantageous in that it can have significant impact in re-establishing equanimity, thereby giving physical education greater harmony with intellectual education in the fullest sense of achieving human beings' capacities and potentialities (Fairs, 1968). Aristotle has much to say about the body and soul in education in the *Politics*. He ponders whether priority should be given to the soul or the body. His response is that the "two modes of training" must be in harmony with each other to the highest degree because we may fail to reason the best principle and likewise may be lead astray by our habits (Aristotle, *Politics*, 1995, pp. 289–290, 1334ᵇ6). He goes on to add that reason may be our "ultimate end of our nature", which will develop naturally over time through the educational process, but even before we pursue these aspects in our education we need to make sure our bodies are in good condition so the soul will benefit. Subsequently, the health of the soul/mind is contingent on the health of the body, for which physical education has a necessary part to play in the curriculum. St Thomas Aquinas (1265–1274/1993a) further develops Aristotle's position that the nature of personhood is an integral composite of body and soul whereby the soul needs a body to acquire knowledge, thereby validating our sense of personal psychosomatic relationship and of corporeal and spiritual (hylomorphic) unity.

The ancient Greeks, amongst other great minds, well knew that the experience of movement gives meaning to our existence and constitutes what it means to be a human being, and so the real value of physical education as Whitehead (1990, 2001, 2008, 2010) asserts lies in the development of both embodied and intellectual faculties so that students can achieve effective liaison in progressively more complex and demanding situations. In direct contrast to the Platonic–Cartesian tradition of understanding the relationship between the body and mind, Merleau-Ponty (1945/1962) does not view the body as a special kind of object separate from the mind that can only comprehend the world via the reasoned mind, but views the body as "being-in-the-world" in the sense that our embodiment precedes reflective thought. Anderson (2002, p. 94) reinforces this point further by arguing that the "… experience of movement is thus humanizing, just as is the reading of Shakespeare or Willa Cather – and just as are Cather's and Shakespeare's acts of writing" and to denigrate our experiences of movement is to misunderstand the important of non-theoretical knowledge. The implications here are significant because such a position implies that there no longer exists a philosophical division between the object and subject because the world begins from the body and provides the means in which we can develop a sense of our own identity and at the same time come to know the world via physical action. This is confirmed by Merleau-Ponty (1945/1962, p. 162), who emphasises that our body is a "meaningful core" which engages with the world through the body, which in turn provides the "… link between here and a yonder, a now and a future …".

According to Schilling (1993), traditional notions of education which have an exclusive intellectual knowledge focus are mistaken because schools are not just places that educate the minds of young people – they are also concerned with the bodies of young people both biologically and socially. Consequently, the low status of physical education is linked to the low value accorded to young peoples' embodiment and corporeal experiences in education. Therefore, it seems clear to me at this juncture that physical education could benefit significantly from the establishment of a legitimate understanding of the body in education before attempting to develop philosophical justifications for its inclusion within educational institutions. According to Armour (1999), if a legitimate body focus can be argued for in education then it is more likely that a "body-linked" subject like physical education will achieve the recognition it aspires to. She goes on to add that there are four arguments why the body should be a concern for education and therefore a legitimate concern for physical education. These are: (1) pupils are embodied; (2) embodiment is increasingly central to self-identity; (3) numerous social factors influence pupils' embodiment; and (4) physical education can have a significant role in the establishment of pupils' embodied identity (Armour, 1999, p. 10). Furthermore, acknowledging the primacy of the body in physical education has many practical and theoretical advantages. It is not a panacea, but at least it becomes difficult to envisage the "embodied pupil" in a dualistic sense. Anderson (2002) makes the strong point that we should not apologise to academics and intellectuals for having an essentially practical and overtly physical subject. However, we should celebrate and promote this feature directly as an intrinsic value of being human. In essence this is the advantage physical education has over other subjects.

In this chapter, I provided a brief overview of the main philosophical arguments contravening the educational value or significance of physical education as a means to construct an apology and coherent conceptualisation of sport and physical education. I argued that the reason why physical education has struggled for legitimacy within the curriculum at most levels is due to a variety of damaging claims made by critics who have argued that physical education activities within the curriculum are basically trivial compared to other forms of knowledge that are considered to be educationally worthwhile. Probably, the most serious criticism levelled against the nature of physical education can be attributed to R. S. Peters' earlier work on educational activities and their justification within the curriculum. To counter such arguments I argued that it is not the activities or what certain curriculum areas ask young people to do which makes such activities educational. What makes them educationally valuable is the experience per se, not the subject, because education ought to be concerned with continued growth and about helping someone to discover, engage in and determine what things are worthwhile for them. Furthermore, I also argued that it is a mistake to just view the nature and purposes of education to be the development of theoretical knowledge and understanding in a cognitive perspective because it represents an impoverished view of the nature of personhood. My point being that a person's essential being is not just confined to his or her rationality, but also involves an embodied dimension. In essence this is one of the unique educational features that physical education has to offer because it has the potential to develop both embodied and intellectual capacities so as to enhance an individual's understanding of the world in which they interact. Such an approach is significant to physical education because each student is treated as a whole being, permitting the person to experience him- or herself as a holistic and synthesised acting, feeling, thinking being-in-the-world, rather than as separate physical and mental qualities that bear no relation to each other. Consequently, the philosophical position of the body and our conception of human nature will have a direct bearing on how we think human beings should behave and be educated and, in this case, how we think individuals should be educated physically.

So what has been the body's place in history? Certainly, for the last 2000 years or more philosophical and theological positions of the body have had a profound influence on how we view human nature. According to Fairs (1968, pp. 21–22) the historical development of the body "... testifies to the perennial influence of Platonic metaphysical dualism ...", particularly in the shaping of religion and philosophy. Inevitably this has meant that an inextricably body-linked subject like physical education has become devalued because the body has been considered to be an obstruction to knowledge, whereas subjects with a strong rational emphasis that can intentionally develop the mind through a wide-ranging cognitive perspective are valued as superior because they develop the natural rational tendencies of human beings through the cultivation of the intellect. To understand the basis for the development of the metaphysical dualistic tradition I will now turn to theological and philosophical accounts of human nature from the medieval period, because both theologians and philosophers from this era considered the nature of human beings' relationships of the soul to the body and so on. This is why it is to this period I now turn to investigate the changing concepts of the body, particularly its influence upon the attitudes concerning the education of human beings physically.

Notes

1 Philosophically, the use of this term "physical education" is contentious; however, I use it here due to its universal standing in most educational systems to identify a learning area and all the associated derivations that may be available, such as Health and Physical Education, Physical Education and Sport, Personal Development, Health and Physical Education and so on.

2 My use of the term "apology" is intentional, and is nuanced somewhat from its theological tradition specifically for the purposes of this book. Generally speaking, in the theological tradition apologetics is engaged in to provide rational arguments for fundamental doctrines that Christians and non-Christians find problematic. Some of these questions may be as follows: Do faith and reason conflict? Does God exist? How can God allow evil to exist? Is Christianity the only true religion? (See, for example, Kreeft and Tacelli's (1994) book on Christian apologetics.) In the same way apologists in the theological tradition use reason to counter their opponent's questions and objections to arguments; in one sense, my intention is the same, notwithstanding certain contextual modifications, that is, *mutatis mutandis*, in physical education. Clearly, the intent of my reasoned arguments is not meant to lead to faith in the theological sense – although faith and reason are clear allies; however, the point that I wish to emphasise here is that a cogent philosophical argument is effective because it is based on logic or *logos*. Indeed, these are the same rules of reason used in both apologetics and in any other field of argument.

3 The term "profession" is used on purpose because as I see the practice of teaching belonging to commonly accepted professions like medicine and law. Clearly, teachers need knowledge of what they intend to teach so they have *something* to teach others. Likewise, I also wish to emphasise that teaching requires context sensitive judgement, ongoing reflection and interpersonal sensibility that share some similarities with the practices of medicine and law. I am also cognisant that some see teaching as a vocation alongside the priesthood, ministry, nursing and so on, because teaching requires a certain degree of genuine care and concern about the students they teach. Of course, this raises all sorts of issues concerning the place of theory in professional teacher education courses, whether teaching ought to be viewed as a profession, a semi-profession, a vocation or something else entirely different. Although interesting, space does not permit an extensive exploration here.

4 For relevant literature, see: Bergmann-Drewe (1999); Carr (1979a, 1983a, 1983b); Evans (1990); Freeman (2012); Green (1998); Hardman (2006); Kirk, (1994a, 1995, 1998a, 2006b, 2009, 2010); Laker (2000); Locke (1992); Marshall and Hardman (2000); McNamee (1998, 2005); Meakin (1983); Hawkins (2008); Parry (1987, 1988b, 1988d); Sparkes *et al.* (1993); Stroot (1994); Stroot *et al.* (1994); Tinning and Fitzclarence (1992); Tinning *et al.* (1994); and Thorpe (2003).

5 I will offer a detailed critique of the nature of play, games and sport in Chapter 4.

6 In Chapter 2 I offer a detailed critique of philosophical and theological positions of the body.

7 When citing classical texts such as the *Republic, Nicomachean Ethics, De Anima* and so on I will list the pagination first as it appears in the translation used, followed by Bekker or Stephanus numbers as is common practice in philosophy.

8 Except for Plato, who was ambivalent towards the body and subsequently held two distinct and paradoxical philosophical concepts of the body.

9 McNamee (2005) argues that at an analytical level, to claim that X is education or not education on the grounds of a pre-eminent criterion (cognitive depth and breadth) neglects to recognise the fact that there are competing conceptions of education. He goes on to argue that despite the fact that these conceptions embody particular evaluative elements regarding the nature of persons and society they all share the formal notion that education is the development of humankind towards the living of full and valuable lives. Physical education therefore can contribute to the living of valuable lives and hence is of educational value.

10 It is important to note that R. S. Peters' (1970) views surrounding the educational merit of practical pursuits within the curriculum changed significantly in "Education and the educated man". Although R. S. Peters does not specifically refute his earlier disparaging remarks about practical pursuits within *Ethics and Education*, he does argue that practical pursuits *could be* educationally valuable in and of themselves, if those who engaged in these activities were either transformed by theoretical understanding and/or pursued to the point of excellence. Unfortunately, it was too late as the damage had already been done and in a sense played a significant role in casting physical education out into the educational wilderness. For an excellent paper that discusses this topic, see MacAllister (2013).

11 At the time of writing this book, according to the Australian Bureau of Statistics (ABS) approximately, two-thirds (64 per cent, or 11.1 million people) of the Australian population aged fifteen years and over reported that they had participated in sports and physical recreation twelve months prior to the census. This information was retrieved from www.abs.gov.au/ausstats/abs@.nsf/Products/5A4BFF9E0C9B2C8EC A25796B00151513?opendocument.

12 Mountakis (2001) is right to argue that physical education aims to develop the whole student through all three domains – psychomotor, cognitive and affective – within an educational context. Whereas sport, particularly elite sport, aims at the

maximisation of performance in organised competitive environments. Clearly the latter is devoid of any educational content and hence sets it apart from physical education.

13 In the first section of Chapter 4 I provide a detailed critique of the "tricky triad", which I argue is the basis of much conceptual confusion in physical education.

14 I am cognisant that some may find the combining of the terms "sport" and "physical education" as problematic, but my intention is twofold. These are as follows: first, I do not want to engage in "languages-games", which as I have already argued, is a futile activity, and more importantly, will inevitably distract from my central thesis of this book. In saying this, Kirk's (2010) conceptual account of "physical education-as-sport-technique" in *Physical Education Futures* highlights how the dominant practice in physical education has been a disproportionate focus on the teaching and learning of specific "skills" and/or "techniques" related to playing a diverse array of games and sports. Consequently, my combining of the terms "sport" and "physical education" is apt in this instance, and hence justifies its conceptual usage herein; and lastly, I want to emphasise the significant role sport has played, and still plays, in physical education. Indeed, physical education within schools, particularly secondary schools, is still overwhelmingly dominated by the practice of teaching and learning sports related skills and/or techniques. In fact, I would go as far as to argue – maybe somewhat controversially – that to most practitioners, sport and physical education are synonymous in the same way that Kirk (2010) argues that physical education is "physical education-as-sport-technique". Indeed, this view has become solidified, both from extended reflection on the inadequacies of my own first-hand experiences and practice as a physical education practitioner, and reaffirmed from the observations of undergraduate pre-service teachers and experienced physical education practitioners teaching in a diverse array of primary and secondary schools over the years.

15 I provide a detailed historical overview of the games ethic tradition within education and physical education in the first section of Chapter 5.

16 See also Chapters I and II of *Whose Justice? Which Rationality* and Chapters VI to IX of *Three Rival Versions of Moral Enquiry*.

17 For instance, the term Health and Physical Education (HPE) is commonly used by most states and territories in Australia except for NSW, which uses the term Personal Development, Health and Physical Education (PDHPE) to designate this curriculum learning area within schools.

18 For relevant literature, see: Arnold (1984a, 1984b, 1988a, 1992, 1994, 1997, 2001, 2003); Aspin (1975); Bergmann-Drewe (2000); Carr (1998); Kirk (2002); Loland and McNamee (2000); McIntosh (1979); Meakin (1981, 1982, 1986); Morgan (1994, 2006, 2007a, 2007b, 2007c); Simon (1991); and Shields and Bredemeier (1995). Likewise, see Chapter 5 that follows for more detail.

19 I make my case for the role of sport and physical education in cultivating character in Chapter 5.

20 See for example, Siedentop (1994).

21 Case in point is the Victorian Certificate of Education (VCE) Study Design for Physical Education (Victoria, Australia) which has an external end-of-year examination worth 50 per cent and two prescribed school based pieces of assessment worth 25 per cent each. Contrary to what is claimed in the rationale ("integration of theoretical knowledge with practical application through participation in physical activity") it is not until much later in the prescription of "School-based Coursework (Units 3 and 4)" do we see that practical activities are only used as a means to an end, such as collecting data to be used in laboratory reports, data analysis and so on in written assessment tasks. See Victorian Curriculum and Assessment Authority (VCAA) (2010) study design for physical education.

22 See Honderich (2005) "Essence" for an explanation of essentialism.

23 The claim that there is no meaningful essence to the concept of physical education is surely false. Something can be socially constructed and still have an essence. For instance, the essential nature of a snowball is that it is round; however, that its constituent snow may have the property of roundness does not entail that snow is round, or that a snowball must be exactly spherical for it to be classed as a snowball. In a way the same applies to physical education. Even though there may not exist an essential core to physical education that is universal or *a priori* knowable does not mean that there are no easily recognisable core practices or particulars.

2 Philosophical and theological positions of the body

Changing concepts of the body and its influence upon sport and physical education

If we believe the works of some philosophers and theologians, the body is our link with the embarrassing animal part of human beings that must be mastered, forgotten and schooled so as not to lead us away from divine salvation. On the other hand, in educating human beings the Athenians of the Periclean Age were dedicated to balance and harmony to the point where much attention was given to it, along with philosophy, in the good life. However, with the collapse of the Roman Empire such ideals were forgotten as society gradually became feudalistic and consequently sport and physical education during this period was non-existent. As one of the few institutions remaining intact, the Christian Church exerted a powerful and profound impact upon the development of European civilisations; so the period beginning with the tenth century (Middle Ages) is noteworthy as we see the re-emergence of the metaphysical questions that were almost always linked to the religious beliefs of the time. The early medieval philosophers recognised and incorporated the works of Greek philosophy, in particular Plato and Aristotle's metaphysical concepts, to form a philosophy uniquely Christian in purpose. According to Copleston (1993), the two great ancient Greek philosophers – and later, neo-Platonism – exercised a great influence on the formation of Christian ideas and as a result the early Christian writers were interested in linking the intrinsic value and relevancy of ancient Greek philosophy with Christian theology. This means that medieval theologians were also students of philosophy as they tried to resolve deep metaphysical questions surrounding the Triune God. The subject of the corporeal nature of Jesus Christ, the influence of neo-Platonism and the position of the Church combined to create a distinct but inconsistent Christian view of the body and its worth (Mechikoff, 2010). Generally speaking, the philosophical views of the body during the Middle Ages reflected theological beliefs; as a result this period is significant to my thesis because no other period considered the nature of personhood so extensively, especially the perceived worth and value of the body, which in turn directly influenced the nature, development and scope of sport and physical education. The influence of Greek philosophy had a profound influence on how Christians viewed the body and soul during the Middle Ages. For instance, some factions in the Christian Church came to embrace Plato's view of the body as a corruptible influence on the soul and therefore not to be trusted. As a result, some Christians came to regard the body as an instrument of sin. This can be seen in the monastic life of early Christian monks who sought enlightenment by rising above all thoughts of the body, even to the extent of ignoring and neglecting essential physical needs. With such an attitude toward the body it would appear that physical education and sporting activities are altogether absent from the Middle Ages; however, this was not entirely the case. The Scholastics, on the other hand, and particularly St Thomas Aquinas, disagreed with the majority viewpoint (ascetic dualism) because they argued that the body is for the soul's good and therefore happiness requires the wellbeing of the body. Aquinas was influenced by Aristotle's view of personhood as an integral composite of body and soul whereby the soul needs a body to acquire knowledge. According to Mechikoff (2010), the theory of the unity of man was adopted by the Scholastics of the thirteenth century and supported by Orthodox Christians who argued that because God was omnipresent (including the body), therefore the body was good and consequently was not an instrument of sin.

The reason why theology and philosophy during the Middle Ages is so important has to do with the close connection the two enjoyed – not to mention the extensive literature on the body and soul – so that it is only natural to review the influential works of this period. For instance, theology during this period contained philosophical elements and the history of medieval philosophy is predominantly found within medieval theology. As stated by Pasnau (2002), the history of medieval philosophy *is* the history of medieval theology, without the theological content. This is further confirmed by Kenny (1993, p. 20) who states:

> … the greatest medieval philosophers were theologians first and philosophers second, it is to their theological treatises rather than to their commentaries on De Anima that one turns for their insights into philosophy of mind.

Consider the telling passage by Aquinas (1265–1274/1993a, First Part, Question 75) from the prologue to his treatise on the body and soul: "Now the theologian considers that nature of man in relation to the soul; but not in relation to the body, except in so far as the body has relation to the soul." Therefore, both theologians and philosophers of the medieval period did not see a division between theology and philosophy, which is why they took human nature seriously as their central focus and hence both studied the soul, the relationship of the soul to the body and so on. This is why it is to this period I will turn to investigate the changing concepts of the body, particularly its influence upon the attitudes concerning the education of human beings physically.

The history of philosophy will attest to a vast array of complex and intricate difficulties in attempting the momentous task of illuminating and resolving the mind–body problem. Shaffer (1965) comments that the problem remains a "source of acute discomfort" for philosophers, as considerable attention has been given to resolving this problem but yet there is still no solution that stands out as markedly superior. Likewise, this same problem has become a preoccupation for some philosophers of sport concerned with corporeal embodiment and the question of the relationship of mind and body and its application to or expression in sport, and as a result it has been actively pursued in the relevant literature.[1] However, philosophical efforts concerned with embodiment in education by physical educationalists to my knowledge are scarce and antiquated. In particular, attempts to overcome the dominant discourse that seems to compartmentalise education into the education of the mind and education of the body are paradigmatic examples of contemporary education's tendency to view the person as a dualistic being composed of two separate entities: superior mind and inferior body.[2] It therefore seems appropriate to canvass anew the basis of contemporary perceptions surrounding the philosophical-anthropological positions of personhood because when the body is disparaged and made subservient to the mind in a relationship, then physical education will be relegated and marginalised compared to traditional forms of intellectual education. The metaphysical dualistic tradition is one of the most damaging and significant events in the history of physical education, in which Plato, as the chief architect of dualism and Descartes his accomplice, are the key symbols in the betrayal of the body in Western culture. Consequently, if we want sport and physical education to be given a legitimate place within educational institutions it will be necessary to reconcile the dualism of the mind and body which lies at the foundation of Western philosophy and our culture from Plato to Descartes and on into the twenty-first century. Hence, it would appear to be logical, given the multitudinous spaces in which humans move, that sport and physical education could benefit greatly from the understanding of corporeal embodiment that is acknowledged and accepted in the phenomenological works of Merleau-Ponty and other existential phenomenologists; these theorists argue that a person's body is not simply another object in the world, but a mode of meaningful communication and interaction with it. Therefore, for the purposes of this chapter I will be concerned with the critical discussion of four issues: first, I survey the philosophical and theological views of the body in the Middle Ages, in particular Aristotle's position on the body that had a profound impact upon St Thomas Aquinas' treatise on the body and soul; second, I review René Descartes' conception of personhood, which has been enormously influential in philosophy and Western culture; third, I outline how Merleau-Ponty's account of phenomenology is ideal for combating the Platonic–Cartesian tradition; and, lastly, I discuss the ramifications of shifting the two metaphysical positions in sport and physical education from "having a body" to the lived-body experience of "being a body" which emphasises the inherent unity of human beings.

Aristotle's view of personhood: the soul as the actuality of the body

Some factions of the early Christian Church embraced Plato's view of personhood, some accepted Aristotle's idea of a composite substance and some rejected Greek ideas altogether due to their pagan connection. However, it is Aristotle's philosophical position of personhood that is in direct contrast to the views espoused by Plato in the *Phaedo* that is noteworthy, since he emphasised the unity of human beings; this is important here to my thesis because it provides cogent justifications for the psychosomatic relationship between mind and body that sport and physical education so desperately needs. By holding such a position we can overcome the tendency of contemporary education to view agents as dualistic entities and bring into focus the sometimes ignored and forgotten dimension of our corporeal embodiment in education, which values the worth of the body in conjunction with the mind in a unified and harmonious relationship. It is to Aristotle's works that I now turn to gain a better insight into why his views of the body and soul were so influential.

Aristotle (1986, p. 126; 402a) at the beginning of *De Anima* points out that knowledge of the soul can make a significant contribution to understanding nature, because the soul is the "first principle of living things". He goes on to argue that the problem about substance and what a thing is, is not easy to ascertain because each subject employs different methods and frames their definitions differently. To Aristotle (1986, p. 156; 412a), some natural bodies have life and some do not; however, every natural body that partakes in life would be a substance in the way that a composite (form and matter) is. The body cannot be the soul because the soul gives the body life; and so the body, then, must be matter to the soul, whilst the soul will be the actuality of such a body. Therefore the soul is the realisation of the body and is inseparable from it even though there may be some parts that nothing prevents from being separable because they are not being the actualities of any body (Aristotle, 1986, p. 158; 413a). Aristotle identifies having a soul with being alive and goes on to outline the various ways in which the soul is responsible for each of the ways of life in which the soul as a hierarchy of parts emerges. Even though Aristotle comments that he is unsure whether the soul is the "... actuality of a body in this way or rather is a sailor of a boat" he does not tell us whether "another kind of soul ... can be separated ..." from the body, and as a result he remains equivocal (Aristotle, 1986, pp. 158–160; 413a–b). According to Copleston (1993), it is clear that Aristotle does not adhere to Platonic dualism in the *De Anima*, for he makes the soul to be the actuality (entelechy) of the body, so that the two form one substance. He goes on to add that Aristotle insisted that the Platonic School of thought failed to provide a satisfactory account of the soul's union with the body, it seems to suppose that the soul can fit itself into any body. This cannot be the case, because Aristotle stated that every substance is spoken of in three ways: as form, as matter and as the composite which in this case is the ensouled thing. It is not that the body is the actuality of the soul, but that the soul is the actuality of some body and as a result the soul is neither without the body or a kind of body (Aristotle, 1986, p. 161; 414a). Aristotle goes on to comment that the soul belongs to a body and for this reason is present in a body of an appropriate kind. Therefore, to the Aristotelian, it is for the good of the soul to be united with the body so that it can exercise all of its faculties. Such a position was adopted by the medieval Scholastics such as St Thomas Aquinas, who is considered as the representative of the medieval intellectual synthesis, particularly in relation to the evaluation of the body.

The body and soul according to St Thomas Aquinas: the essential bodily component in the unity of substances

In addressing the topic of body and soul, Aquinas (1265–1274/1993a, I, Q75) states quite clearly that man is composed of a "spiritual and corporeal substance" in his exploration of the nature of the soul. His reply is that the "... soul, which is the first principle of life, is not a body, but the act of a body ..." (1265–1274/1993a, I, Q75, A1). However, there appears to be much confusion about whether Aquinas argues that the soul is one thing and the body another as per the opening of the pro-logue to his *Treatise on Man*. According to Pasnau (2002), when Aquinas declares that human beings are composed of a spiritual and corporeal substance these are mere statements of a view and therefore not arguments in favour of substance dualism. The crux of Aquinas' (1265–1274/1993a) argument comes in Question 75, Article 4, where he concludes that "... a man is not a soul only, but something composed of soul and body". This assertion has more to do with how we should demarcate where one object ends and another begins. Aquinas (1265–1274/1993a, I, Q75, A4) reasons that human beings must engage in sensation because sensation is plainly an operation carried out by the body and as a result, the nature of person-hood is not just about a soul, but soul and body. Certainly, this does not mean that sensation is the only operation that identifies human beings with their bodies as well as souls. There are still other operations that we attribute to human beings and which obviously require a body. For instance, what about playing cricket, baseball, football, walking and so on? It would be incorrect to deduce that Aquinas is arguing that the body is a mere instrument. Indeed, Pasnau (2002) makes the point that Aquinas is concerned not with those essential operations that every human being must engage in, but with operations that every human being is capable of engaging in, in order to count as human. Therefore, to Aquinas sensation and thought are essential human operations, whereas in this case playing cricket, base-ball, football and walking are not essential to being human in this same sense, but the body is required because without the body we could not engage in sensation. This is further confirmed by Aquinas (1265–1274/1993a) who argues in Question 75, Article 3, that:

> ... sensation and the consequent operations of the sensitive soul are evidently accompanied with change in the body; thus in the act of vision, the pupil of the eye is affected by a reflection of colour: and so with the other senses.

It is noteworthy to mention that Aquinas' (1265–1274/1993a, Q75, IV) position totally rejects the notion that he is a substance dualist because his views depend on accommodating the idea that the capacity for sensation is an essential part of being human, which is contrary to Plato's views espoused in the *Phaedo*. Fur-thermore, the capacity for sensation, even in its essential respects, requires the body, which is also contrary to Descartes' conception of Cartesian dualism.

After considering the nature of the soul in Question 75, Aquinas shifts his focus to the relationship of soul and body, particularly the soul's union with the body in Question 76. In the first article of Question 76, Aquinas concentrates on how this union is accomplished by recounting Aristotle's argument from *De Anima*, Book II, Chapter 2, "... that the soul is the actuality of some body", immediately followed by the challenge that if the intellectual soul is not the form of the body, then some other account needs to be given that explains intellectual cognition as mine or yours. He goes on to add, that because the body engages in sensation, and sensation requires the body, the body must be part of me. The goal of Question 76, Article 1, was not to refute directly any of the popular theories that existed at the time, such as monopsychism, but rather was an indirect refutation that non-reductive theories cannot account for the unity of soul and body (Pasnau, 2002). In terms of coming to grips with Aquinas' thinking about the unity of soul and body, the example offered by Aristotle in *De Anima*, of the material of an axe and its capacity to cut, can be useful in a limited capacity (p. 157; 412b). This example may be a convenient illustration of the hylomorphic theory of substance; however, Aquinas went to great lengths to emphasise that because the axe is an artefact, not a substance, the shape of an axe is an accidental form, not a substantial one. The use of artefacts may not be an entirely satisfactory guide to understanding Aquinas' thinking about substances, because artefacts lack the unity that human beings and other natural substances have. Aquinas (1265–1274/1993a, I, Q76, A4) does make a distinction by arguing that substantial forms make a thing exist, whereas accidental forms make a thing be such. The same applies to the body and soul. The human soul does not change something that already exists, but brings it into being (Aquinas, 1265–1274/1993a, I, Q4, A3). Therefore, a substantial form is that which makes a thing be what it is and without which it could not exist. This is extended further by Aquinas (1265–1274/1993a, I, Q76, A8) when he argues that substantial form should be applied not only to the whole, but to each part of the whole. Here the parts are dependant on the survival of the human being as long as it exists. Consequently, a corpse is not a human being, and similarly for all the parts of the corpse. This assertion is consistent with Question 2, articles 1 and 2, in which Aquinas establishes that the body is part of a human being since the body is needed for essential human functions, as well as the establishment of the soul's existence on the basis of its capacity for continued operation. As a result, a person's existence is contingent upon his ability for ongoing function, which is confirmed at death since the body ceases to exist and therefore ceases to function. If we look at a human being and ask whether the body is separable from the whole person, it would appear to be the case because we can lose arms and legs without the person ceasing to exist (Pasnau, 2002). From such a perspective it certainly would appear as if the body can be separable from the whole person; however, Aquinas rather focuses on whether the living substances such as arms and legs could survive without the whole, which in this case they cannot. This is the insightfulness of Aquinas, because the soul exists throughout our body giving it life, rather than as some mysterious non-extended force located at some point within the body moving the body like a sailor piloting a ship. This account has the advantage that it explains the unity of soul and body in such a way to allow for the human soul's unique independence relative to the body. A goes on to reply to Question 76, Article 1 by arguing that the only accept theory of human nature is the principle "… by which we understand, whether be called the intellect or the intellectual soul, is the form of the body". Aristotle (1986, p. 161; 414a), states that:

> Now that by which we live and perceive is spoken of in two ways, just as with that by which we know … and in the same way by that which we are healthy we mean on the one hand health and on the other some part of the body or a whole body. Of these knowledge and health are indeed shape and a kind of form and an account, and as it were activity of the recipient, know-ledge of the knowing faculty, health of the healthy faculty … but the soul is that by which we primarily live and perceive and think.

Aquinas (1994) goes on to explain in his commentary on Aristotle's *De Anima* that both body and soul are principles of life, but the soul comes before the body because the soul is the form of the living body and the primary principle of our life and feeling and movement and understanding. He goes on to argue that it is by the body that we come to know whether we are healthy: only insofar as the body has health are we said to be healthy. Likewise, just as our souls come to know insofar as they have knowledge, thereby knowledge itself is that by which the soul is said to be in a state of knowing. To Aquinas it seems reasonable to propose that the body and the intellect are a unified whole because our intellect makes use of the body as a means of obtaining information. However, Aquinas seems unsatisfied with the causal relationship, and actually questions whether the intellect is united to the body as its "motor", which he notes is Plato's view of the soul–body relationship in Question 76, Article 3; as a result Aquinas' own type of hylomorphic theory seems able to give human beings the sort of unity required of a genuine substance. Aquinas in Question 76, Article 8, defends his claim that the soul, like all forms, exists as a whole in every part because every part is alive, and to say that a body has a soul is basically to say that it has life. The benefit of Aquinas' account of the unity of body and soul is that it provides an explanation of the human soul's "peculiar autonomy" relative to the body (Pasnau, 2002, p. 94).

After Plato, the most famous exponent of dualism was René Descartes. His conception of personhood has been enormously influential in philosophy and Western culture. As a result, it will be necessary to review Cartesian dualism in order to discover its flaws and in turn offer cogent arguments rejecting the rigid Cartesian conception of the mind as a distinct and superior substance somehow controlling the body. I will argue in favour of a phenomenological anthropology in which a person's body is not simply another object in the world; rather, our bodies are modes of meaningful communication and interaction with it. I will now turn my attention to a critique of Cartesian dualism.

roblem according to René Descartes: the
n of human beings into both a body and a

p. 12; §17) starts his *Meditations* with a clear statement
iry ... to demolish everything completely and start again
ions if I wanted to establish anything ... that was stable
)escartes, to reach knowledge it is necessary to eliminate
could be doubted and keep only those of which we could be
certain. Hence, calling everything into radical doubt is the method adopted by
Descartes to reach certain truths because once the "... foundations of a building
are undermined, anything built on them collapses of its own accord ...'"; and so
to cast doubt on the very foundations of one's own beliefs we arrive at the absolute. As a result Descartes first considers his senses, which he believes are the
origin of many of his ideas (Descartes, 1641/1986, p. 12; §18). His argument
that all senses ought to be considered uncertain is confirmed when he states:

> Whatever I have up till now accepted as most true I have acquired either
> from the senses or through the senses. But from time to time I have found
> that the senses deceive, and it is prudent never to trust completely those who
> have deceived us even once.

> (Descartes, 1641/1986, p. 12; §18)

Descartes makes it clear in the First Meditation that as long as there is doubt that
some of our sense-based beliefs are inconclusive and that there is difficulty in
determining what is true and what is false, then we ought to be cautious in trust-
ing any particular sense-based belief. In the Second Meditation Descartes
attempts to lay down the foundations that will allow him to reconstruct his own
knowledge on a secure basis. He does this by recognising the one thing that
cannot be doubted, which is that "I" certainly exist, and goes on to conclude that
"... *I am, I exist*, is necessarily true whenever it is put forward by me or conceived in my mind" (Descartes, 1641/1986, p. 17; §25). He continues to argue
that thinking is "inseparable from me", and therefore it must be our essential
nature to be a thinking thing; however, then he asks: "A thing that thinks. What is
that?", to which his response is that a thinking thing (mind) cannot be a body, as I
can conceive of myself without a body, and as a result it must be a purely mental
substance (Descartes, 1641/1986, pp. 17–19; §26–29). It is not until much later,
in the Sixth Meditation, when Descartes (1641/1986) examines material things
and the distinction between the mind and body, that we get a real sense of his
radical view of the body. He continues his idea that the body "... is simply an
extended, non-thinking thing ... in which I find in myself faculties for certain
special modes of thinking, namely imagination and sensory perception" (Descartes, 1641/1986, 54; §78). Descartes goes on to add that there is great difference
between the mind and the body because the body is by its nature divisible, while
the mind is indivisible. His argument is based on the idea that when we consider

the mind we are unable to distinguish any parts within a mind because we understand ourselves to be single and complete; whereas when it comes to the body, if a part of the body is removed, such as a foot or arm, nothing has therefore been taken away from the mind and as result the mind is not affected by all parts of the body. In accord with such assertions, Descartes advanced a rather strict mechanistic physiological view of the body by regarding the body as a kind of "clock" or "machine" which obeys the "laws of its nature" when it completely fulfils the wishes of the clockmaker. This is further confirmed, when he states:

> ... I might consider the body of man as a kind of machine equipped with and made up of bones, nerves, muscles, veins, blood and skin in such a way that, even if there were no mind in it, it would still perform all the same movements as it now does in those cases where movement is not under the control of the will or, consequently, of the mind.
>
> (Descartes, 1641/1986, p. 58; §84)

Accordingly, Descartes viewed human beings as composed of two distinct substances of mind and body, in which the essential characteristics differ radically. For instance, the body is viewed as an unthinking, extended, material substance, whereas the mind was a thinking, unextended, immaterial substance. In addition, the analogy of the body as machine further confirms the body as an unconscious machine that conforms to the laws of nature, but the true essence of a person is the mind which is a conscious and free substance not disposed to the mechanical laws of nature. As a result, the mind and body are viewed to be radically distinct and independent.

According to Meier (1975), the presumption of such an extreme bifurcation of mind and body causes immediate difficulties when we reflect on lived human experiences, because although specific human activities may be performed unconsciously and mechanically, such as reflex action, selected aspects of conscious perception – such as sensations like pain, hunger, thirst and the expression of emotions and passions – significantly challenge the dualistic structure as a result of the intimate union between mind and body. In this case, Descartes was aware of the sense experiences in the Sixth Meditation since he asserts the interrelationship of mind and body is intuitively obvious because of a person's ownership of clear and distinct notions of their union:

> Nature also teaches me, by these sensations of pain, hunger, thirst and so on, that I am not merely present in a ship, but that I am very closely joined and, as it were, intermingled with it, so that I and the body form a unit. If this were not so, I, who am nothing but a thinking thing, would not feel pain when the body was hurt, but would perceive the damage purely by the intellect, just as a sailor perceives by sight if anything in his ship is broken. Similarly, when the body needed food or drink, I should have explicit understanding of the fact, instead of having confused sensations of hunger and thirst. For these sensations of hunger, thirst, pain and so on are nothing

but confused modes of thinking which arise from the union and, as it were, intermingling of the mind with the body.

(Descartes, 1641/1986, p. 56; §81)

In addition, to these "confused modes" of self-consciousness, numerous other occasions have highlighted the union of the mind and body. Of course, it is not unreasonable to argue that the mind has the ability to consciously suppress sensual appetites. However, Meier (1975) raises the interesting point that particular mental states, such as excitement, appear to have a noticeable physiological affect on the cardiorespiratory system and in the intensity of performance of physical activities. To explain consciously directed action, Descartes clearly acknowledged that the body diverges from its mechanical function "under the control of the will", which is contingent upon the mind; however, such assumptions can only occur if there is some form of structural unity of the mind and body. Meier (1975) goes on to comment that the admission that the mind indeed consciously influences the movements of the body, and conversely is affected by physiological states or activities, clearly demonstrates a crucial problem of Cartesian dualism: How can an extended material substance be influenced by a spiritual substance that has no extension and consequently no spatial location for interaction? Descartes, in a feeble attempt to resolve this problem, states that the mind is connected to the body, but the nature of this interaction is muddled and confused. Aware of the necessity to better explain his mind–body interaction more efficiently, Descartes goes on to state in imprecise and in non-specific general terms that a person experiences a basically unexplained primary notion of the interaction of the mind and body, which is only vaguely understood, but is known by the senses. According to Meier (1975, pp. 55–56), to resolve the problem Descartes asserts that the interaction of the mind and body is limited to one central and specific location of the body, "the pineal gland, situated near the top of the brain ... wherein the mind can exercise control of the body's movements and conversely be affected by the animal spirits agitated by physiological change...", and as a result the question of how there be an interaction between a substance that is spiritual and a substance that is material was frustratingly not answered.

The problem with relating mind and body in the manner attempted by Descartes is that it appears to be artificially created. Meier (1975) makes the strong point that it is extremely difficult, if not *a priori* impossible, to meaningfully synthesise two elements of such discontinuous and diverse natures into a functioning, complex whole. Consequently, any attempts to advance a position of man as composed of two radically distinct substances is simply a fatal error. Ryle (1949, p. 17), in his famous attack on Cartesian dualism, argues that "the dogma of the Ghost in the Machine" is "... entirely false, and false not in detail but in principle ... it is one big mistake and mistake of special kind ... namely a category-mistake" (see Chapter I: Descartes' Myth). He goes on to illuminate what is meant by the phrase "category-mistake" by utilising a series of analogies, such as the foreigner visiting Oxford or Cambridge University for the first time. The foreigner, after being shown the various colleges, libraries, faculties, playing fields and so on, asks: "But where is the University?" To Ryle (1949), the foreign visitor has mistakenly attributed the University as an extra member of the class to which these other institutions belong and as a result the problem arises from the foreigner's inability to use certain concepts such as "University" and so on appropriately. Likewise the representation of a person as a ghost within a machine is just another example of a category mistake, because to liken a human being's thinking, feeling and purposive actions solely in a reductionist and atomistic way is to misunderstand the human body as a complex organising unit in which the mind must be another part of the complex organising unit, albeit made of a different "sort of stuff" and "sort of structure". Ryle goes on to argue that the dogma of the ghost in the machine is as absurd as conjoining terms of different types, such as a consumer who may say that they bought a left-hand glove and a right-hand glove and a pair of gloves. Consequently, the ghost in the machine problem maintains that there exist bodies and minds, physical processes and mental processes, mechanical causes of corporeal movements and mental causes of corporeal movements. I agree with Ryle that the contrast between mind and body can sometimes rest upon a category mistake, which is shown in linguistic expressions that seem to be logically absurd. This is further reaffirmed by Ryle (1949, pp. 23–24) who states:

> The "reduction" of the material world to mental states and processes, as well as the "reduction" of mental states and processes to physical states and processes, presupposes the legitimacy of the disjunction "Either there exist minds or there exist bodies (but not both)". It would be like saying, "Either she bought a left-hand and right-hand glove or she bought a pair of gloves (but not both)".

According to Ryle (1949, p. 24), to use the linguistic expression that there "exist minds" and to say that there "exist bodies" does not mean that they are two different species of existence because the term "existence" is not some generic word like the use of the term "rising", which has different senses such as "the tide is rising", "inflation is rising" and so on. He goes on to add that just as the differences between the mind and body were represented in a common framework of categories of "things", "processes", "causes and effects", in which minds are "things", but different types of "things" from bodies, so the foreign visitor expected the University to be an extra building, rather like the others but considerably different. Such an analogy is useful in that it highlights how Descartes' theory represented minds as extra centres of causal processes rather like machines, but also considerably different because these occurrences (mental activity) signified non-mechanical processes and as a result minds must be non-spatial.

Furthermore, Maslin (2001) goes on to highlight a variety of issues surrounding dualism from which I will only list three problems. First, for the Cartesian dualist possession of a mind is all or nothing. There is no in-between or due consideration given to ourselves and the diverse range of living creatures that exist. Second, the existence of minds basically has nothing to do with what takes place in the brain and nervous system generally and as a result existence is deprived of a function. Finally, probably the most piercing attack on dualism is attributed to Kant. Descartes claims that one and only one soul is associated with and acts through the human body, but Kant asks: how do you count souls? For instance, incorporeal substances don't by their nature occupy an area of space at a given time and so this justification of identity cannot apply. For argument's sake let's assume that they did: How would we distinguish one soul from the next? As a result we are left with an incoherent mess surrounding the concept of the soul. Kant argues that just because we are self-conscious is not enough. Kant (1781/2007, p. 336; A363) writes:

> The identity of the consciousness of myself at different times is therefore only a formal condition of my thoughts and their coherence, and proves in no way the numerical identity of my subject.

The point Kant is making is that any thought or mental state which is mine is indeed one and the self same "I" who has these experiences and at no time can they be used to prove that what I basically am is a simple, non-composite, incorporeal substance, a Cartesian soul (Maslin, 2001). Subsequently, concepts that have no application within the realm of experience are empty of content and so the concept of a person as an incorporeal soul would seem to be basically meaningless. However, if we think of people as familiar bodily entities from our experience then we are more likely to have a genuine and meaningful concept of the person. This is primarily linked to the idea that when we think of embodied beings we can always differentiate one person from another at a given time or over a period of time primarily because embodied beings cannot occupy the same space at the same time or the same spaces at successive times.

I will now turn my attention to Merleau-Ponty's phenomenological perspective of what it is to be human, which is in direct contrast to the Platonic–Cartesian tradition. The implications here are significant: because such a position implies that there no longer exists a philosophical division between the object and subject since the world begins from the body and provides the means by which we can develop a sense of our own identity and at the same time come to know the world through our embodiment. It seems clear to me at this juncture that physical education could benefit significantly from the establishment of a legitimate understanding of the body in education before attempting to develop philosophical justifications for its inclusion within educational institutions. It is to this I now turn.

Merleau-Ponty's phenomenological perspective of the body

Rather than emphasising and advocating an inherently dualistic distinction that is flawed, an approach that accounts for both consciousness and embodiment is significantly more productive in a subject like physical education, which has a clear and distinct body focus. Subsequently, Maurice Merleau-Ponty focused his attention to a significant extent on resolving the Platonic–Cartesian problem of how human beings can experience themselves as a "meaningful core" that makes sense of the world from "being-in-the-world" from a phenomenological perspective. Phenomenology to Merleau-Ponty (1945/1962, p. vii) is a search for a philosophy that can offer an account of "space, time and the world" as we "live" in it, rather than theorising about it. Central to what it is to be a human being is the idea that "... I am the absolute source ... of my existence ... for I alone bring into being for myself ..." my own personal engagement with the world, rather than as a detached subject or consciousness advanced by Descartes (Merleau-Ponty, 1945/1962, p. ix). Consequently, "I" has meaning because I cannot be aware of myself as a subject without also being aware of other subjects, and as a result, to accept the existence of other subjects as well as myself is to accept that there is a world in which all these different subjects experience, each from their own perspective, that which provides the "permanent horizon" for all our experiences. Therefore, I am not as a subject, outside of time and space but necessarily "incarnate" or "embodied" in a certain historical situation. Merleau-Ponty (1945/162, p. xiv) reinforces this point when he writes:

> ... it is necessary that my existence should never be reduced to my bare awareness of existing, but that it should take in also an awareness that one may have it, and thus include my incarnation in some nature.... The true *Cogito* does not define the subject's existence in terms of the thought he has of existing, and furthermore does not convert the indubitability of the world into the indubitability of thought about the world, nor finally does it replace the world itself by the world as meaning. On the contrary it recognizes my thought itself as an inalienable fact, and does away with any kind of idealism in revealing me as "being-in-the-world".

Therefore, my experiences are experiences of the world, and the world is what gives meaning to my experiences. I cannot disconnect and filter out the world itself from the world as meaningful to me because a human being is a "being-in-the-world". It is impossible to withdraw completely from the world, but we can change the way we perceive the world by no longer viewing the world in a scientific way. Instead Merleau-Ponty (1945/1962) urges us to train ourselves to perceive the world differently and in a sense create "a new cogito" between the thinking self and what it is like to experience ourselves from the first person perspective. Subsequently, the "essence of consciousness" is the rediscovery of our attempt to understand our own lives in the world and so in a sense the "essence" of phenomenology is to understand how perception actually works in our interactions with the world around us; and as a result our "essence" cannot be segregated from our "existence" (Merleau-Ponty, 1945/1962, pp. xvii–xviii).

According to Matthews (2006, pp. 19–20), phenomenology as Merleau-Ponty sees it combines a form of subjectivism with a form of objectivism in the sense that it acknowledges that all experience is someone's experience because "how things appear" means "how they appear to a particular 'subject'". Since the being of subjects is being-in-the-world, an account of a subjective experience is not an account of "pure being" because my experiences of the world are "inseparable from subjectivity and intersubjectivity"; therefore our engagement in the world exists independently of our experience in it, but in a sense it describes our existence in the world, our various modes of being-in-the-world, which come before conscious reflection and theorising.

It is noteworthy at this juncture to mention that Merleau-Ponty viewed human beings as an "incarnate" subject, a unity not union of physical, biological and psychological processes. He asserted that the human body is not an "enclosed mechanism" or object subject to the inclinations of the soul; rather, the body is a subject in itself, gaining its subjectivity from itself as an embodied consciousness. Merleau-Ponty (1942/1963, p. 202) reinforces this point further when he writes:

> To say that the soul acts on the body is wrongly to suppose a univocal notion of the body and to add to it a second force which accounts for the rational significance of certain conducts.

Consequently, the human body is a fundamental unity, a single mode of being, which is both difficult to articulate and to examine. Meier (1975) makes the point that human beings seem to be able to use their body as a type of instrument, but not in the same sense as we use a chair. Consequently, there is a real sense that the body is not simply another object in the world; rather, it is "anchored" in the world as a person's mode of communication and interaction with it. As a result, the rigid Cartesian conception of the mind as a distinct and superior substance somehow controlling the body, rather than being logically impossible, may be remedied. Merleau-Ponty provides an alternative approach in dealing with the mind–body problem by arguing that an account of personhood and reality cannot be delineated with total lucidity, which is asserted in idealistic positions of human beings that argue that consciousness is different and separate from the extended, material body and the world. Merleau-Ponty (1945/1962, p. 231) states:

> Whether it is a question of another's body or my own, I have no means of knowing the human body other than that of living it, which means taking up on my account the drama which is being played out in it, losing myself in it. I am my body, at least wholly to the extent that I possess experience, and yet at the same time my body is as it were a "natural" subject, a provisional sketch of my total being. Thus experience of one's own body runs counter to the reflective procedure which detaches subject and object from each other, and which gives us only the thought about the body, or the body as an idea, and not the experience of the body or the body in reality.

Consequently, incarnation and embodiment cannot be achieved solely from *a priori* grounds or even segregated into clearly demarcated aspects of being.

Merleau-Ponty argues that when we study humans as an embodied subject, we should study human beings as a unity of physical, biological and psychological relationships. He states:

> ... matter, life, and mind could not be defined as three orders of reality or three sorts of beings, but as three planes of signification or three forms of unity. In particular, life would not be a force which is added to physio-chemical processes; its originality would be that of modes of connection without equivalent in the physical domain, that of phenomena gifted with a proper structure and which bind each other together according to a special dialectic.
>
> (Merleau-Ponty, 1924/1963, p. 201)

The body is the primary mode of communication in the relationship with the world and is the central locus of expression and meaning-producing acts. This is further highlighted and reinforced by Merleau-Ponty (1945/1962, p. 273):

> My body is the seat or rather the very actuality of the phenomenon of expression (*Ausdruck*), and there the visual and auditory experiences, for example, are pregnant one with the other, and their expressive value is the ground of the antepredicative unity of the perceived world, and, through it, of verbal expression (*Darstellung*) and the intellectual significance (*Bedeutung*). My body is the fabric into which all objects are woven, and it is, at least in relation to the perceived world, the general instrument of my "comprehension".

Through corporeality we are open to the world and it is by means of this "dialectic" communication that meaning arises. For instance, human beings cannot be reduced or broken into specific component parts to be studied without important loss of significance because the body is a "meaningful core" in the world and as a result must remain united for it to have meaning.

Consequently, "meaning" in this sense is constructed and constituted by the body's engagement in the world and hence must always be worldly, because there is no world without the body. Matthews (2002, 2006) makes the point about Merleau-Ponty's work that to be an embodied subject is to be an active being in a world with needs; these needs in turn motivate actions in relation to which elements in the surrounding environment are meaningful. He goes on to add that to be in the world is partly to be in a world of one's own, since we do not create the things in the world in the sense of bringing them into existence, but our needs and thoughts about the world are embedded in our nature as a biological organism, and give a unity of meaning to those objects which makes them into a single world. It is noteworthy at this juncture to mention that, contrary to Descartes, the burden of meaning is not caused by a universal consciousness but by bodily experience, and as a result Merleau-Ponty rejected the argument that the body is merely a passive receiving station for objects. Merleau-Ponty's account of embodiment is radically different from the extreme bifurcation adopted by Descartes, which depicts human beings as two diverse and distinct substances with the body predisposed to the control of the mind. According to Meier (1975), the theory of the body is implicitly a theory of perception because human beings can only learn to know "expressive unity" by being engaged in the body's action as it relates to the sensing world. He goes on to add that the characteristic features of human beings as embodied consciousness have no clear points of demarcation because the distinction between the subjective and objective extremities is clouded in the experience of living in the world and the meaning-woven body. Consequently, a human being's engagement in the world develops personal meaning in the process of actively embodying him or herself.

Although my critique of phenomenology as Merleau-Ponty sees it has not been exhaustive, it was nevertheless my intent to provide a philosophical account of the mind–body problem that unifies the body and at the same time recognises the body as a "meaningful core" as a means to establishing a legitimate understanding of the body in education so that an inextricably body-linked subject like physical education will achieve the recognition it desires. It is my assertion that "being a body" is radically different from "having a body" or "using a body". For instance, my body is more than a mere machine or set of physico-chemical systems; it is something I could not do without because as a living being my body is not a mere object in the world but something I live, something I inhabit and the means of my own subjective experience. Phenomenology according to Merleau-Ponty combines a form of subjectivism with a form of objectivism in the sense that all my experiences are my own experiences in terms of how they appear to me and therefore must be descriptions of subjective experience (Matthews, 2002). For an embodied being-in-the-world a description of subjective experience is not a description of some inner thought process, but a description of our engagement in a world which exists independently of our experience of it. Phenomenology in this sense is a kind of "anti-philosophical" philosophy because it does not try and rise above our practical involvement with the world in order to understand why the world is the way it is, but "describes our existence in the world, our various modes of being-in-the-world, which comes before conscious reflection and theorizing" (Matthews, 2002, p. 20). The ramifications of this radical shift is significant to my thesis because embodiment is more often objectified and reduced when it should be expressed or celebrated as a meaningful form of knowledge. As a result, the phenomenological conceptions of Merleau-Ponty and others like Whitehead are significant for three reasons. First, such ideas are critical to resolving the mind–body problem persistently besetting sport and physical education. Second, it permits a human being a unique environment in which to experience his or her full and meaningful humanity as incarnate consciousness. Lastly, the power of this kind of knowing is in harmony with important principles commonly pursued in education: freedom to explore, discover, express, invent and create (Kretchmar, 1995). Taken from this viewpoint our body and its motility can be seen to have equal claim for attention in education alongside other activities which give life meaning.

The meaning of the radical shift in the two metaphysical positions of lived human experiences in sport and physical education: "being a body" rather than "having a body"

There is no question that physical education is inextricably linked to the body and consequently the philosophical position of the body and our concept of human nature will have a direct bearing on how we think human beings should behave, be educated, and in this case, how we think they should be educated physically. In much of contemporary sport and physical education theory and practice, there appears to be an almost implicit form of Cartesian dualism, despite occasional claims to the contrary. Take for instance Weiss' (1979) dualistic conception of personhood. In his account, he repeatedly emphasises that the fundamental task of the athlete in sport is to "correct the disequilibrium between the mind and body" so that athletes become one with their bodies in training and comes to "accept their bodies as themselves" (Weiss, 1979, pp. 189–191). He goes on to emphasise throughout his analysis that the mind has power over the body, by arguing that "to be fully a master of one's body ... man uses his mind to dictate what the body is to do" until it proceeds in accord with the mind's expectations (Weiss, 1979, pp. 189–190). The dualistic structure evident in the preceding statements demonstrates rather a common tendency to view the body as an entity that needs to be restructured, disciplined, managed and conquered, and that clearly depicts human beings as "having" a body rather than fully "being" a body. Furthermore, in accordance with such an orientation science seems to have an exclusive sanction to analyse, examine and manipulate human beings corporeal nature; so it is not a surprise that the approach adopted by sport scientists is almost totally atomistic, instrumental and mechanistic as a result of the human body being viewed from a biomedical engineering model. This is further reinforced by McKay *et al.* (1990, p. 60) who argue that the human body is seldom portrayed as a "... pleasurable site for ecstatic, aesthetic, vertiginous, autotelic, sensuous and holistic experiences", but portrayed as a biomechanical object that must be managed, maintained, conditioned and repaired for instrumental reasons, such as improving performance or physical appearance. Consequently, the athlete is regarded as an instrument or reduced into parts to be studied from a biological–scientific perspective with the express purpose of altering or controlling his or her corporeal aspects.

However, as my review of Merleau-Ponty's phenomenology of the body in the previous section demonstrates, it is incorrect and impossible to provide an account of embodiment solely from *a priori* grounds or even to attempt to segregate the body into two distinct and independent substances. By rejecting the Cartesian conception of personhood, which depicts the body as a machine or instrument that needs to be mastered, the phenomenologist perspective permits human beings to experience the depth and richness of the central feature of his or her humanness and in a sense "create a new truth" about his or her active corporeal existence. Anderson (2002) makes the point that movement in sport and physical education is analogous to the practice of music in the study of music, and so sport and physical education without engagement in movement is like a music programme without musical instruments. Consequently, human movement is the place where we can both find meaning and express our own particular identity and our uniqueness because the body is actively involved in the world, it is the central locus of expression and meaning-producing acts (Anderson, 2001, 2002). This is further reinforced by O'Neill (1974, p. 114), who argues that "... nothing is more expressive than the human body, our hands and fingers, our dancing feet, our eyes, our voice, in joy and sorrow". Embodiment and expression should not be taken lightly because the experience of movement is not only humanising, it provides a more authentic means of making sense of our world and the power of expressing our being-in-the-world. Furthermore, the educational implications of Merleau-Ponty's phenomenological account of human experiences connects strongly with the notion that learning also involves the exploration of the world from where one is, as well as coming to a clearer understanding of how things relate to each other and to ourselves in the world. It is an ongoing process. The key here is that we "come to" understand something (if successful) from our own point of view as a result of experiencing it (Stolz, 2013a). To use Merleau-Ponty's (1945/1962, p. x) own analogy, we come to know "what a forest, a prairie or a river is" because we have already experienced the countryside as a place we have explored, not because of the abstract symbols of the geographer's map. These meaningful movement experiences can be captured by human actions in sport and physical education and in short represent, express and confirm his or her capabilities, intentions and means of being.

Engagement in sport and physical education, therefore, should be chosen purely because it is set apart from serious duties like work and projects which make up the purposes of our ordinary life; this is essentially why we play, because we are immediately released from these duties momentarily. The reason why playing sport and engaging in physical education activities can have a serious function and therefore an educational function has more to do with the fact that there is no clear equivalent in ordinary life. For example, there is nothing in ordinary life which resembles cricket or soccer. A good cover drive in cricket or long pass in soccer is simply useless in any other human pursuit, and this is exactly why people play games. Ordinary life does not provide enough opportunities at all for such pursuits and as a result engagement in sport and physical education activities permits human beings to attain an insight into the depth of his or her basic existence, an avenue of discovery and self-expression, an awareness of his or her capabilities and limitations so he or she becomes conscious of what he or she is and what he or she is not. Whitehead (1990) reinforces this point further when she argues that our embodiment affords us two almost inseparable modes of continuous liaison with the world: that our body responds through movement according to the demands of our environment and is also perceptually sensitive to the nature of this environment. Borrowing from Merleau-Ponty, Whitehead (1990) goes on to add that beneath the intentionality of the act our motility plays a significant part in giving meaning to objects (operative meaning), and when the actual interaction occurs there is "at one and the same time, a reaffirmation of the operative meaning of the object, and an actualisation of a mode of the individual's motile capacity"; and since we are essentially a being-in-the-world our continuous liaison is basically a form of "operative liaison" that gives us an appreciation of our environment and a realisation of our capacities. She argues that operative meaning and operative liaison have been neglected and ignored, with respect both to the contribution they can make to perception as a whole and to their potential for developing an enriched interaction with the world that could be nurtured by education. Such a position was also advocated by the ancient Greeks, who accorded the body equal dignity with the mind in a psychosomatic relationship by educating the whole person. If a similar position was adopted today a radical change in the curriculum would subsequently be needed and the dominant educational discourse that disproportionately focuses on and favours intellectual development at the expense of other forms of knowledge would give way to a much broader curriculum programme in which intellectual development would be only one of a whole range of balanced activities intended to enrich our interaction with the world. This is where sport and physical education has real value because it has the capacity to develop a specific mode of relating to the world. This value is conveyed by Whitehead (1990, p. 7) when she writes:

> This involves building from the pre-reflective operation of the embodiment that provides the essential ground for our interaction with the world, towards an ever more articulate operative liaison – one that is not lived with the usual casual presumption, but in which the mover is acutely aware of the totality of his embodiment in its reciprocal interaction with the patterns of force and resistance in the world.

It is only in pre-reflective lived embodiment that the mover becomes more aware than usual of their conscious relationship with the environment and it is in this "fusion", as it were, that embodiment is lived on two levels: pre-reflective and reflective. According to Whitehead (1990, p. 8), the aim of physical education should be to develop these embodied faculties so that students can achieve effective liaison in more complex and demanding environments. She goes on to add that the development of innate human characteristics from their habitual use to their cultivated and multifaceted use is similar to the concerns of intellectual education. In this case, just as certain mental capacities are nurtured and challenged to operate in increasingly more complex contexts, the development of both embodied and intellectual faculties also shares the capacity to enhance an individual's understanding of the world in which they interact. In a sense we come to be "more-at-home" in our embodied capacities because the experience gives rise to a greater awareness of the intimate relationship we have with the world and the development of a general self-confidence in these abilities. Likewise, in the intellectual realm, acquiring knowledge such as scientific concepts and principles gives an individual a sense of "being-at-home" in the scientific realm. The nurturing and fostering of innate intellectual capacities and the self-assurance gained from the mastery of knowledge is seen to be valued in education and there is no reason why the development of subjects linked embodiment like sport and physical education should not be viewed the same way. Both (intellectual and embodied) advance the development of distinctly human capacities, thereby enriching our being-in-the-world, mastery and progress towards understanding the fundamentals of an area of knowledge; and of course promoting self-assurance. Whitehead goes on to argue that what she means by the term "development" in this context is similar to and includes attention to depth and breadth in the progress towards mastery and understanding of the fundamentals of both of these areas. Both types of capacities can be developed singularly or in a diverse array of combinations; however, if we focus on the mastery of just one narrow area at the expense of broadening our understanding of other bodies of knowledge and therefore become too narrowly specialised in just one area I think quite rightly we would be hesitant to call ourselves "educated" or even "intellectually educated". Conversely, it too would be problematic to call someone "educated" or "physically educated" if they were highly skilled in one narrowly specialised area like cricket, soccer and so on, but closed off from developing a broader understanding of other physical activities or bodies of knowledge. Such a view is merely an extension of Peters' conception of education, which opposed both a narrow specialisation and an instrumental view of knowledge by arguing that an "educated man" is someone who has breadth of understanding but is also capable of "connecting up these different ways of interpreting his experience so he achieves some kind of cognitive perspective" (Peters, 1973, p. 240). In reference to the use of the term "cognitive perspective" in this context, it certainly does not mean that a person views all things from a cognitive perspective. For example, to view all things from just a mathematical perspective would be too narrowly focused; this certainly does not mean that we cannot have a mathematical appreciation of the world, but it should be balanced alongside other modes of viewing the world. By adopting such an approach we can come to appreciate more fully the complexities of our environment. It is interesting and somewhat ironic to note that Peters' (1970, p. 6) claim that "… 'education is of the whole man' is a conceptual truth in that being educated is incompatible with being narrowly specialised …" exposes the lopsidedness of the dominant view of education as being concerned with the development of the mind at the expense of the body. If education is to be "of the whole man" it needs to be concerned with all a person's faculties and capacities which, to borrow from Merleau-Ponty, is to promote a person's existence as an embodied being-in-the-world. The body is not just another object in the world; rather, it is "anchored" in the world as "man's" primary mode of meaningful communication and interaction, and hence must always be worldly and human. If we are serious about achieving a well-balanced education that is not defective we need to develop the embodied being alongside the intellectual and other innate human capabilities. We can present a strong case for our cause because the primacy of perception indicates that the basis for our cognition is through bodily experience. As Merleau-Ponty

(1947/1964, p. 17) reveals, perceptual capacities underpin all intellectual capacities, which is reinforced further when he writes:

> ... we can only think the world because we have already experienced it; it is through this experience that we have the idea of being, and it is through experience that the words "rational" and "real" receive a meaning simultaneously.

Consequently, our embodied capacities warrant serious attention throughout education. By radically shifting from a Cartesian to a phenomenological conception of personhood, we provide a mechanism by which we can vigorously defend sport and physical education as legitimate educational activities that are just as important as traditional views of education which emphasise intellectual development at the expense of other modes of inquiry. Certainly, this view by no means denies the importance of intellectual education, but it does not grant it *a priori* pre-eminence over every other mode of human inquiry or even seek to separate it from other modes in which it is interwoven. As I have argued in Chapter 1, education should be of the whole person and develop all of a person's capabilities and faculties. Following an extended analysis of the mind–body problem, I concluded that Merleau-Ponty's incarnated consciousness and Whitehead's operative meaning and operative liaison are more compatible and commensurate with our understanding of human nature compared to Descartes' dualistic conception. Therefore, the view of the body as a machine and its segregation into a mind and a body have been replaced by a radical shift of embodiment, from "having a body" to the lived-body experience of "being a body" which emphasises the inherent unity of human beings.

If our embodied experience underpins all that we call "intellectual" then why is sport and physical education marginalised within the curriculum? Its marginalisation would appear to arise from an unwillingness to count any non-theoretical knowing or "knowing how" as important. This is further reinforced by the traditional view of education, which emphasises cognitive development and as a result places a significant onus upon propositional forms of knowledge – or "knowing that" – that are prejudicial to the body. It is to this I now turn, to examine the unique place of physical education within educational institutions and what it means to be "physically educated".

Notes

1 For relevant literature, see: Belaief (1977); Gerber and Morgan (1979); Meier (1975); Morgan and Meier (1995); O'Neill (1974).
2 Philosophically, the debate surrounding physical education as "education of the physical" or "education through the physical" was and is still an important debate to be had in physical education.

3   The unique place of physical education within education

The fluid concept of education and the process of being "physically educated"

A precursory survey of traditional educational systems would show that the most familiar type of school curriculum offers both practical as well as academic-type courses and is just as concerned with learning in practical forms of knowledge or "knowing how" as it is with the initiation into theoretical forms of knowledge or "knowing that". Upon closer inspection it becomes clear that, for some teachers, parents, educational leaders and educational theorists, practical pursuits and activities are perceived to have less educational worth and status than academic-type subjects. For instance, it is not uncommon for some to associate practical pursuits and activities within the curriculum with the less academically able individual, who is alleged to be unable to cope with academic study but can manage to play cricket, paint, dance and so on. In education there are some who argue that education must necessarily involve experiences and activities of learning which involve some engagement with or acquisition of knowledge in some recognisable sense of that term. The question of knowledge and the curriculum in education as an issue owes much to the 1960s and 1970s work of R. S. Peters (1966) *Ethics and Education*, R. F. Dearden (1968), *Philosophy of Primary Education*, P. H. Hirst and R. S. Peters' (1970) *The Logic of Education* and P. H. Hirst (1974), *Knowledge and the Curriculum*. These classic texts are paradigmatic of the centrality of epistemological theorising that occurred in post-war literature on educational philosophy. Of these educational philosophers, Peters (1966) developed arguably the most powerful statement about the nature of education (see Chapters I, II and V). Briefly speaking, his thesis was that education should transmit and initiate the unlearned into what are intrinsically worthwhile forms of knowledge that are constitutive of the rational mind.[1] In addition to this significant epistemological contribution, his associate Hirst (1974) developed a "forms of knowledge" thesis that had a tremendous influence not only on educational theorists thinking about knowledge and understanding in Britain, and further afield in most English language speaking countries, but most pertinently on educational leaders, curriculum policy makers, curriculum decision makers and so on. Despite the time that has transpired since this work was published, its immense significance has been highly instrumental in casting physical education out into the educational wilderness. As a result it is relevant to my task to revisit the forms of knowledge thesis to better understand how, or perhaps how not, to think philosophically about physical education as an educational process.

The primary reason, of course, for all of this philosophical uncertainty has to do with the concept of "knowing how", which is located in an area of constant philosophical dispute of an epistemological kind. It is difficult, then, to know quite where to start in order to deal with such complex and diverse areas of philosophical inquiry, particularly given the ambiguity of the conceptual term "knowing how". My thesis is that practical subjects within the curriculum like sport and physical education[2] are often undervalued because the concept of practical knowledge is not appreciated and ultimately misunderstood, as well as there being a general unwillingness to count any non-theoretical knowing as important. This is further reinforced by the traditional view of education, which places a significant onus upon propositional forms of knowledge in the development of the mind, to the point where practical pursuits in the curriculum are deemed to have no serious part to play in this development and relegated to the periphery in education. For instance, the argument goes that the nature of play, games and sport which are central features of physical education practice and utilised as an educational mechanism are not concerned with the attainment of theoretical knowledge, because they are only concerned with "knowing how" in the form of practical knowledge. Hence, the very nature of play, games and sport renders them non-academic and non-educational. At the risk of labouring the point, as I have argued in earlier chapters, such an approach seems to be based on a narrow and question-begging criterion that only seems to reinforce a form of Cartesian dualism that is severely problematic. It is noteworthy to mention at this juncture that we seem to easily forget that physical education has featured in most school curricula in some form or another continuously from the time of Plato and Aristotle and so we should not doubt its educational pedigree. Its educational longevity in the curriculum, I think, has more to do with the fact that physical education is an inextricably body-linked subject that directly deals with the brute actuality of our embodiment in education; this should be taken seriously because movement experiences in and through physical education can provide opportunities that are humanising and that provide authentic opportunities to concretely reinforce the point that a person's essential being is more than just his or her rationality; he or she is a being-in-the-world.

Therefore for the purposes of this chapter I will be concerned with the critical discussion of three issues: first, I outline some of the most well-known post-war accounts of practical knowledge that have been influential in the literature surrounding the conceptual term "knowing how"; second, I review a well-known educational philosophical theory of the curriculum commonly known as the "forms of knowledge" thesis, which won widespread post-war popularity and basically cast physical education out into the educational wilderness and because of this dominance such accounts have attracted much criticism from postmodern and poststructuralist sources about the value of traditional epistemology in education. Furthermore, I intend to draw upon some of these accounts to argue for an alternative conception of education, one which can accommodate practical as well as theoretical or academic-type pursuits. Lastly, I consider the question of whether there actually is a claim for there being a unique place for physical education within education and what form this may take.

Some well-known post-war accounts of knowledge: the epistemology of "knowing how" and "knowing that"[3]

The philosophical language when referring to knowledge forms varies considerably. For instance, we talk of knowing that $2+3=5$, how to get to Flinders Street Train Station, how to bowl the various deliveries of off spin in cricket, who the current Prime Minister of the Australian Commonwealth is, that I have feelings of pain and so on. Despite certain overlaps in linguistic structure these expressions can take three basic forms that have entered the parlance of philosophy. First, those expressions in which what is known is fact – such as $2+3=5$ or who is the current Prime Minister of the Australian Commonwealth – are normally referred to as propositional forms of knowledge and commonly referred to as "knowing that" that represent theoretical knowledge about how the world in fact is (Franklin, 1981; White, 1982). Second, expressions which make reference to how to carry out a practical activity of some kind – like how to get to Flinders Street Train Station, how to bowl certain variations of off-spin bowling in cricket – are usually referred to as practical knowledge or "knowing how" that is involved in actually doing things (Franklin, 1981; White, 1982). In the third form, what is known as an object of some kind – such as a train station, cricket ball or Prime Minister, as well as feelings of pain – is commonly known as "knowledge with an object" or "knowledge by acquaintance". The problem with such an approach is that there now appears to be three quite distinct mutually exclusive forms of knowledge; however, the relationship between the three forms is complex and a brief glance at each will have to suffice at this point.[4] Traditionally, epistemology has focused almost exclusively on propositional forms of knowledge because it aims at an objective truth, whereas practical knowledge has suffered since the latter emphasises what an agent is able to actually do, which is why it is often expressed as "knowing how" as opposed to what people know in a propositional sense. This kind of one-dimensional approach owes much to the empirical philosophers of Hobbes (1651/1999) and Locke (1689/2001), who provided an atomistic conception of the world. Such accounts of the world have come to be challenged because they are not the only possible model for knowledge and are quite limited in their understanding of the various senses of knowing that relate to our own experiences. Some of these experiences could range from knowing how to ride a bike or how to play cricket or soccer, to knowing the meaning of a joke and so on. Furthermore, Ayer (1957) makes the point that we are misled by the term "knowledge" because it features both in theoretical and practical knowledge (see Chapter 1). He goes on to argue that propositional knowledge has become the paradigm to the point where practical knowledge has come to be explained in theoretical terms as well. My thesis is that we need to acknowledge that there are certain implied or inferred elements of human knowledge that cannot be verbally articulated, so my position can be strengthened considerably by expanding on Polanyi's (1958, 1962, 1966a, 1966b, 1967; Polanyi and Prosch 1975) understanding of knowing by tacit inference or "tacit knowing". Polanyi argues that it is a futile task to seek strictly impersonal understandings of knowledge, which some accounts of science (positivism) strive for, because the act of knowing exercises a personal dimension in relating evidence to an external reality. He goes on to add that we need to seriously reconsider our understanding of human knowledge by starting from the premise that "we know more than we can tell" (Polanyi, 1966a, p. 4). For instance, we can know and identify a person's face amongst a vast sea of people but at the same time we usually cannot verbalise how we recognise a face we know. For Polanyi, knowledge is personal because the knower relies on a framework, or a set of "subsidiaries", that is essentially unknown to the knower. Such a framework is unknown not because we can't identify and analyse it at some point in time but because it has more to do with its function in knowing. This is further confirmed by Polanyi and Prosch (1975, p. 39) who state: "... subsidiaries are – for this reason and *not* because we cannot find them all – *essentially* unspecifiable". To Polanyi, this framework is central to his overall theory of personal knowledge and his theory of meaning. For instance, in his earlier works he uses the concept of "dwelling in" to describe the application of his framework by using the function of the human body as a metaphor, which he states as: "When we accept a certain set of presuppositions and use them as our interpretative framework, we may be said to dwell in them as we do in our own body" (Polanyi, 1958, p. 60). He goes on to explain "dwelling in" as:

> Like the tool, the sign or the symbol can be conceived as such only in the eyes of a person who *relies on them* to achieve or signify something. *This reliance is a personal commitment which is involved in all acts of intelligence by which we integrate some things subsidiarily to the centre of our focal attention.*
>
> (Polanyi, 1958, p. 61)

According to Hawkins (2008), the notion of "subsidiarily" and "focal" attention is significant here in this phrase because the knower uses this subsidiary to attend focally to the object of his attention and tacit knowing is an aspect that remains implicitly unexpressed and can only come to be known through engagement with that to which we are focally attending. Much can be gained by using those aspects of Gestalt psychology that can provide a means to better understand tacit thought, particularly as it relates to how we know particulars without being able to identify these particulars, as presented in the case of physiognomy (Polanyi, 1961, 1962, 1966a, 1966b). To Polanyi (1966a, p. 6), the restructuring of Gestalt to better understand the logic of tacit thought is further confirmed when he states:

> ... I am looking at Gestalt, on the contrary, as the outcome of an active shaping of experience performed in the pursuit of knowledge. This shaping

or integrating I hold to be the great and indispensable tacit power by which all knowledge is discovered and, once discovered, is held to be true.

Such an approach gives us a better insight into the power of tacit knowing and changes how we come to know to the point where it improves the standing of the class of performative activities that have been previously marginalised like sport, physical education and so on. Consequently, to Polanyi (1966a, p. 7) "knowing" therefore covers both practical and theoretical knowledge, which we interpret through the use of "tools, of probes, and of pointers" as instances of the "art of knowing". He goes on to add that certain psychological experiments of note in the 1940s and 1950s have demonstrated that tacit knowing always involves the relationship between two events, both of which we know, but about which we can only say that we "know" much more than we can articulate. For instance, in one of the experiments the subject quickly learned to connect a first term (shock syllables and shock associations) with what followed in a second term (electric shock) as a means to determine the shock producing particulars for the purposes of avoiding an electric shock. What this demonstrates about tacit knowing is significant, because it shows that we can come to know without being able to identify those aspects in which we know and illustrates the functional relationship that exists between the two terms or events of tacit knowing. This is further confirmed by Polanyi (1966a, p. 10), who states: "we know the first term only by relying on our awareness of it for attending to the second" and as a result the functional relation between the two terms represent the first aspects of tacit knowing.

In the second aspect of tacit knowing Polanyi begins to introduce the language of anatomy to refer to a first term or event as "proximal" and a second term or event as "distal" as an explanation for how we attend to appearances and features of that thing. He states:

> We may say, in general, that we are aware of the proximal term of an act of tacit knowing in the appearance of its distal term; we are aware of that *from* which we are attending to another thing, in the *appearance* of that thing. We may call this the *phenomenal structure* of tacit knowing.
>
> (Polyani, 1966a, p. 11)

The relationship between the two terms of tacit knowing is important because it combines the functional and phenomenal aspects with a contextual meaning. For example, in the case of the experimental setting the sight of certain syllables prepares us for the electric shock which gives their meaning to us. To further expand his idea of the phenomenal aspects of tacit knowing, Polanyi uses the analogy of the blind man feeling his way by tapping with a stick as a means to explain how we interpret what would normally be in isolation meaningless feelings into meaningful ones. He goes on to refer to this as the "semantic aspect" of tacit knowing. From the three aspects of tacit knowing that Polanyi (1966a) outlines so far (functional, phenomenal and semantic), it is only the fourth aspect, the "ontological aspect", which tells us what tacit knowing is a knowledge of because it establishes a meaningful relationship between the two terms. Thus, the first term represents the particulars found in the proximal term so we can say that a person comes more and more to know by relying on his awareness of the particulars by "dwelling in them", and in attending to their joint meaning they become meaningful.

To Polanyi, our body is the "ultimate instrument" of all our external knowledge, irrespective of whether it is intellectual or practical, because we rely on our body to act as a type of transformative tool or stick – as a sentient extension of our body in the case of the blind man. Consequently, Polanyi's work is significant to my thesis for four reasons: first, it demonstrates how we come to know more than we can articulate; second, tacit knowing makes intelligent use of our bodily elements and argues that we possess a practical knowledge of our bodies; third, tacit knowing achieves a form of integration (proximal and distal) that takes on a more positive character that involves an active "dwelling in" what we are attending to as a means to understand joint meaning; and, fourth, it provides an account of how we are able to perform quite complex bodily movements quickly, autonomously and what appears to be automatically with very little awareness or understanding of why we are able to do them. This is further confirmed by Polanyi and Prosch (1975, p. 41) who highlight how we can easily "paralyze" the performance of a skill by focusing our attention away from the performance and attending to other less important matters than "dwelling in" the moment of the act:

> For the same reasons we cannot learn to keep our balance on a bicycle by trying to follow the explicit rule that, to compensate for an imbalance, we must force our bicycle into a curve – away from the direction of the imbalance – whose radius is proportional to the square of the bicycle's velocity over the angle of imbalance. Such knowledge is totally ineffectual unless it is known tacitly, that is, unless it is known subsidiarily – unless it is simply dwelt in.

There is something to be said about those aspects of knowing that are not easy to explain, such as how a highly skilled batsman could possibly respond in action with a cover drive to a ball being bowled at him at 150-plus kilometres per hour.[5] Such an example helps to challenge ideas about the philosophy of cognition as an inner process between input information and behavioural output. Instead it is important to understand that the batsman in question does not think then act as if they are independent steps in a process. As a result, such flexible, intelligent action in real time is less a matter of producing well-thought-out planned action based on perceptual input and then executing it, but more like a form of time-constrained prediction that does not contain an accurate perception of where the ball already is (Sutton, 2007). According to Land and McLeod (2000), elite performers "initial anticipatory saccade" (looking ahead of the ball to pick up advanced cues) starts earlier than novices, and the authors concluded that the better you are the less time you spend watching the ball and the more you leap into the future (predict the bounce). This type of "know how" goes by many theoretical terms, from tacit knowing, to procedural memory, to kinaesthetic memory, but despite the contentious nature of the various literatures, each basically takes into consideration the embodied skills which have been acquired in the past, and are retained and employed on cue in the present "to influence ourselves" (Sutton, 2007). There is something about how we come to know through personal experience that cannot be explained which should not be underestimated, and it is interesting to note how our thoughts (attending to less important matters) can sometimes get in the way of successful performance. For instance, there is the often reported dilemma found in elite-level sporting activities that an excessive form of "proceduralization" (theoretical or technical aspects) can detract from skilful performance in the moment by trying to remember past or anticipate future performances, particularly in situational contexts that require simplicity of performance and a specific focus on the perception–action cycle. In the case of the batsman, there is an assumption that the successful execution of skills required for batting involves considerable practice, to the point where they become habitualised "embodied skills" that are independent of more explicit forms of knowing such as verbalising. This is further reinforced by Sutton (2007, pp. 767–768) who notes in the context of cricket:

> *Having* such batting skills and embodied memories, and being able to employ them, is utterly different from *knowing* about them, or being able to describe them, or even remembering your earlier exercise of them … because the movements are in one sense new and fresh every time a shot is played, and because … nothing in the occurrent activity *refers* in any straightforward way to its history or to the source of the skill.…

This highly peculiar kind of skilled performance demonstrates the complexity of skilled performance and exemplifies the importance of an interdisciplinary approach in the study of our embodied performance.

From a philosophical perspective the most relevant critique to understanding this kind of embodied intelligence can be found in Hubert Dreyfus' (Dreyfus, 1991, 1993, 1996, 2002a, 2002b, 2005; Dreyfus and Dreyfus, 1986) work, which combines the insights brought forward by Merleau-Ponty's phenomenology of embodiment with dynamical approaches in neuroscience. Dreyfus (2002b, p. 417) argues that there can only be two distinct kinds of intentional behaviour: "deliberative, planned action and spontaneous, transparent coping". He goes on to outline how in the first four levels of skill acquisition we need to consciously and deliberately follow rules in the initial stages of learning, particularly in the early novice stage (first stage) but the move through the stages to expertise status (fifth stage) is characterised by a gradual relinquishing of the associated rules and priorities of activities as we gain experience in coping with real situations (Dreyfus, 2002a; Dreyfus and Dreyfus, 1986). It is important to note here that to Dreyfus expert performers who have attained mastery do not rely on explicit reasoning behind their action or even have conscious control over or conscious access to the processes by which they act because "... an expert's skill has become so much a part of him that he need be no more aware of it than he is of his own body" (Dreyfus and Dreyfus, 1986, p. 30), to the point where the expert "... not only sees what needs to be achieved: thanks to a vast repertoire of situational discriminations he sees how to achieve his goal" (Dreyfus, 2002a, pp. 371–372). Central to Dreyfus' approach is Merleau-Ponty's account of how human beings tend towards getting a maximal grip on an object without thinking about it according to their situation. To Merleau-Ponty, maximum grip comes from perception and manipulation. For instance, when we are looking at an object we tend to move to the "optimum distance" to take in the whole and finer and finer discriminations (intentional arc) to aid perception. This is further confirmed when he states:

> For each object, as for each picture in an art gallery, there is an optimum distance from which it requires to be seen, a direction viewed from which it vouchsafes most of itself: at a shorter or greater distance we have merely a perception blurred through excess or deficiency. We therefore tend towards the maximum visibility, and seek a better focus as with a microscope.
> (Merleau-Ponty, 1945/1962, p. 352)

In the sporting context, Dreyfus (2002a) provides an interpretative description of the phenomenon in focus by using the example of a tennis swing. In the novice performer much of their effort is on acquiring (pre-reflective thought) and laying down some of the finer aspects of the movements (intentional arc) whereas for the expert, prior experience has sculpted his swing to the point where pre-reflection is no longer required and he can be more absorbed in the game because optimal maximum (muscular) gestalt has been achieved. He goes on to state that:

> ... the final gestalt need not be represented in one's mind. Indeed, it is not something one *could* represent. One only senses when one is getting closer or further away from the optimum.
> (Dreyfus, 2002a, p. 379)

This same holds for the final gestalt of body and racket in the example of the expert performer because the skilled agent through experience has sculpted his swing to the point where he cannot represent how he turns his racket when he returns the ball. At one stage in his skill acquisition he may have once recalled being told to hold his racket in a certain way and may have had some success in executing this but now experience has "sculpted" his swing to the contextual situation in a far more subtle and effective way than what he could have achieved as a novice or beginner. This is further confirmed by Merleau-Ponty (1945/1962, p. 177) who states:

> Whether a system of motor or perceptual powers, our body is not an object for an "I think", it is a grouping of lived-through meanings which moves towards its equilibrium.

Subsequently, skilful coping does not require mental representations of its goal or even normally express what the optimum may be because the acting agent's body responds to the environment by tending toward equilibrium with it. As Dreyfus (2002a, p. 379) argues, "it can be *purposive* without the agent entertaining a *purpose*"; or as Merleau-Ponty (1945/1962, pp. 160–161) puts it:

> A movement is learned when the body has understood it, that is, when it has incorporated it into its "world", and to move one's body is to aim at things through it; it is to allow oneself to respond to their call, which is made upon it independently of any representation. Motility, then, is not, as it were, a handmaid of consciousness, transporting the body to that point in space....

According to Moe (2005), the "background knowledge of the body" is a valuable alternative to the traditional (classical cognitivism) way of thinking about intentional movements in sport to the point where there may be some educational merit in exploring how movements are experienced, performed and evaluated from an accurate phenomenological perspective. In a way, phenomenological methodologies in general complement learning aims rather than contradict them in educational discourse, particularly when experiential learning is linked with personal experience (personalisation) and based on the integration between performance and analysis of performance.[6] The benefits of such programmes demonstrate a mix of practical ability and critical thinking that have been lacking in physical education programmes in the past; such an approach enables students to "learn about what knowledge is useful and most importantly why it is useful" as well as develop our understanding of practical knowledge, most importantly in physical education programmes (Thorburn, 1999). Subsequently, physical education could profit greatly from a (re)conceptualisation of what it means to be "physically educated" from a Merleau-Pontian phenomenological perspective.

Preoccupation by philosophers with propositional forms of knowledge as knowing has been to the detriment of other forms of knowing and understanding that deal with the "how" and "why". Accounts that have this kind of limitation are incomplete because they neglect the question as to why there is both theoretical and practical knowledge, and so I plan to limit my outline to post-war epistemological theories of knowing how and knowing that. One philosopher who paid attention to the distinction between theoretical and practical knowledge was Ryle.

Ryle's positive account of knowing how: knowing how as a contradistinction to knowing that and understanding intelligent performance of a specific kind

Gilbert Ryle (1949) in his seminal work, *The Concept of Mind*, brought these expressions to our attention through an extensive discourse on how to describe people as exercising qualities of mind (see Chapter II: Knowing how and knowing that). Ryle starts out by highlighting the important distinction between being intelligent and possessing knowledge, which we tend to speak of and treat as intellectual operations of cognition. He makes it clear that the object of his thesis is to illustrate how there are "... many activities which directly display qualities of mind, yet are neither themselves intellectual operations nor effects of intellectual operations ...", and at the same time correct the "intellectualist doctrine" which tries to define intelligence in terms of acquiring truths (Ryle, 1949, p. 27). He goes on to add that "intelligent practice" is not secondary to theory; on the contrary, theorising is just one practice amongst others. Ryle (1949, p. 28) goes on to state that:

> Theorists have been so preoccupied with the task of investigating the nature, the source, and the credentials of the theories that we adopt that they have for the most part ignored the question [of] what it is for someone to know how to perform tasks.

In ordinary life we are more concerned about the proficient operations of practices than with the truths a person may acquire and retain. For instance, we speak of learning how to ride a bike; and we can also learn that something is the case. Part of what it is to know how to perform an operation is that the agent must perform it well in the sense of correctly or successfully against certain standards or satisfy specific criteria. This point is significant as its means that intelligent performance is not just about satisfying some public criteria which a well-trained monkey could perform but applies to those individuals who detect and correct mistakes to improve on their performance to get them right. This is further reinforced by Ryle (1949, p. 29) when he states:

> This point is commonly expressed in the vernacular by saying that an action exhibits intelligence, if, and only if, the agent is thinking what he is doing while he is doing it, and thinking what he is doing in such a manner that he would not do the action so well if he were not thinking what he is doing.

It follows then that the agent in performing the operation characterised by intelligent performance must be preceded by certain propositions about what can be done and put into practice what these propositions are, but Ryle cautions his audience that this certainly does not mean the double operation of considering and then executing. Ryle (1949, p. 32) goes on to criticise the "intellectualist doctrine" as absurd due to the endless regress required to show that an operation must be controlled by a prior intellectual operation, because "... 'thinking what I am doing' does not connate 'both thinking what to do and doing it' ..." in some pattern of interconnected processes but thinking about what I am doing to Ryle is the same as "doing one thing and not two". Why is it that people are so drawn to the idea of doing and then theorising about doing? According to Ryle (1949, pp. 33–34), part of the answer he attributes to the dogma of the "ghost in the machine", because doing is an overtly physical act and cannot itself be a mental operation and as a result this has contributed to the mythical bifurcation of "unwitnessable mental causes" and their "witnessable physical effects".

According to Winch (2009, 2010), Ryle was concerned with the intellectualist claim that all intentional action is caused by mental events in a non-material medium and to avoid this he argued that knowing how and knowing that should be distinct.[7] Ryle (1945, p. 8) contends that the intellectualist legend must be rejected and goes on to add that "... when a person knows how do things of a certain sort (e.g., make good jokes, conduct battles or behave at funerals), his knowledge is actualised or exercised in what he does". Although it is commonly believed that knowing how to do something is somehow reducible to a set of "knowings that" – such as principles, rules, reasons and so on that govern performance – this is not always the case. In Ryle's (1945, p. 11) words, "... intelligent application in practice of principles, reasons, standards, etc., is not a legatee of the consideration of them in theory; it can and normally does occur without any such consideration". Consequently, the evaluation of how good someone is at performing an action depends on how well they actually perform the action, rather than on what they may know (Winch, 2009).

Does this mean that Ryle holds the untenable position of behaviourism, that knowing how to do something exhibits some type of mental operation and thereby is the same as intelligence? Certainly one could gain this impression when he describes a person by one or other of the epithets such as "clever" or "silly", "prudent" or "rash", imputing in the person the ability to do certain sorts of things and thereby according knowledge or ignorance as a result of his actions (Ryle, 1949, p. 26). Although Ryle (1949) at times may appear to be unclear, he does make it clear that some intelligent performances "... are not controlled by any interior acknowledgements of the principles applied in them" (Ryle, 1949, p. 31). Subsequently, his view is consistent with the claim that there are many different types of actions and that when someone knows how to do something we can evaluate whether or not they have indeed performed, but also entails how well they have been performed.

If intelligent performance is to do one thing (not two) and apply certain criteria in the operation of a performance, the question then becomes how we can tell or even characterise that an agent is acting skilfully or with intent and not by accident or good fortune? Ryle responds by arguing that to determine whether the performer was lucky or skilful we need to take into account his subsequent record, explanations offered or excuses, plus other information to build a picture of "heterogeneous performances" that could assist in deciding whether the performance was a matter of sheer good luck or due to mastery of a skill. He states:

> The boxer, the surgeon, the poet and the salesman apply their special criteria in the performance of their special tasks, for they are trying to get things right; and they are appraised as clever, skilful, inspired or shrewd not for the ways in which they consider, if they consider at all, prescriptions for conducting their special performances, but for the ways in which they conduct these performances themselves. Whether or not the boxer plans his

manoeuvres before executing them, his cleverness as a boxer is decided in the light of how he fights.... Cleverness at fighting is exhibited in the giving and parrying of blows, not in the acceptance or rejection of propositions about blows....

(Ryle, 1949, p. 48)

Such an example illustrates what is normally classed as intelligent performance and highlights how an agent does not execute some additional intellectual operations. Furthermore, the learning of the simplest tasks requires some form of intellectual capacity that requires the agent to have the ability to understand operations and instructions of a propositional nature. Just as a spectator who does not understand how to play chess also cannot follow the play of others, understanding is part of knowing how of a specific kind. The use of the terms "understanding" and "following" in this context are different exercises of knowing how, which may be executed without having to be performed. To Ryle (1949), then, knowing how then is a disposition, but not a one-way disposition like a reflex or habit, because knowing how not only involves intentional acts of doing and correcting mistakes according to specific kinds of criteria, but also in imaging how to do things correctly, in instructing others, in criticising and appreciating movements that performers make and so on indefinitely. For the purposes of this chapter, I will now turn my attention to the work of Franklin, who provides the most notable criticism levelled against Ryle's conception of knowing how.

The ambiguity of knowing how: a misleading explanation of practical knowledge

According to Franklin (1981), Ryle's distinction between knowing that, which is clearly meant to represent theoretical knowledge about how the world in fact is, and knowing how, as presented as practical knowledge involved in actually doing things, is not actually a distinction between knowing that and knowing how, because the latter can be theoretical as well. Franklin's argument rests on a linguistic analysis of the terms. For instance, "We know how volcanoes operate" is quite different from "We know how to operate". These examples suggest that the distinction between theoretical and practical knowledge might "... not be the conjunction (*that* versus *how*), but whether there is a finite verb or an infinitive (*operate* versus *to operate*)" (Franklin, 1981, p. 194). He goes on to argue that the paradigmatic form of practical knowledge would seem to consist mostly of "*wh*-forms"[8] plus an infinitive in which "how to" covers a variety of cases in which two conditions are central: (1) knowledge of the principles suitable to some activity; (2) the actual physical or mental capacity to exercise a skill. The problem is that these two conditions do not necessarily correspond deftly or even accurately, as the following example will attest. For instance, to use the expression "I know how to speak German" must mean that I have knowledge of how to exercise the language skill according to the second condition, whereas a champion swimmer who is left a paraplegic after an accident still knows how to swim theoretically, as in the knowledge of the principles associated with swimming, and as a result must satisfy the first condition. Therefore, to Franklin (1981, p. 197), expressions such as "I know how to drive a car" are ambiguous because they could be either (1) or (2) and in a way condition (1) is in a sense between (2) because theoretical knowledge is closely familiar with (1), because the agent may know (theoretically) the principles appropriate to the activity of how to drive a car but may not to be able to perform them.

Wright (2000) argues that a failure to recognise that knowing how is an ambiguous concept could be detrimental to a coherent understanding of what actually is practical knowledge, particularly as it relates to physical education. She goes on to add that the knowing how that is exhibited in performance is not necessarily referring to just propositional knowledge in the form of knowing what the procedure is, because it does not necessarily follow that one can carry out the procedure. For instance, knowing how to bowl off spin in cricket[9] could be simply explained away in terms of knowing that certain procedural aspects are true, but in this case it would be a mistake to refer to this verbal account as practical knowledge because it lacks a performative element. It may well be the case that a student comes to a strong theoretical sense of knowing how from learning how to bowl off spin, to the point where they share the same amount of knowledge as the teacher or coach and could explain and teach the technical aspects, but what is mainly of interest in physical education is whether and to what degree of success the student has according to recognisable standards. In this case a strong theoretical understanding is not a sufficient or even logically necessary condition of good performance because we wouldn't "define a good chef as one who cites Mrs. Beeton's recipes, for these recipes describe how good chefs cook, and anyhow the excellence of a chef is not in his citing but in his cooking" (Ryle, 1945, p. 13). In the case of practical pursuits within the curriculum such knowledge would not be considered necessary for effective performance because the focus shifts towards evaluation in relation to knowing how, particularly for complex or non-basic performances relating to specific tasks. The problem for practical pursuits within the curriculum has been how to evaluate the diverse array of circumstances that may differ according to the contextual situation.

This issue becomes apparent in intellectualist accounts of knowing how that are reductive, and it abstracts away from our understanding of knowing how as practical modes of presentation in a contextually relevant way. Although person A may know that X is a way to F, it does not follow that person A can use their own judgement and discretion to successfully perform X and F, let alone F-ing well. For example, person A may well know that X is a way to bowl off spin in cricket and demonstrate this in a practical mode in a contextually relevant way but may fail to bowl successfully because they have misjudged the type of wicket, ignored relevant field placements set by the captain for a specific batsman, failed to react to the batsman and make adjustments accordingly and so on in a game context. In one sense person A knows how to bowl off spin in cricket but there is more to bowling off spin in cricket than knowing that X is a way to bowl off spin. We need to be able to distinguish between someone knowing the procedure or technique for a way of doing something and from the judgement and discretion to respond to the exigencies of particular contextual situations. Consequently, I think there is a need to acknowledge that some accounts given by certain theorists used to explain practical knowledge have been unsuccessful or incomplete and in a way reaffirm the importance of theoretical knowledge. Such a position, for instance, can be found in Powell (1968), who denies practical knowledge is a form of knowledge at all. He argues that to be able to engage in "practical skills" like surgery, plumbing, hurdling and ship-handling requires a sufficient familiarity with "factual, logical and procedural" features so that the thinker "knows what he is talking about" and therefore has a close acquaintance with sets of knowledgeable "particulars" rather than the possession of a skill of wide applicability. To Powell, theoretical knowledge is valued only because it can notice errors and at the same time say how they should be corrected, particularly if a person's thinking is subject to the "context-bound character of the intellectual skills" of that field of inquiry. Therefore in such an approach theoretical knowledge only becomes practical in its application. For instance, this is a common occurrence in the applied sciences (like exercise science), which have traditionally valued the knowledge gained from scientific experimentation so it in turn can be used for improving performance. The assumption behind this approach is based on the idea that there must be a connection between practical and theoretical knowledge. As a result, explaining practical knowledge then becomes a question of extrapolating this connection. Indeed, to adopt the extreme position that there is no such thing as practical knowledge would be problematic, as this eliminates entirely the bodily movements which are required to execute what theoretical knowledge demands be done.

If practical knowledge cannot be explained according to propositional forms of knowledge, how can it then be explained?[10] In this case there are other accounts of knowing how which may be understood in terms of practical reasoning as a basis for practical knowledge.

The logic of practical reasoning: knowledge in movement

When it comes to the arguments surrounding practical reasoning, most take their starting point from Aristotle's practical syllogism. Some of his general comments are of great interest to philosophers primarily because they identify a peculiar character of practical reasoning which others have either tended to ignore or misrepresent. Unfortunately, most of Aristotle's passages on this topic are fragmented and his treatment could be described as being unsystematic; however, his fullest example of a practical syllogism can be found in the *Nicomachean Ethics*. Aristotle (2004) presents two premises: "... all sweet things should be tasted" and since "*x* is sweet" (one of the particulars) and if the agent has the "... power and is not prevented, must immediately act", which leads to, or ends in, action. When the two premises are combined, "... if there are two universal judgements present in the mind ... and at the same time desire is present ... the desire carries his body forward" (p. 175; 1147a30). To Aristotle, practical reasoning involves the agent acting under a general rule of action that, like theoretical reasoning, has to conform to logical standards. As a result practical reasoning is valid only if the conclusion follows from the premises, which usually takes the following form: (1) a major premise which expresses some end, purpose, want, intention, desire and so on; (2) a minor premise setting out the means to achieve the end; (3) practical conclusion to be performed to achieve the end. It is worth mentioning at this juncture that practical knowledge (*phronēsis*) to Aristotle was generally aimed at a conclusion concerned with what to do (namely, its relation to action), as distinguished from theoretical knowledge and mere means-to-an-end reasoning or craft necessary of virtue.

David Carr (1978a, 1978b, 1979b, 1980a, 1980b, 1981a and 1981b) has written extensively about the conceptual problems surrounding the nature of human action and knowledge in movement and so his work is particularly important to physical education. His paper (1981b), "Knowledge in Practice", provides a sophisticated study through his analysis of practical inference as the logic of knowing how. Carr (1981b) starts out by arguing that it seems reasonable to assume that physical ability must be a necessary condition of knowing how to do something, and paradoxical descriptions, such as an elderly and arthritic piano teacher knowing how to do what they cannot perform, still have meaning because to know how to do something such as playing a piano assumes that one should at some time have possessed the physical ability and so the present possession of the ability does not appear to be necessary. Carr goes on to outline two general conditions governing the logic of knowing how which are considerably more complicated than that of physical ability (possession of the physical power to ϕ): (1) with respect to simple tasks or actions; (2) with respect to complex or non-basic actions. In condition (1) even though a person may be able to (has the physical power to) perform a simple or basic action such as raising an arm or opening their mouth, it would seem unusual to describe such actions as movements of knowing how, and therefore these would not be commonly associated with the term knowing how. In condition (2), even though we may again say that a person is able to (has the physical power to) perform complex or non-basic actions, these performances must satisfy certain standards before they can be accurately described as actions of knowing how. For instance, a beginner to basketball may get a basket at their first attempt from the free-throw line, but it may be questionable whether this can be attributed to knowing how, rather than accident or good fortune. In this case, he or she does "know how" in one sense, but as Ryle's account of intelligent performance outlines, to determine whether the performance was a matter of sheer good luck or due to mastery of a skill requires an historical account of past performances to gain a full picture of "heterogeneous performances" and so what seems to be missing is the notable evidence of the mastery of certain specific practical standards.

Carr (1981b, p. 54) argues that the distinction between knowing how and physical ability is misleading because it rests somewhere between knowing how that is "mental" and knowing how that is "physical" and is far from clear; however, the expression "knows how" has connections with "... sophisticated mastery of complex rule-governed practical procedures ...", which is different from that of "is able to" and "can" and so is best restricted to such contexts. He goes on to argue that there are two senses implied in "*A* knows how to ϕ": a strong and weak sense. For instance, a person may come to know how to play football (soccer) in the sense of becoming familiar with the laws (theoretical underpinnings) and the acquisition of the physical abilities necessary to play football. In this case, knowing how, in the weak sense, to play football would apply to an understanding of the laws (theory), whereas knowing how, in the strong sense, means both an understanding of the laws and having mastered the relevant physical abilities. Therefore, to Carr practical knowledge cannot be analysed according to theoretical knowledge since it is a function of practical (directed towards action) rather than theoretical reasoning. This is further confirmed when he states:

> ... reasoning presupposed to knowing how is reasoning about what to do rather than about the way things stand in the world and that, in consequence, practical knowledge is quite wrongly construed as concerning theoretical knowledge.
>
> (Carr, 1981b, p. 55)

Carr (1981b) goes on to identify a set of conditions that we can use to describe a person as knowing how to do something or other. He then goes on to argue that a simple common-sense response to any investigation into the nature of knowing how in the strong sense would have to involve a description of knowing how to the point where, if the agent in question intended to perform whatever the agent said he or she knew how to do, he or she would have some success in satisfying his intention. This of course would not be enough, since we would not normally describe a simple or basic action as knowing how, as we would need to include performances of non-basic actions of some sophistication and complexity in our explanations of knowing how. So what conditions would justify a claim of an agent as knowing how? According to Carr (1981b, p. 58), in the standard case, the following three conditions need to be met:

A knows how to ϕ only if:

(1) *A* may entertain ϕing as a purpose;
(2) *A* is acquainted with a set of practical procedures necessary for successful ϕing;
(3) *A* exhibits recognisable success at ϕing.[11]

By formalising his argument Carr's intention is to demonstrate that knowing how to do something shares a conceptual connection with the three conditionals of knowing that.[12] For instance, knowing that *p* must include the following:

A knows that *p* only if:

(1) *A* believes that *p*;
(2) *p* is true;
(3) *A* had reasonable grounds for holding that *p*.

There does appear to be a certain formal similarity between knowing how to ϕ (practical knowledge) and knowing that *p* or believing that *p* (theoretical knowledge). For example, knowing that *p* presupposes a belief that *p*, and likewise an application of knowing how to ϕ normally follows from ϕing having been intended as a purpose (Carr, 1981b). Likewise he goes on to add the second suggested condition of knowing how is analogous to the third premise of knowing that. Obviously, there are going to be some differences in making such a claim. For instance, characteristics of knowing how normally involve actions rather than propositions; to some, actions are physical occurrences and as a result it is mistaken to regard them as capable of being used in inferential statements. Carr (1981b, p. 59) responds to such claims by stating:

> Since that which an agent knows how to do is not a proposition but an action, it can be neither true nor false, although a truth value may be assigned to a report of his knowing how to do something. Nevertheless, I believe it possible to view the remaining conditions of knowing that and knowing how ... as formally analogous.

It is noteworthy to mention at this juncture that Carr's conception of practical reasoning strives to make use of practical inferences as a means to find truth rather than discover it in a world of complex human purposes, and as a result he calls on the conceptual term of "satisfactoriness" found in Kenny's (1966) work on practical inference as a cogent validating principle.[13] Carr (1981b) acknowledges that coming to know or performing complex tasks is essentially a matter of learning to reason practically, just as teaching someone is similarly a matter of practical reasoning and showing how certain ends are logically related to specific means.

   Carr finishes by emphasising the point that knowing how should not be understood in terms of a kind of theoretical reasoning that precedes or accompanies action, but rather as practical reasoning that differs from theoretical reasoning in a number of different respects. Theoretical knowledge strives for truth that is supported by reason and confirmed by experience, whereas practical knowledge is primarily concerned with the employment of purposeful actions, performed in a non-rational way, which can be confirmed by a reasonable degree of success according to the standards of the activity. In addition, as argued earlier, knowing how in the strong sense of playing football (soccer) is more than the knowing of the laws of the game in some theoretical way, but is rather a "... description of a set of constitutive rules of a *practice* ... " which brings with it more than a theoretical understanding of an activity (Carr, 1981b, p. 60). Carr (1981b) finishes with a notable analogy to make his point that it would be a profound mistake to assume that the best way to transform an apprentice into a master plumber is through say the teaching of hydraulics, because the practical knowledge that the apprentice requires comes from the initiation into and mastery of practical not theoretical knowledge.

The relevance of Carr's account of practical reasoning is significant to physical education, primarily because it demonstrates how practical knowledge cannot or should not be explained as a form of propositional knowledge because it would dispense with the performative criteria that is such a crucial feature of practical knowledge. Likewise, it would also be a mistake to assume that practical knowledge can be reduced to mere physical ability, which would remove the need to learn how to reason practically. It is also noteworthy to mention at this juncture that one needs to be cautious not to overstate the logical status of practical reasoning as a form of practical knowledge because technically it is not strictly a valid form of reasoning according to propositional forms. For instance, there is no logical fault in acknowledging the premises but an agent may decide not to "taste all sweet things" or pursue some end. The idea that the conclusion of the argument is an action should not be taken too far, and as I have outlined, practical knowledge should not be explained in propositional terms or even an applied theory but can be used in an analogous way that is rational but not truth functional. According to Winch (2010), dispositional accounts of knowing how only offer a partial explanation of what it is to be an expert practitioner as much more can be gained by judging performance when actions are subject to both constitutive norms (what makes them action of type X rather than type Y) and evaluative norms (what makes X graceful, efficient and so on) in a contextually relevant way. Knowing how to do something in most cases is to know how to act in such a way that intelligence concepts like "clever" or "silly", "prudent" or "rash" are applicable to the action and the know how that it expresses (Winch, 2010). Judging whether a person knows how to do something involves a good deal more than the mere acquisition of procedural knowledge or skill. It also involves episodic accounts of judgement that have taken account of the particular context in "order to act well or expertly" (Winch, 2010, pp. 563–564).[14]

According to Reid (1996a), in reference to Carr's account of theory and practice in physical activities, propositional knowledge usually functions as technical knowledge or as the technical component of practical knowledge. Wright (2000) makes the point that being able to reason in a practical way is a process that normally happens in physical education anyway, particularly as it relates to understanding "how" and "why" certain movement patterns fit into games. She goes on to add that there is considerably more to understanding practical knowledge than the ability to reason effectively because one may still lack the necessary skills to carry out an action. This would be problematic because physical skills are just one feature that characterise the inherent nature of physical education; as a result it would be a serious mistake to place too much emphasise on practical reasoning to justify physical education, because it neglects, first, the common features of practical knowledge such as practical performance, mastery of techniques specific to the activity and some degree of success in the performance and, second, neglects the richness and diversity of physical education activities that do not fit neatly into a means–end account. Certainly, I am not arguing or denying that those engaged in physical education-type activities do not reason practically with respect to complex or non-basic actions. As I alluded to earlier in my critique of Ryle's account, intelligent performance is to do one thing not two, and to determine whether a performance can be classed as intelligent according to certain standards specific to the task requires the accumulation of heterogeneous performances that can assist in deciding whether the performance was a matter of sheer good luck or due to mastery of a skill. Therefore, to single out practical reasoning as the central feature of practical knowledge is to only look at one part of the picture instead of the whole. Practical knowledge I think can apply to simple tasks or actions just as much as those that demand a great deal, like complex or non-basic actions. It is only when one views the diversity of each activity, say from individual to team sports, that one gets an appreciation of the different skills and techniques required to participate in them, and as a result an understanding of the activity will be necessary. Williams (1999) makes the point that it is impossible to define exhaustively the nature of knowledge because it is not just the case that we think, act, and so on as separate entities, but rather that all of these aspects are logically interwoven. Consequently, when it comes to practical knowledge a comprehensive view has to be considered if we are going to acknowledge the diversity of physical activities that take place within physical education.

So what are the common features in practical knowledge that could be used to distinguish propositional knowledge from practical reasoning? Borrowing from the accounts presented on practical knowledge it appears to me that there are three features implicit in physical performance. These are as follows:

(1) Intention to act out ϕ as a purpose;
(2) Mastery of the means or methods adopted for successful ϕing;
(3) Being judged as consistently successful and flexible according to special criteria in the performance of ϕing that are context specific to the social practices (normative practices) of ϕing.[15]

I am the first to acknowledge that there is an implicit element that simply cannot be verbally articulated or explained when it comes to practical knowledge, such as creative or expressive forms of movement, and cannot be easily reduced to technical or propositional form. I think it is important to realise that there are many aspects to practical knowledge that should not be segregated in case we seriously alter our understanding of it. I am in agreement with Wright (2000, p. 281), who argues that when practical knowledge is viewed holistically it is "... the performance that is all important in assessing whether people have practical knowledge or not ...", and it means more than "can do" and involves aspects such as "... agency, intentionality, and initiation into valued social practices ...". Therefore, we cannot and should not rule out certain physical education activities such as simple tasks or actions because they are deemed to have no educational value compared to intellectual or academic pursuits in the curriculum according to some question-begging account. These attitudes are prejudicial to theory against practice and basically lack understanding of the complexities of practical knowledge, not to mention an understanding of the nature of theoretical or propositional knowledge and its place in education. For instance, one of the key features of any education is to obtain a level of competence so we can say that person A knows how to do X, but this is not enough because we should also introduce and initiate students into the standards and excellences of that activity. This cannot be done if we do not have available to us the conceptual framework in which to talk generally about the differences between a novice and expert performer in the particular area of activity in which we are concerned about.

To Sutton (2007, p. 772), the distinction between knowing and doing, explicit or conscious thought and embodied or kinaesthetic memory which underlies skilled performance may seem to reinstate the old dichotomies of dualism, but we should not be "blinded" by the claimed independence of habit and thought because genuine expertise requires "sculpting" and "shaping" (practice), as well as a need for some theoretical understanding of more complex kinds of integration and links between knowing and doing. He goes on to add that the primacy of embodied performance and the secondary role of thought (and talk) may seem to be incidental by-products of being actively immersed and embedded in the moment of the task rather than a contributing factor of that skill; however, this is not the whole story because experts too require concentration, mental focus, conscious effort and so on. As a result, the focus here is on the embodied intelligence and the diverse forms of interaction and mutual influence that occur between thinking and doing from a phenomenological and cognitive science perspective. Sutton (2007) concludes that what is central to, for example, the skill of batting requires both developing and exerting high levels of skill – skill that does not restrict and close off the intellect from our embodied performances, but establishes networks that allow the flexibility to link "… thought and action, knowledge and motion, conceptual memory and procedural memory" (p. 779). Since practitioners, coaches, scientists and so on do not understand fully the specific mechanism about how exactly we respond in real-time embodied performance, it would be a conceptual mistake to compare theoretical knowledge with practical knowledge or vice versa. To appreciate the place of practical knowledge requires an understanding of human achievement in gaining practical knowledge. For instance, because a task or action is simple does not mean that it was necessarily easy to master and have consistent success at; so an appreciation of these qualities often requires personal experience and, in the end I think, is essential to an understanding of practical knowledge.

I will now turn my attention to a review of a well-known educational philosophical theory of the curriculum commonly known as the "forms of knowledge" thesis, which won widespread post-war popularity and led to physical education being cast out into the educational wilderness. As a result of the dominance of this thesis such accounts have attracted much criticism from postmodern and poststructuralist sources about the value of traditional epistemology in education. Subsequently, I intend to draw upon some of these accounts to argue for an alternative conception of education that can accommodate practical as well as theoretical or academic-type pursuits.

Post-war educational epistemology: the "forms of knowledge" thesis and the inadequacies of the post-war conception of physical education in education[16]

P. H. Hirst (1974), in his chapter titled "Liberal education and the nature of knowledge", is attributed with providing a philosophical theory of curriculum commonly referred to as the "forms of knowledge" thesis, which went on to become the endorsed or accepted position – albeit with a few modifications – of a host of philosophers of education associated with the London Institute of Education.[17] First, for the purposes of this chapter, and second, for convenience, I shall refer to supporters of some kind of forms of knowledge view as "the liberal education paradigm". The central tenet of this paradigm views education as the pursuit of knowledge that is determined "... objectively in a range, in structure, and in content by the forms of knowledge itself ..." and in the development of the mind in "... rational knowledge, whatever form that freely takes" (Hirst, 1974, pp. 31–43). The basic elements of this liberal conception of education consisted of students being initiated and inculcated into seven main areas of knowledge[18] that form the mind and can be clearly distinguished because of their logical form and can be tested against experience and therefore have distinct verification procedures according to particular public criteria (Hirst, 1974). Hirst's earlier forms of knowledge thesis delineated a set of epistemological criteria that clearly focused exclusively on modes of purely theoretical or intellectual understanding, which basically excludes physical activities. Likewise, so did Peters (1966), who basically labelled the content of sport and games as largely a matter of "knack" with limited educational use in his sophisticated account of educationally worthwhile activities (see Chapter V). Carr (1997) makes the pertinent observation that the liberal education paradigm resulted in theorists and scholars of physical education attempting three possible responses for the justification of physical education activities within the curriculum. These are as follows: (1) agree with the liberal education paradigm and concede that physical activities have no educational value and subsequently provide non-educational justifications for the inclusion of physical activities within the curriculum; (2) argue that the liberal education paradigm is fundamentally sound and attempt to adapt the content of physical education programmes to meet the paradigm; and, (3) argue that the liberal education paradigm is partially or completely flawed and provide an alternative conception of education which can accommodate practical as well as theoretical pursuits. Carr goes on to comment that the first option has usually been considered by theorists and scholars of physical education to be quite damaging, and undermining of its professional status within educational institutions. What is interesting to note is that around the 1970s and 1980s it appeared that the second option seemed to gain popularity as it brought forward sophisticated attempts to demonstrate that some or all forms of physical activity could be justified as moral or aesthetic education.[19] However, as noted above, it is not surprising that the third option came to be the most attractive course of action for most of the more seriously minded theorists and scholars of physical education.[20] Carr (1997) makes the point that the liberal education paradigm drew the distinction between educational and non-educational activities in the wrong place, and without doubt this can be attributed to the confusion surrounding the distinctions between education and training, intrinsic and extrinsic value, theory and practice, the liberal and the vocational and so on. Carr (1997) even acknowledges that his views are close to the liberal education paradigm, particularly in relation to epistemological issues to do with the development of the rational mind; however, he goes on to identify "two potential flaws" in the liberal education paradigm pertaining to the educational/non-educational and theory/practice dichotomies: first, such an approach presents an artificial separation of the theoretical and practical and, second, it preserves a kind of dualism which has been heavily criticised by opponents of dualism like Ryle and others. He goes on to add that these dichotomies are so "coarsely woven" that it may be more convenient to review the pragmatist charge that advocated for a liberal prejudice against a range of practical activities in favour of traditional epistemological sympathies of an academic nature. Carr's position about the longstanding problem of the place of physical education within the curriculum becomes clearer when he argues that it may be easier to resolve this issue by not demonstrating the educational value of certain physical activities within physical education programmes that appear to be directed towards a range of goals, not all of which are strictly educational. He states:

> Clearly the skills of shorthand typing or swimming do not have the same educational value of history or geography – they are not, that is to say, included in the curriculum for reasons of "personal illumination" – but they have all the same a valid place in any school curriculum concerned to equip pupils for after-school life.
>
> (Carr, 1997, p. 203)

Instead, Carr's argument rests on a distinction between education and schooling that post-war liberal traditionalists such as Peters and Hirst did not acknowledge. He goes on to add that by recognising that "... schools have a plurality of goals and purposes – only one of which is educational ..." – we come to the point where physical education activities need to be "redistributed" because of their "heterogeneous" nature across the educational/non-educational distinction, which will no doubt raise some serious questions, not only about the "point and purpose" of teaching physical education activities, but more importantly the ways in which they should be taught (Carr, 1997, p. 203).

According to McNamee (2005), accounts by Reid (1996a, 1996b, 1997) and Carr (1979a, 1997) failed to confront the liberal education paradigm because

Reid was unsuccessful in providing arguments for the specific epistemological aspects of the activities of physical education and Carr's position was a broad rehearsal of "Petersian" education. He goes on to add that a more useful starting point in responding to the liberal educational paradigm is to challenge the claims made by Peters' account of "seriousness" which is used to differentiate knowledge considered to be of educational value versus those forms which are not. In taking up this challenge, McNamee (2005, p. 7) asks the question: "Why ... should a wide-ranging cognitive content similarly be viewed as a logically necessary condition of educational activities?". In a way, claims of "seriousness" are some of the same justifications made by theorists and scholars of physical education for the subject, as are its transformative qualities which can contribute to a quality of life. As a result they fail simply because these are hypothetical arguments, contingent upon satisfaction derived by those who participate in these practices. Of course, one needs to acknowledge that some people despise and loathe sport and physical education, just as we have those who are passionate participants, and hence this explains why such justifications break down. In order to overcome some of these differences McNamee (2005, p. 7) provides what he considers to be the strongest philosophical case for what it means to be physically educated when he states:

> ... what one knows must characterise the way one acts in the world, then as physical educators, it is our duty to both habitualise children into patterns of activity and engagement with social practices such as hockey and basketball, and to open up to our students the significant sporting inheritance of our cultures so that they too may come to savour its joys and frustrations *and* to know a little about the aspects of the cultures which sporting practices instantiate (for no one would seriously deny their enormous significance in modern societies).

Such a position is influenced by a MacIntyrean (2007) account of philosophy, which can be identified from the use of terms such as "social practices" and "cultures/traditions". Such views essentially preclude the identification of universal and/or objective forms of knowledge and here we start to see the demise of the traditional epistemological account once preferred by philosophers of education in resolving issues surrounding questions about the structure of knowledge and its educational significance and a move towards postmodern and poststructuralist accounts of education.

The demise of post-war educational epistemology: the postmodern and poststructuralist challenge

What is of interest to my thesis is that the one-time pro-rationalist position held by Hirst in the mid-1970s to the 1980s now appears to have been radically revised to the point where he acknowledges that the rationalist approach to knowledge was a "great mistake", as it viewed "... theoretical knowledge as the only type of knowledge ... in determining both the ends and means of rational practice ... of the good life" (Hirst, 1993, p. 193). There can be no doubt that postmodernism and poststructuralist critiques have led to widespread scepticism among philosophers of education about the value of traditional epistemology in education. In a way it almost seems *de rigueur* on the part of some post-modernists and poststructuralists to be intentionally distrustful and suspicious about any absolutist discussion of objective knowledge and truth and to prefer relativist or at least pluralist ideals clothed in the language of "rival traditions", "social practices", "narratives", "social construction" and so on (Carr, 1999). For instance, postmodernists and poststructuralists would argue that there is no objective truth, because it is an intractable concept in which truth is better under-stood as something that is socially constructed due to our interpretation of our environment as a meaningful being-in-the-world. As a result human beings are the absolute source of our experience of knowing in the world, which comes to us in many different forms as different agents make sense of world. This school of thought has been greatly influenced by the phenomenologist Merleau-Ponty. It would appear that Hirst's defection from his rationalist transcendental approach to education seems to have occurred under the influence of certain postmodernist and social constructivist philosophical trends in favour of an appeal to a kind of relativism. This picture starts to emerge when he makes ref-erence to education as primarily an initiation into certain substantive social prac-tices in which such practices "... are rationally engaged in ... individually or collectively which have been socially constructed ..." and deemed significant by some social group (Hirst, 1993, p. 195). He goes on to state that education will involve practices in at least three distinguishable domains: (1) varied basic prac-tices necessary for any individual to be rationally viable in their given everyday physical, personal and social contexts; (2) practices from a wider range of optional practices available for the construction of each individual rational life; (3) critical reflection of the first two categories (second order) (Hirst, 1993, pp. 195–196). To Parry (1998a), the language of "practices" used by Hirst in his modified account of education is still a type of rationalism, albeit in reduced form to his earlier accounts, and does nothing to resolve or justify the place of physical education within the curriculum. He goes on to make a sharp observa-tion about Hirst's usage of the term "rational practices" and asks:

> Is a rational practice one which contributes to the development of rationality; or simply a practice that can be engaged in rationally? If the former, then the case remains to be made for PE activities; and, if the latter, then it is not clear what is excluded, so that no educational justification is forthcoming.
>
> (Parry, 1998a, p. 72)

Like any philosophical thesis of education, one may challenge the liberal educa-tion paradigm by searching for inconsistencies or incoherence within it. Like-wise, one could totally abandon the paradigm and in doing so (re)conceptualise some or all of the conceptual accounts to find an approach to physical education more conducive to its educational claims. Despite the ongoing battle surrounding the contentious nature of knowledge, I think the postmodern and poststructuralist critiques of traditional epistemology in education have highlighted significant questions about the nature and meaning of knowledge and truth that by no means have been finally settled. The importance of and significance of embodiment in education in its various ways of "knowing" and "doing" I think could offer credible philosophical conceptions and justifications for the inclusion of sport and physical education within educational institutions.

The unique place of physical education within education: (re) conceptualising the idea of physical education and what it means to be "physically educated"[21]

Postmodern theories, particularly the broad philosophical school of thought known as continental philosophy, have unquestionably been significant in renewing an interest in sport and physical education discourse surrounding the crucial role embodiment can have in educational institutions. This scholarly interest in the "meaning" of movement in sport and physical education discourse has been limited to the influential work of Arnold (1979a), *Meaning in Movement, Sport and Physical Education*, Best (1978), *Philosophy and Human Movement*, Gerber and Morgan (1979), *Sport and the Body: A Philosophical Symposium*, Kretchmar (2005a), *Practical Philosophy of Sport and Physical Activity* and Metheny (1968), *Movement and Meaning*. Unfortunately, the current literature and its status within physical education discourse is scarce and has not been widely established; however, some of the recent and more notable authors who have made contributions to the literature of phenomenology in physical education have taken thematic approaches varying from "operative meaning and liaison" to "physical or movement literacy".[22] Other discipline areas, particularly philosophy and sociology, have also addressed this topic – often using quite different terms and concepts – and so I will limit my critique to the following philosophical conceptual approaches in physical education discourse: Arnold's (1979a, 1988a) three dimensions of movement in education, O'Loughlin's (1998, 2006) embodied intelligence and practice in education, Egan's (1997) somatic understanding and Merleau-Ponty's lived experience (1942/1963, 1945/1962, 1947/1964, 1948/2004). Therefore, for the purposes of this section, I plan to outline some of the significant conceptual insights made by such works, in an attempt to ascertain whether physical education could benefit from these understandings within the curriculum, and if so, what form this may take. I discuss each briefly in turn.

The three dimensions of movement in education: education "about" movement, education "through" movement and education "in" movement

Arnold (1979a, 1988a) in his seminal work proposes three conceptual dimensions of movement as a justification for its legitimate place within general education as a

response to Peters' and Hirst's claims made against the contentious place of physical education within the curriculum.[23] He has some success in setting forth a legitimate account of physical education as a stand-alone subject to be studied within
the curriculum with his three conceptual dimensions of movement. To Arnold
(1979a), education "about" movement is best understood as a specific subject that
draws upon on a diverse array of discipline areas such as physiology, psychology,
sociology and so on, and comprises its own theoretical body of knowledge, and is
regarded as a serious area of research that can be applied in practical situations. A
practical example could be: How can I train in order to delay the onset of fatigue
in a physical activity? The solutions to such a problem can be found in the various
disciplines engaged in and subsequently "about" movement, which is predominantly concerned with the theoretical foundation in which coherent understanding
can take place about what is performed. In the second dimension of education
"through" movement, movement can best be understood as a family of physical
activities that are normally found and associated with the conceptual term "physical education". Accordingly, physical education can be justified within the curriculum as long as its activities are instrumental in serving directly and indirectly the
aims and purposes of education. For example, there is considerable scientific evidence to suggest that physical activity can have positive health benefits, and since
physical education activities include some form of physical activity their value
rests in the contribution it can make to the improvement and maintenance of
healthy students in the school context. In the third dimension, education "in"
movement brings together the view that physical activities when experienced from
the "inside" (or participatory perspective) permit the actualisation of the agent in a
set of distinctive and bodily-orientated contexts which ultimately provide opportunities for the agent to learn about him or herself and the world in which he or she
lives in a meaningful way. Education "in" movement involves the engagement of
the agent in physical activity itself so that the lived experience can enrich and bring
greater understanding of and meaning to what the agent does by appropriate
means. The key aspect of education "in" movement that is pertinent in this case is
the point that movement activities should not be viewed as "objects" studied in
isolation as a means to other ends, but rather participated "in" and pursued because
they are full of meaning that has personal intrinsic value worth pursuing for its
own sake.

The problem with Arnold's three dimensions of movement in education is
that the "about" and "through" dimensions have tended to dominate at the
expense of the "in" dimension in school programmes. As a result, this turns
physical education into a theoretical subject, thereby legitimising it according to
a theoretical model of education but delegitimising it as practice. Kretchmar
(2000b) confirms this point when he argues that theorists and scholars of physical education have long agreed that meaning has a significant role to play, but
there exists considerable scholarly disagreement over which model is perceived
to be the most successful pedagogical method in practice. Thorburn (2008) confirms that most school-based physical education programmes characteristically
lack the integration of practical activity with subject knowledge. He goes on to

add that this has basically resulted in students becoming disengaged in the learning process due to the limited number of practical opportunities afforded them to learn from personalised experience. To overcome these problems Thorburn argues that a Merleau-Pontian phenomenological framework could improve what he refers to as "authenticity" issues surrounding students' learning in physical education by integrating more effectively students' lived-body experiences with experiential learning. It would appear that the benefits of the phenomenological route have educational potential. What makes phenomenology educationally desirable in this case is its capacity to take an explicitly body-linked subject like physical education and describe how our embodiment has a significant role to play in student learning.

Bodies in education: practical consciousness and multisensorial education

According to O'Loughlin (1998), there has been a tendency in postmodern conceptualisations to, first, view the subject of the body as a conceptual object of discourse and, second, to misunderstand the significance of the social dimension of embodiment. She goes on to add that if we want the body to be taken seriously within education we need to shift education's focus within research, practice and curriculum by helping individuals access the realm of "practical consciousness" and in the process also assist agents in understanding how it is they react somatically to others. To O'Loughlin (1998, p. 291), practical consciousness refers to the complex but usually ignored circumstances of awareness of the "... embodied subject's attention to the habituated space ..." of themselves and others. For agents to come to an awareness of this realm requires an understanding of a "myriad of bodily positioning, gestures, orientations and verbal and non-verbal expressions" which are not explicitly part of discourses (O'Loughlin, 1998, p. 291). At the moment education seems to ignore the body altogether or render the body problematic, which can be seen by a "disembodied/ embodied" divide that exists in the curriculum. For instance, education seems to privilege knowledge that is disconnected from human experience against those subjects seen to be connected with bodily activity. O'Loughlin (1998) acknowledges that sport (assuming physical education as well) is often assumed as providing the best opportunity for realising a practical consciousness due to it being one of the most corporeal of the curriculum areas. Furthermore, the body in physical education seems to be confined within a relatively narrow set of disciplinary parameters that seem to focus on the body as a biomechanical object that must be managed, maintained, conditioned and repaired, and which establish routines of exercise, diet control and so on for instrumental reasons to improve performance. To redress the imbalance of knowledge as disembodied she argues that an embodied and multi-sensorial approach needs to be taken to the curriculum and to pedagogy by providing a diverse array of opportunities for exploring the multiplicity of experiences and behaviours through different spaces and environments. Embodiment in education has tended to be relegated to the margins of educational research, particularly surrounding what it means to be become educated. Why this is the case has more to do with the body being ignored altogether or considered to be problematic, particularly in accounts of how we come to understand knowledge.

Somatic understanding: the crucial elements of mimetic culture and its implications for education

Egan argues that the somatic is a distinctive kind of understanding (Egan, 1997, Chapter 5: Ironic understanding and somatic understanding). It begins only prior to language development and continues to be developed and modified by other modes of understanding for the rest of our lives. Egan (1997) borrows from Donald's (1991) characterisation of mimetic cultures, due to the similarities that exist with somatic understanding. He argues that mimetic representation (cultural forms and mental characteristics) and somatic understanding have survived to the present day either through evolutionary coding or by cultural transition because "memesis" forms the core of an ancient root that is distinctly human.[24] He goes on to add that memesis is distinguished from mimicry and imitation because it involves the invention of intentional representation and performance of such acts which communicate complex intentions beyond what is comprehensible among other animals. Crucial to any understanding of mimetic culture is an agent's own body and how it moves in space. Therefore the main elements of somatic understanding can be summarised by six descriptions and will yield a particular kind of distinctly human understanding that, once developed, is a form of non-linguistic understanding. These are as follows: (1) intentionality – purposeful action; (2) generativity – actions that can be broken into components and then reused for other purposes to represent something new, such as a child in the process of imitational practice of the basic actions of lifting, laughing, waving and so on of a parent which can then be used in a different sequence to re-enact these events; (3) communicativity – mimetic acts are normally performed publically to communicate; (4) reference – an ability to distinguish between play-acting and a real event; (5) unlimited objects – no limits on the events that can be represented; (6) autocueing – internally generated cues that are voluntary (Egan, 1997, pp. 164–165). The importance of emphasising somatic understanding is significant to my thesis because most postmodernist theories of education are built on assumptions that student understanding is essentially linguistic understanding. Egan rejects the postmodern position of an "essentially linguistic" conception of human experience and argues that from a very young age (pre-language) children have an understanding of the world which is not the same as a biological (animal) understanding; we are human beings before we acquire language. The ramifications here are significant given that the postmodern conception of educational theories asks for the fullest possible development of each understanding; and so it becomes even more important to develop and preserve somatic understanding due to the unique insights that can be gained from embodied experience. Furthermore, the mimetic skills that can be exemplified by games due to their universal structure – such as modelling social strata, acting out certain roles through imitation, support ritual, cooperation and so on – could be used for pedagogical practices; however, once developed they take on the unique human characteristics of intentionality, generativity, communicativity, reference and so on.

The philosophy of Merleau-Ponty and its significance for physical education

In direct contrast to the Platonic–Cartesian tradition, Merleau-Ponty does not view the body as a special kind of object separate from the mind, but views the body as "being-in-the-world" in the sense that our embodiment precedes reflective thought. Anderson (2002, p. 94) reinforces this point further by arguing that the "... experience of movement is thus humanizing, just as is the reading of Shakespeare or Willa Cather – and just as are Cather's and Shakespeare's acts of writing", and to denigrate our experiences of movement is to misunderstand the importance of non-theoretical knowledge. The implications here are significant, because such a position implies that there no longer exists a philosophical division between the object and subject, because the world begins from the body and provides the means in which we can develop a sense of our own identity and at the same time come to know the world via physical action. This is confirmed by Merleau-Ponty (1945/1962, p. 162), who emphasises that our body is a "meaningful core" that engages with the world through the body, which in turn provides the "... link between here and a yonder, a now and a future ...".

The body has posed a significant problem and challenge with educational theorists, particularly with explicitly body-linked subjects like physical educaiton. According to O'Loughlin (2006), embodiment has been for the most part absent from educational research specifically in those areas that focus on the process of "becoming educated", mainly because we have tended to accept that the body does not play a part in the construction of knowledge. She goes on to argue that to fully understand what is really involved in the making of different types of epistemic subjects requires a concentrated focus on the body as a multidimensional locus of all possible action. Unfortunately, the current trend in the social sciences and regrettably to some point even in physical education discourse[25] has focused on the discursively constructed body[26] as an object of scrutiny. For example, in its current educational form the latter stresses the health of the body through the development of healthy habits, the establishment of regular exercise routines and so on. While there is some recognition of the socially constructed nature of experience, what is missing in this case is how pre-reflective experience of our corporeal nature enables meaning to develop. As we have seen, on Merleau-Ponty's view of phenomenology human experience is essentially meaningful. As Merleau-Ponty puts it, we are "condemned to meaning" and as a result our involvement with our natural and human milieu implies that we cannot regard this milieu as value or meaning free.

To say that physical education is inextricably linked to the body is, to some, is to state the obvious, but the philosophical position of the body and our concept of human nature will have a direct bearing on how we think human beings should behave and be educated, and particularly in this case how we think they should be educated physically. As argued earlier in Chapter 2, much of contemporary sport and physical education theory and practice would appear to rest upon subtle forms of Cartesian dualism, despite claims to the contrary. This is evident by the way the body is treated as a disembodied object of study in most physical education programmes within schools, particularly the academic tradition of physical education. Subsequently, the performer is regarded as an instrument or reduced into parts to be studied from a biological–scientific perspective, with the express purpose of altering or controlling his corporeal aspects.

Rejecting the Cartesian conception of personhood, which depicts the body as a machine or instrument that needs to be mastered, permits human beings the opportunity to experience the depth and richness of our humanness (that being a "lived body") and in a sense creates a "new truth" about our active corporeal existence. Anderson (2002) makes the pertinent point that movement to physical education is analogous to the practice of music in the study of music, and so sport and physical education without engagement in movement is like a music programme without musical instruments. Consequently, human movement is the place where we can both find meaning and express our own particular identity, because the body is actively involved in the world and also the locus of expression and meaning-producing acts.

Embodiment should not be taken lightly, because the experience of movement is humanising, providing a meaningful way of making sense of being-in-the-world. These meaningful movement experiences can be captured by our actions in physical education and in short represent, express and confirm our capabilities, intentions and ways of being. Physical education activities can have a serious educational function in that they provide human beings with an insight into the depth of their basic existence, an avenue of discovery and self-expression, and an awareness of their capabilities and limitations so they become conscious of what they are and what they are not. The power of this kind of knowing is in harmony with important principles commonly pursued in education: freedom to explore, freedom to discover, freedom to express, freedom to invent and freedom to create (Kretchmar, 1995). Whitehead (1990) reinforces this point further when she argues that our embodiment affords us two almost inseparable modes of engagement with the world: our body responds through movement according to the demands of our environment; it is also perceptually sensitive to the nature of this environment.

If education is to be of the whole person it needs to be concerned with all of a person's faculties and capacities. Merleau-Ponty's view of phenomenology complements this view because it is the whole human being that experiences the world, not just the mind or the brain, even though I need a functioning mind or brain in order to experience at all. If human beings were not embodied, we could not experience the world. As Merleau-Ponty (1947/1964, p. 17) reveals, perceptual capacities underpin all intellectual capacities, for as he says:

> ... we can only think the world because we have already experienced it; it is through this experience that we have the idea of being, and it is

through experience that the words "rational" and "real" receive a meaning simultaneously.

At the heart of Merleau-Ponty's account of phenomenology is a description of "perception", or the world perceived from our experiences of being-in-the-world. In this context, being-in-the-world necessarily involves the unified whole in which the elements have no separate existence from each other, but contribute to a whole in a meaningful way. According to Merleau-Ponty (1945/1962), if we understand perception properly as the experience of an embodied subject, we assign meaning or value to objects perceived based on our practical and emotional relation to them, which is just as real as the objects' properties. For instance, to a frightened child who has been burned, the light of a candle changes its "appearance" and he or she becomes "literally repulsed" by it, just as the candle is "bright" (Merleau-Ponty, 1945/1962, p. 60). The educational implications of Merleau-Ponty's phenomenological account of human experiences connects strongly with the notion that learning also involves the exploration of the world from where one is as well as coming to a clearer understanding of how things relate to each other and to ourselves in the world. It is an ongoing process. The key here is that we "come to" understand something (if successful) from our own point of view as a result of experiencing it. To use Merleau-Ponty's (1945/1962, p. x) analogy, we come to know "what a forest, a prairie or a river is" because we have already experienced the countryside as a place in which we have explored, not because of the abstract symbols of the geographer's map.

This is further reinforced by Hughson and Inglis (2002), who attempt to understand and capture the corporeal experiences of soccer players' movements through language, while recognising that the phenomenon of corporeal movement is essentially non-verbal in character. They go on to add that Merleau-Ponty's philosophy of corporeal movement makes a "... profound contribution to a very vexing problem, both within the philosophy of sport and philosophy in general ..." because it captures the "evanescent qualities" of corporeal experience in concepts and of language (Hughson and Inglis, 2002, p. 2). According to Hughson and Inglis (2002), Merleau-Ponty's philosophy presents a more nuanced account of particular modes of corporeal experience, one that seems to grasp the uniqueness of experience in a concrete way rather than discredit it under other less phenomenologically sympathetic philosophies. Subsequently, Merleau-Ponty's philosophy makes a significant two fold contribution: first, it grasps the nature of experience in general and locates the body as the focal point in the production of the lived experience and, second, it captures the uniqueness of embodied experience in the language of the philosopher (Hughson and Inglis, 2002). Hughson and Inglis (2002), after an extensive and complicated critique of Merleau-Ponty's terminology of "body-subjects", go on to apply this approach with the view of demonstrating how the "player-body-subject's" experience of soccer play might be reconstructed through philosophical analysis. On the basis of their critique they proceed to outline a phenomenological model for exploring the relationship that holds for, and underpins, forms of soccer play in general.

This relationship is framed by three fundamental components in which each part is interdependent and represents a totality: (1) body-subject; (2) practical knowledge and actions; and (3) spatial form of the activity (Hughson and Inglis 2002, p. 8). Although the triadic relationship was originally intended for soccer play, its structure has considerable application in other areas like physical education discourse. The important point to take away from this framework is how the performer makes sense of his or her embodiment from a phenomenological perspective. For instance, an expert or proficient tennis player has a greater affinity with his swing than a novice or beginner as he has already achieved maximum grip and is able to understand kinaesthetic feedback more efficiently and adjust more quickly in a refined way.[27] In this case, incorporating the educational aspects of teaching tennis with the phenomenological perspective for learning has more to do with providing experiences with the phenomenon such as the tennis swing (spatial form), with the overarching aim of increasing the body-subjects' (students') skilful understanding (knowledge and action) of the situation. These experiences enable the student to become familiar with the spatial form of the activity and at the same time come to understand how kinaesthetic feedback is crucial in obtaining maximal grip in his or her situation. Merleau-Pontian phenomenology places the body as the central focal point in the production of the lived experience and provides the means to capture the phenomenon of the non-verbal characteristics of movement and their meanings in, by and through physical education.

Phenomenology and physical education discourse

Van Manen's (1997) approach to the "lived experience" shares similarities with Arnold's third dimension of education "in" movement due to the emphasis he places on understanding something "from the inside" as a means to gain a deeper appreciation of our everyday experiences from the first person perspective. In van Manen's approach, we have a good example of phenomenological study of human experience because he provides, on the one hand, a description of the quality of human experience and, on the other hand, a description of meaning as a being-in-the-world. For instance, phenomenology asks: What is this or that kind of experience like? It is important to realise that the basic idea of the lived experience could take two forms. First, it attempts to describe and interpret an immediate description of the agent's lifeworld as a being-in-the-world, whereas, in the second, it attempts an intermediate description of the agent's lifeworld involving a more active element of interpretation. Van Manen goes on to emphasise that the nature of the lived experience has a temporal structure that can never be grasped introspectively but rather only retrospectively, and thereby it has an interpretative element that relates the particular to the universal, part to whole, episode to totality. According to van Manen (1997, p. 101), our lived experience can be described and interpreted by four fundamental "lifeworld" themes or "existentials" useful as guides in the reflective process: spatiality (lived space), corporeality (lived body), temporality (lived time) and relationality (lived other), by which all human beings experience the world, although not all in the same modality. He goes on to provide an example of a father and son going for a bike ride to highlight his point that the significance of the lived experience gathers meaning when the father assigns memory to the experience and interprets the quality of the space, mood and shared world associated with "going for a bike ride with my son" as something special and unique, and in the reflective act determinates it as a meaningful aspect of his life. Investigating experience as we live it aims at establishing a connection with the original experience.

This is further reinforced by Thorburn (2008, pp. 272–273) who argues that the first step in implementing a phenomenological approach in physical education is to recognise the distinguishing characteristics of the lived experience using an "… autobiographical writing approach, and then analyse the criteria by which students' learning can be measured following practice". Likewise, to Connolly (1995, p. 27) the lived experience is a place where we can conceptualise "… a praxis that celebrates subjective lived experience, and that places the body as the centre of things" in which the body, body-subject, lived experience provides us with a method "for feeling, seeing, knowing, and understanding our lived experiences and the meaning(s) of those experiences". According to Connolly (1995), phenomenology and physical education share a "common ground" through three sensitising concepts: lived experience, intersubjectivity and "insider" stories (or lived experience descriptions). She goes on to outline three ways in which phenomenology can be used effectively in physical education: (1) when the body does something in physical education we create opportunities for narrative descriptions (insider stories) which can generate a "voice of the body" that has a unifying potential about what the body does, or how it feels to do something; (2) eidetic features give significant meaning to the experience which when made explicit can be used heuristically as a pedagogical method in physical education; (3) shifting the focus to the body as the integrating centre of things forces us to refute dualism and to realise that as humans we are at our best when we are consciously aware of our embodiment. It is important to note that neither physical education nor phenomenology on its own can do this, but it is only through making the connection between physical education and phenomenology explicitly clear that we can begin to see the value of using physical means to educate in physical education. After all, physical education offers us a means to discover the corporeal movement of the body and phenomenology offers us a means of articulating our relation to our own bodies, particularly from a Merleau-Pontian point of view. This is further confirmed by Connolly (1995, p. 39), who states:

> If we are to make the wisdom of the body intelligible, *we must find ways of telling our stories, listening to our stories, and making our own stories meaningful for ourselves and others.*

To ignore this dimension is to close off those embodied experiences of the world that arise naturally through bodily movement which Merleau-Ponty (1945/1962) calls the "phenomenal body" and which refer to what "I" experience as a natural system of one's own body taking place in the domain of the phenomenal. An example of this occurs when my hand moves around the object it touches, anticipating the stimuli and tracing out a form which I am about to perceive visually. Our perception ends in objects because our own body as experienced by us "from the inside" makes contact with the object through touch, stimuli and tracing out its form from the first-person point of view. Simply put, we cannot come to understand our embodiment if we do not engage in the world as a being-in-the-world. The phenomenal body is what we experience as a first-person subject of experience and as a result we can only exist in connection with a lived body. We cannot make contact with the world just by thinking about it, but only through experiencing it with our senses and acting in it, in ways that range from the most complex to the most primitive unreflective movements. The student experiences and apprehends his body neither as an abstract object nor as an instrument, but as a "lived-body" subject that senses and does the sensing in a meaningful way. Subsequently, movement becomes significant not by knowledge about the body or what it does in a disembodied way. It is through doing and being on the "inside" of physical education that we become aware of our embodiment. The educational implications are that, because we have experienced our embodiment through a family of physical activities in physical education, we can then come to know or learn about the various scientific (biomechanics, physiology and so on) analyses of the body and make sense of them in a meaningful way. Consequently, one of the primary roles of physical education is about making movement experiences as significant as possible, by exploring different physical learning environments from the students' perspective so students gradually come to understand how things relate to each other and to themselves. To do this we need to locate the body as the focal point in the production of the lived experience, and also recognise the role corporeal movement and embodiment plays in learning, in, by and through physical education.

Historically, the discipline area of physical education has struggled for legitimacy at most if not all educational levels due to the damaging claims made by critics who argue that physical education is a trivial pursuit and thereby non-serious compared to other forms of knowledge and understandings that are considered to be educationally worthwhile. For instance, the argument goes that the nature of sport and physical education is not concerned with the attainment of theoretical knowledge because it is only concerned with "knowing how" in the form of practical knowledge. Hence its own nature renders it non-academic and non-educational. The phenomenon of play poses some unique problems mainly because we are discussing something of which everyone has an intuitive understanding, but when it comes to explaining what it is and what it is for we come to much ambiguity. Despite its universality, scholarly investigations of its nature, structure and purpose have produced a diverse array of ad hoc, occasionally antithetical characterisations that have either condemned or celebrated play. Therefore, it is hardly surprising to note the same diversity of theories which have attempted to explain the multifaceted, paradoxical and highly elusive phenomenon of play in educational discourse. Consequently, in the next chapter I discuss why philosophers talk so much about play and games as a means to make sense of play and its educational significance.

Notes

1 I provided a detailed critique of Peters' (1966) work in Chapter 1.
2 In this case I will argue for practical pursuits in the curriculum like sport and physical education; however, I am cognisant of the status of other practical pursuits in the curriculum like drama, dance, art, manual arts and so on which also experience prejudicial attitudes.
3 Some parts of the first five sections of Chapter 3 have been adapted from my paper (Stolz 2013b), "The philosophy of G. Ryle and its significance for physical education: Some thoughts and reflections". *European Physical Education Review*, 19(3), pp. 381–396.
4 I have limited my critique to three forms of knowledge specifically for this book, but it is important to point out that it is not possible to give a full account of all forms of knowledge here. Knowledge can be classified in many different ways which sometimes depends on the author. For instance, White (1982) outlines three broad conceptual classes of knowledge: "knowing how A X's", "knowing that", and "knowing by acquaintance". Another example can be found in Maritain (1995), who distinguishes three divisions of knowledge: sense knowledge, philosophical knowledge and spiritual knowledge.
5 Based on my conservative calculations, a delivery at 150 kilometres per hour travelling from bowler's hand to bat equates to about 0.4828 seconds or 482.8 milliseconds reaction time (it could be less due to a number of variables) and movement time in which a batsman has to complete a shot. Another example worth considering is a batter in baseball responding in action to a pitcher who throws a fastball at 90 to 100 miles per hour (or 145 to 160 kilometres per hour respectively). Of course the calculations will be less than the cricket estimates provided as the distance from the pitcher's mound to the home plate is less than from the bowler to the batsman in cricket.
6 It is interesting to note that the principles of integration and personalisation in educational discourse can be found in the following examples: Queensland Studies Authority (QSA) *Physical Education Senior Syllabus*, Queensland Studies Authority, Brisbane, 2010 and Scottish Qualifications Authority (SQA) *Arrangements Document for Higher Still Physical Education: Higher Level*, Scottish Qualifications Authority, Edinburgh, 2004.
7 Stanley and Williamson (SW) (2001) set out Ryle's argument against the intellectualist claim that knowing how is a species of knowing that using *reduction ad absurdum*. According to SW, Ryle's argument can be set out as follows:

(1)   If one Fs, one employs knowledge of how to F.
(2)   If one employs knowledge that p, one avows the proposition that p.
(3)   Knowledge how to F is knowledge that, for some proposition $\phi(F)$.

In a nutshell, if knowing how was a species of knowing that, then to engage in any action one would have to contemplate a proposition, but the contemplation of a proposition is itself an action which in itself would have to be followed by an infinite number of propositions of ever increasing complexity to the point that knowing how could never be exhibited.
8 This is a linguistic term that applies straightforwardly to *know*. Two of them being, *how* and *why*.

9 I use a cricket example here because it is what I am most familiar with. For those who may not be familiar with my cricket example provided, substitute off-spin bowling with something like baseball pitching or tennis serving.

10 Practical knowledge may have an informative or explanatory function, but I wish to review practical reasoning and its alleged connection with practical knowledge.

11 Ryle by contrast holds that performance is central to practical knowledge, but Carr's schema infers either an empirical or conceptual necessary condition of some kinds of action and as a result Ryle's account needs to be adapted accordingly.

12 These three conditionals have their origins in Plato's account of knowledge. See for example Plato's *Theaetetus*.

13 The term "satisfactoriness" can best be described as the most satisfactory plan which will best serve our purposes and gratify our desires.

14 For instance, to ascribe the characteristics of an expert soccer player will be multifarious, but will possess a set of appropriately mastered skills, knowledge and understanding of the rule-governed features of the game through to the ability to apply these skills in an intentional way whilst continually thinking and adjusting to the endless number of variables – the condition of the field, the weather, the position of defenders and fellow team-mates and so on – in which a player interacts with and responds to consciously or unconsciously. Whitehead (2001, p. 131) captures some of these features of intelligent action nicely in her conceptual account of physical literacy by describing a physical literate person as an individual who is perceptive in "… 'reading' all aspects of the physical environment, anticipating movement needs or possibilities and responding appropriately to the these, with intelligence and imagination" and who uses all their embodied capacities of "… perception, experience, memory, anticipation and decision making" in response to the physically challenging situation. The implications for physical education are that the concept of "reading" can be nurtured and developed in the educational setting. However, in order to bring this about Whitehead (2008, 2010) argues for a kind of heuristic approach that is guided by teachers so that students come to a greater understanding of embodied experience in order to enhance or improve physical performance.

15 I have listed three features as I believe there is considerable overlap and repetition in some accounts. As a result, from my review of the literature I have recognised three common features. Others, such as Wright (2000, pp. 279–281), uses the term "criteria of practical knowledge" in which she lists four kinds of criteria: (1) performance is the result of intentional human action; (2) performance has normative aspects because it implies success according to performance criteria that is not based on truth criteria; (3) success is context specific; (4) acknowledgement of success is dependent upon acting intentionally not based on simple good luck.

16 My use of the term "post-war" is used to demarcate a period in history which brought about the rise and fall of educational epistemology that was significant to physical education.

17 As alluded to earlier in this chapter, Hirst's close colleague Peters also had a profound dominance in the philosophy of education but it is now common knowledge that both played an equal part in influencing educational thinking about knowledge and understanding, particularly from the 1960s to the mid-1980s.

18 These are as follows: (1) understanding formal logic and mathematics; (2) understanding of the physical sciences; (3) awareness and understanding of our own and other peoples' minds; (4) moral judgement and awareness; (5) objective aesthetic experience; (6) religious understanding; (7) philosophical understanding. See Hirst and Peters (1970, Chapter 4: The Curriculum).

19 Two notable attempts are Aspin 1975, "Ethical aspects of sport and games and physical education" and Carlisle 1969, "The concept of physical education".

20 For some of the more notable authors, see the following: Arnold (1979a, 1979b, 1979c, 1988a, 1988b, 1989b, 1990, 1991, 1992, 1997); Carr (1978a, 1979a, 1983a,

1983b); Kirk (1983, 1988, 1992a, 1992b, 2010); Kretchmar (1996, 1998, 2000a, 2000b, 2005a, 2008a, 2008b); McNamee, (1992, 1998, 2005); Meakin (1983, 1990); Parry (1998a, 1998b, 1998c, 1998d); Reid (1996a, 1996b, 1997, 1998); Siedentop, (1992, 1994); Thompson (1983).

21 Some parts of the final five sections of Chapter 3 have been taken from Stolz, (2013a), "Phenomenology and physical education". *Educational Philosophy and Theory*, 45(9), 949–962.

22 For other notable authors on this topic, see: Kentel and Dobson (2007); Kretchmar (2000a, 2000b, 2007b); Loland (1992, 2006); Meier (1975, 1976, 1979, 1980); Sheets-Johnstone (1999); Smith (2007); Stevenson (1975); Stolz (2013a); Stone (1975); Whitehead (1990, 2001, 2008, 2010).

23 See, for example, Arnold 1979a, Chapter 6: Education, movement and the curriculum, and 1988a, Chapter 8: Education, schooling and the concept of movement.

24 The term "memesis" was coined by Donald (1991) and is a representational dimension of imitation which can be best understood as a gesture adopted to represent deeper meaning, like covering one's face to indicate grief.

25 Take for example, Kirk (1998b, Chapter I, 1999), Tinning and Glasby (2002) and Webb *et al.* (2008).

26 According to O'Loughlin (2006), the concept of a "discursively constructed body" draws upon an understanding of corporeal inscription which has historically occurred through external power structures like schools, but this notion of disciplining and regulating the body has taken on new meaning to also include overt consent to regulate and manage oneself.

27 Hubert Dreyfus seeks to combine the insights brought forward by Merleau-Ponty's phenomenology with dynamical approaches in neuroscience in the sporting context. Dreyfus provides an interpretative description of intentional arc and maximal grip by using the example of a tennis swing. In the novice performer, much of the agent's effort is on acquiring (pre-reflective thought) and laying down some of the finer aspects of the movements (intentional arc), whereas for the expert, prior experience has sculpted the agent's swing to the point where pre-reflection is no longer required and the agent can be more absorbed in the game because maximum grip (muscular gestalt) has been achieved. See Dreyfus 2002a.

4 The phenomenon of play and its educational significance in physical education

Why do philosophers talk so much about play, games and sports?

The concept of play has a long history in Western culture to the point where it has influenced our philosophical views of education. Huizinga (1949) in the classical text *Homo Ludens* argues that play has a certain significance that existed before culture existed and continues to pervade our culture today. The concept of play poses some unique problems. The difficulty lies in the fact that we are discussing something of which everyone has an intuitive understanding, but little or no way of conceptually articulating. Despite its universality, scholarly investigations of its nature, structure and purpose have produced a diverse array of ad hoc, occasionally antithetical characterisations that have either condemned or celebrated play. Therefore, it is hardly surprising to note the same diversity of theories which have attempted to explain the multifaceted, paradoxical and highly elusive phenomenon of play in educational discourse.

Historically, physical education has struggled for legitimacy at most if not all educational levels. One factor that has been significant in physical education's current status surrounds the diversity of activities found within its practice. For instance, the practice of physical education within educational institutions are as diverse as environmental habitats, in which activities can range from informal forms of play to more formalised versions of play that involve codified rules and skills. In one sense this is one of the reasons why physical education has featured within the curriculum; however, at the same time this has led to a significant dispute about what the profession is (or ought to be) and significantly contributed to the "grandfather clock syndrome" that has caused the ideas of physical education to swing from one extreme position to another, to the point where the pendulum never stops in exactly the same place nor stays near the middle. When we compare the traditional view of education, which places a significant onus upon propositional forms of knowledge in the development of the mind, with the current status of physical education it is not surprising that practical pursuits in the curriculum are deemed to have no serious part to play in this development and are relegated to the periphery in education. This is because education is deemed to be serious and play is considered to be non-serious. It follows that physical education is non-serious and so non-educational. In a sense, play is non-serious or it would not be play; however, upon further examination play cannot just be reduced to a closed set of systems due to the fact that the motives and reasons for playing are part of what it means to play. For instance, this could be for pleasure, a momentary break from common life and so on. Until we can understand the reasons why we play, I do not think we can understand their paradoxical nature or why in certain circumstances play can be very serious and at the same time have educational merit, given the right conditions. There are clearly elements within educational discourse which worship reason to the point of designating us as *homo faber*.[1] As a result there exists a negative and sometimes quite vulgar interpretative view that perceives play to be an occasional and peripheral phenomenon that is allowed, albeit grudgingly, in a restricted sense in certain places. The adoption of play, games and sports as methods for imparting educational ideas is significant to my thesis as it reflects a profound change in philosophical focus due to the growing interest in the phenomenon of play as an educational mechanism of value, particularly as it relates to competitive games.

Furthermore, it would appear that the transformation of physical education away from the traditional health objectives early in the twentieth century toward physical education as an educational process owes much to the influential legacy of Jesse Williams (1930), who examined physical education and asked two probing questions to obtain a new view of physical education based on unity. These are: (1) Is physical education an education *of the* physical? and (2) Is physical education an education *through* the physical?[2] He argued that education through the physical would produce some distinct gains that had been previously neglected, such as the unification of the body and mind, and that the physical experience is an extension of education that develops all the potentials of an individual's physical, psychological, social and moral values (virtues) gained from participating in directed play and appropriate games (Williams, 1930, 1951).

For the purposes of this chapter I will be concerned with the critical discussion of four issues: first, I outline the multifaceted, paradoxical and highly elusive phenomenon of play. My intent is not to provide an exhaustive explanation of play but rather to come to a better understanding of the interrelationships among the concepts of play, games and sport, and most importantly to determine when games and sports are also part of the play phenomena that occur in physical education programmes. Second, I argue that *homo faber* in his pursuit of mastery and objectivity reveals a conception of human nature that basically rejects unique bodily subjectivity, is unreceptive and closed off to different modes of perceiving and relating to the world, and which has been detrimental to our understanding of practical pursuits. Third, I highlight the ontological dimension of the play phenomenon by arguing that it deepens our experience of the world and is a distinct mode of being-in-the-world because it seeks to provide an understanding of the ways in which human beings subjectively experience the world and make sense of it. And lastly, I discuss how play, games and sport within physical education programmes are an extension and enrichment of education that is uniquely different from other curriculum areas because these activities offer opportunities to explore alternative modes of awareness and to develop insights into and new modes of being and possibilities perhaps not readily available elsewhere in the curriculum. Furthermore, I illuminate how physical education can benefit from using a hermeneutic–phenomenological framework as a methodological basis for linking students' lived-body experiences with the acquisition of increasingly complex subject knowledge within the curriculum.

Making sense of play, games and sport in physical education: the multifaceted, paradoxical and highly elusive phenomenon of play

We all know what play is and what it feels like, but when it comes to articulating what it is and what it is for, we come to much ambiguity. The reason for this ambiguity has much to do with the diversity of play forms and experiences found within play. A review of the literature will illustrate the complexity of this venture.[3] To provide an in-depth analysis of the psychological, sociological or historical accounts of play is far beyond the scope of this book; and so for the purposes of this chapter my intent is not to provide an exhaustive explanation of play but rather to come to a better understanding of the interrelationships among the concepts of play, games and sports, and most importantly to determine when games and sports are also part of the play phenomena. I will now turn my attention to a critique of the multifaceted and highly elusive phenomenon of play as a means to make sense of play, games and sports in physical education discourse.

In our vernacular the word "play" is used in a diversity of contexts. For instance, children play in the playground, an actor plays a part, a footballer plays a certain position or game, the gods play with human beings, he plays by the rules, he is being played, he is a playboy and so on. The use of the word "play" will depend on the context in which it is used and, as a result, meanings can range from the peripheral to the superficial, from the extended to the metaphorical and so on. The sheer variety of play presents a significant problem in coming to a better understanding of the phenomenon of play. According to Sutton-Smith (1997, p. 3), the diversity of play is well-illustrated by the varied kinds of play forms that can be found in the "menagerie of the play sphere". He goes on to list those activities that are often said to be play forms or play experiences, to illustrate the great diversity of play phenomena that can range from the mostly private to the mostly public sphere. These are as follows: mind or subjective play, solitary play, playful behaviours, informal social play, vicarious audience play, performance play, celebrations and festivals, contests such as games and sports, and risky or deep play (Sutton-Smith, 1997). It is noteworthy to mention that to Sutton-Smith the boundaries between each activity are not as discrete as they might imply, because some items typically go by other names, such as entertainment, recreation and so on. The ambiguity of play, as well as the great diversity of play forms, have led to considerable problems in conceptualising what play is. Understandably, the elusive and ambiguous nature of play seems particularly problematic in contemporary Western culture and this has led some to ask: Why is it acceptable for children to play but not for adults? Why do children "play" but adults "recreate"? Why is play used to distinguish childhood from adulthood? Why is play considered educationally important in young children's development and growth but considered a distraction for adults? To Sutton-Smith (1997), the reason why ambiguities exist surrounding play has more to do with a lack of clarity about the "popular cultural rhetorics" that underlie the various play theories and play terms and has more to do with consciously or unconsciously being persuaded by members of a particular affiliation of the worthwhileness of their ideologies. He goes on to add that popular cultural rhetorics are basically "ways of thought" in which most of us participate in one way or another, despite some dominant groups advocating for a particular rhetoric. Sutton-Smith (1997, pp. 9–11) outlines seven rhetorics, characterised as follows: (1) the rhetoric of play as progress, which is usually applied to children's development through play but not adults; (2) the rhetoric of play as fate, which is in total contrast to the prior rhetoric and involves gambling and games of chance; (3) the rhetoric of play as power, which is normally applied to sports, athletics and contests; (4) the rhetoric of play as identity, commonly associated with traditional and community celebrations and festivals as a means of confirming, maintaining or advancing the power and identity of the community of players; (5) the rhetoric of play as the imaginary, usually applied to playful improvisation of all kinds; (6) the rhetoric of the self, which involves solitary activities; and (7) the rhetoric of play as frivolous, which is normally identified with activities of the idle, however in modern times has come to signify a puritanical negative. It is interesting to note that we are normally not aware of these rhetorics most of the time and in a way we take it for granted that children learn and develop through play or that sports are contests in which people compete against each other or that contrary to all of these is the notion that play is a waste of time. Sutton-Smith (1997, pp. 12–13) states that these are the rhetorics that "fill the airwaves of daily life, in churches, in schools, and in the community" to the point where people cannot live without them, even if they can't stand some of them; they are a part of who we are and how we think we should live.

Wittgenstein (1953/2009) was interested in the multifaceted way in which we use language, particularly when we use the same word that has many "... different kinds of *affinity* between them" (p. 35^e; §65). He goes on to use the example of those things we call "games" to make his point that there is nothing common to them all, but there is a "complicated network of similarities overlapping and criss-crossing" of activities with multifarious relationships that can best characterise these similarities as "family resemblances" in which "games" form a family (Wittgenstein, 1953/2009, p. 36^e; §66–67). Unfortunately, the concept of a game does not have rigid limits compared to, say, the concept of numbers and so the use of the word "game" is unregulated and not "circumscribed by rules" in a rigid sense like in the logic of mathematics (Wittgenstein, 1953/2009, p. 37^e; §68). So the question then becomes: How should we explain to someone what a game is taking into consideration its complexity? Wittgenstein responds to his self-imposed question by arguing that strict boundaries are not necessarily needed to come to an understanding of what a game is in terms of making the concept usable and so an inexact description is part of how a person might explain to someone what a game is as an expression of their knowledge. Midgley (1974) makes the useful point that we come to understand when we attach meaning to language on the occasions when we know what we are looking for. In a sense this is what Wittgenstein means when he comments, "Don't think, but look!" in reference to finding examples of the multifarious features of games. For instance, something can be accepted as a chair provided that it is clearly made for sitting on, irrespective of whether it is a stool with three legs, a basket suspended from the ceiling and so on. The general point Midgley is making is that it is easy to come to understand the need for chairs, whereas the need for play is subtle and complex, and something we don't fully understand. In a sense this is what makes Wittgenstein's point about having a "family of meanings" so attractive. What troubles me about entering the "language-game" is that such efforts will reduce this chapter to that of defining play and detract from my task at hand, which is to reflect on our experience of play. In addition, proposing a formalised definition of play would render it susceptible to the same rules and limitations and as a result such a definition would immediately be identified as being too broad or too narrow. There is a distinct difference between the two tasks. For instance, definitions seek specific closure of a rigorous kind achieved by successful definitions, whereas reflection does not seek nor of course achieve this. With this in mind let me continue.

According to Schmitz (1979), play takes on four general varieties depending on whether they can be characterised as informal or formal along a continuum of activities. These are as follows: (1) The least formal form of play is simple spontaneous frolic and commonly associated with young children. It is an immediate and unreflective expression of a kind, such as turning the hose onto the others washing a car which begins an impromptu battle with little or no object. (2) The second variety of play is that of make-believe or pretend and is normally associated with children, but in this form not exclusive to them. For instance, adults can pretend to be Santa Claus or even take on a theatrical role. In this case, the stage role is for the sake of presentation and said to be artistic creativity, whereas in make-believe the representation is for the sake of play. (3) The more formal varieties include sporting skills and involve aspects of knowing to perform a skill, like surfing, mountain climbing, throwing a ball and so on. (4) The final variety of play is completely formal and involves codified games like cricket, football, basketball and so on. Alternatively, in a more extended description surrounding the concept of play, Huizinga (1949) develops three general characteristics: voluntary activity; not "ordinary" or "real" in the sense that it is an activity that is transcendent and distinct from ordinary life; and, lastly, creating a distinct order. Having said this there still is the issue of what play is and so my intent then is not to provide an exhaustive explanation of play but rather to determine when games and sports are also part of the play phenomena, to provide illumination and to legitimate discourse.[4]

The philosophy of sport literature has developed a multitude of theories concerned with the interrelationships present among three forms of human activity: play, games and sport.[5] Despite the extensive literature conducted in this area, apparent consensus is absent and the presumed results can best be described as inadequate. Most of the literature has specifically focused on the necessary features of what sport is compared to the other two members of the triad. Often play is analysed in terms of what it is not. For instance, play is perceived to be non-serious, separated from real life, disconnected, non-productive and so on, which has led to a negative perception of play that is not essential to sport. In addition, it is sometimes portrayed within the literature that play and sport are on opposite ends of a continuum and have nothing in common. According to Meier (1988), we can come to a better understanding of play if we consider the stance of the participants engaged in the activity. The idea is that by doing this, play would be perceived "simply and profitably, as an autotelic activity" because it is voluntarily pursued primarily for intrinsic reasons. This is further confirmed when he goes on to state:

> Consequently, if games or sports are pursued voluntarily and for intrinsic reasons, they are also play forms; if they are pursued involuntarily or engaged in predominantly for extrinsic rewards, they are not play forms.
>
> (Meier, 1988, p. 25)

In this case, the context will be more important than the content. The argument that play and sport are two exclusive entities at opposite ends of a continuum needs to be reconsidered because both play in general and games in particular can be serious. Midgley (1974) makes the point that the relationship between play and seriousness is always fluid. Just because it has the qualities of spontaneous frolic, pretend and so on does not prevent it from becoming serious because any game can at any time run away with the players. Consider the example of a boy walking down a street. By accident he stumbles across an aluminium can and decides to kick it to see how far it can travel. It just so happens that another boy approaches in the opposite direction just in time to observe the original kick and as he reaches the can, he kicks it back in the direction it came. After kicking the aluminium can back and forward for a while between each other the boys decide to make a few modifications to make it more challenging, by adding a designated area, some extra players, and codifying a few rules and so on. This example illustrates how unsophisticated and serendipitous play can become sophisticated play and take on the qualities of games and sports; in a sense it represents the origins of how games and sports came to exist and change over time.[6] To take this idea further and in a different direction it is perhaps noteworthy to mention how sports have metamorphosed from mere frolic play or recreational activities into highly institutionalised and distinct entities in contemporary Western culture. As a result this has brought about the demise of unsophisticated play due to increased commercialisation of contemporary sport. For instance, the advent of the professional sportsperson has led many to abuse sport by overemphasising the importance of victory, rigidly rationalising techniques that improve efficiency at the expense of autonomous freedom, alienating sport from its original play objectives and values, and ultimately reducing sporting performance to a commodity for commercial gain. As regrettable as this may be, this is more a reflection of the social conditions surrounding contemporary professional sport. Does this mean that all sport can be participated in without a "spirit of play"? On the contrary, one can participate in competitive sport and take a playful stance without compromising good performance in the contest. This is further reaffirmed by Kretchmar (1972, p. 113), who argues that the "competitive fullness of sport and the play gesture are, in a most fundamental sense, wholly compatible, but not coextensive" because sport is one of the ways in which we can engage in play, albeit at times in highly polarised ways. In this case, this is what Schmitz (1979) means when he refers to sport as primarily an extension of play, and resting upon the "spirit of play". To Schmitz the spirit in which the contest is pursued is just as important as the outcome of the contest. For example, a player may engage in a contest in order to win and receive an extrinsic reward like money, or players may participate in the contest in order to test themselves against opponents of equal ability in order to learn more about themselves. Only the latter would be considered to be influenced by a spirit of play, due to its connection with an existential stance. Meier (1988, p. 25) makes the compelling point that play is not a necessary or sufficient condition of either games or sport but it may well be an "element that enriches either or both pursuits". He goes on to argue that play or non-play occurrences depend upon the "contingencies surrounding or motivating participation" and so test match cricket may indeed be considered to be a non-play activity; however, a game of backyard cricket which modifies many or even retains all of the same rules of cricket can be considered to be a play occurrence as well. Even though these cases represent two radically different orientations, the sport of cricket is in essence the same, independent of the motives and attitudes displayed by the participants who engage in the activity of cricket in various contexts or settings. However, such factors can be utilised to determine whether or not the sporting activity is also a form of play. These characteristics and relationships are best summarised by Meier (1988, p. 26) in Figure 4.1, which shows the suggested interrelationships among the concepts of play, game and sport.

The following four points relate to the diagram in Figure 4.1: (1) all sports are games; (2) not all games are sports; (3) sport and games may or may not be play; and (4) play may take forms other than games or sports. Meier (1988) goes on to add three more qualifying descriptions as a means to clarify his distinctions between play, games and sport. These are as follows: (1) play involves any activity voluntarily pursued for intrinsic rewards; (2) games are goal-orientated activities in which rules prohibit more efficient means in favour of less efficient means that are an accepted part of the activity persuaded; and (3) sport shares the same characteristics as games, however it requires the demonstration of physical skill and ability.[7]

To better understand the relationship of the tricky triad in physical education is important because it has been the basis for much confusion, particularly about whether play can be used in educational contexts that present work in the guise of play. There has been a general tendency to view each in isolation and as

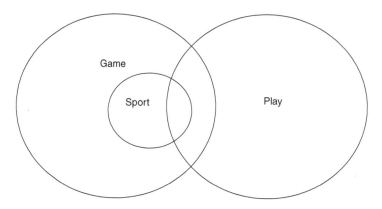

Figure 4.1 The interrelationships among play, game and sport.

distinctly different, even though each can also overlap in a unique way, as seen in Figure 4.1. As argued earlier, sport in a sense is a highly organised and form-alised form of play; however, sport also in a sense is never just play, even though it can be approached with this intent, its overriding feature being its competitive nature. Consequently, the diverse array of movement activities found in physical education goes a long way to highlight its multifarious nature, but what appears to be missing from this account is physical education's explicit educative intent, which neither play nor sport in isolation can provide. For instance, play can be relaxing and reinvigorating without an educational end, just as sport can exist for its own sake without an educational end. My point is that play, games and sport can exist for pleasure, for education or for any other combination and should not be considered to be mutually exclusive entities but can and should exist together.

Since play, games and sport are central elements in physical education dis-course the applicability of this analysis will provide the opportunity to vigor-ously reflect on the interrelationships of this tricky triad and at the same time determine those instances when play, games and sport are present and at times may disproportionately dominate at the expense of the others in practice. For instance, physical education programmes that predominantly focus on pedago-gical approaches such as sport education have a tendency in practice to inadvert-ently exaggerate and overemphasise competition and the outcome of "winning" in sport. Rather we need to consider sport as one of the ways in which we engage in play, by engaging in it voluntarily for intrinsic reasons, because it can provide students with the opportunity to experience human possibility not readily avail-able elsewhere in the curriculum. Some of these opportunities may range from the freedom to try out quasi-adult identities, to being in control of an environ-ment where adult power and presence is limited, forgotten or at least suspended.

What is noteworthy at this juncture is the profound and complex need for play in human life that seems to transcend cultural boundaries. Due to its strong universal appeal the things that satisfy this need do not necessarily share obvious characteristics. Midgley (1974) reinforces this point by arguing that we need play but at the same time we can't say why. She goes on to argue that whatever the purposes or purpose of play may be, art shares equally with play a certain kind of paradoxical quality due to it being somehow set aside from the practical purposes of life and at times asserting a mysterious influence over it. In saying this, Sutton-Smith (1997) argues that the contentious nature and diversity of the theoretical approaches surrounding the concept of play that have entered mainstream culture may have more to do with dominant groups advocating more strongly for a particular rhetoric compared to others. This is supported by Armitage (1977), who argues that play's alleged frivolity may itself be a mask for denigrating play by certain groups as has been done throughout history by those of higher status against those of lower status.

Reflections on *homo faber*: the problem of play and its conflict with contemporary Western culture

The problem of play is that as soon as we assign play as a "non-serious" activity it is extremely easy to refute an argument claiming that play is serious. In fact it is self-contradictory to claim that play is serious. According to Huizinga (1949, p. 6), the reason why play is so difficult to fully grasp is that it lies "outside the antithesis of wisdom and folly", in which "folly" was greatly emphasised in the Middles Ages, which tended to express the opposition between Dionysius and Apollo or the "... two cardinal moods of life – play and seriousness – somewhat imperfectly by opposing *folie* to *sense* ...". The term "play" does have positive connotations, which are usually associated with freedom and pleasure; however, when a culture is geared toward a strong "work ethic" ideology the possibility of play becomes a problem because individuals are more focused on working in order to make a good living rather than the possibilities of engaging in leisurely pursuits. Paradoxically, play is considered to be beneficial and even considered to be educationally worthwhile for young children because of its utilitarian function, as it teaches children skills and is a necessary prelude to socialisation; it is consequently justified because it is useful. But as soon as adults engage in play for an extended period of time and overdo it, it is commonly considered to be a diversion and treated with suspicion due to its power to distract us from the real business of life. This is further confirmed by Neale (1969) who argues that any culture orientated toward work will find the place of play to be incomprehensible and dangerous to the point where the vast majority will respond ambivalently to the possibility of play. He goes on to add that when play evokes ambivalence, play becomes a problem that leads most to overcompensate by working longer hours, taking fewer holidays and mixing work with leisure as a means to maintain their productive personality. In contemporary, achievement-orientated Western culture the strength of the work ethic ideology gives us "highly limited permission to be useless", as excessive emphasis is placed on human beings as labourer or producer in the process of work toward the accomplishment and achievement of useful results, efforts, goods or services (Neale, 1969). For instance, pay rises are tied to productivity increases. To Huizinga (1949), the central reasons for this overemphasis can be attributed to the intensification of work and production that took place during the Industrial Revolution, which essentially became the ideal and then the "idol of the age" that was influenced by technological progress which was itself the consequence of rationalism and utilitarianism. In Huizinga's view the spirit of play has been contaminated and exploited for political purposes behind the illusion of genuine play forms, to the point where we have forgotten to free ourselves from this absurdity. Furthermore, the puritanic tradition of nineteenth-century Protestantism was another source of antagonism, one with a particular religious orientation that placed work and play at opposite ends of the spectrum and accorded a positive value and importance to the former and a negative value to the latter. Keen (1969) makes the point that the fourth and most popular form of "*homo faber*" is the most destructive because we come to associate the significance of work with our personal identity in a society which the secularised Protestant ethic of work continues to influence.[8] He says:

> For *homo faber* there is no vocation except work because there is no God who can appeal to man. Man must manufacture his own dignity by working. Under the impact of industrialization, creativity gives way to work, occupation, and production. It is for this reason that we find the most concentrated points of identity crisis in our society where we find persons ostracized from the world of work – the preemployed, the unemployed, and the postemployed. Those who are excluded from the arena in which values and meanings are produced are exiled from full humanity. Work gives status and identity....
>
> (Keen, 1969, p. 123)

Consequently, our contemporary understanding of the work ethic is deeply embedded in basic assumptions about the nature of humankind. These same presuppositions have begun to increasingly dictate our understanding of humanity, which has come to be expressed in common parlance and is evident when we meet people for the first time or seek to relate to in some capacity and ask: What do you do? Basically, such a question is asking: What type of function in society do you fulfill? Keen (1969) goes on to argue that the influence of *homo faber* is rooted in our striving to become human to the point where human existence can only be won in action, by our fabrication, by our work. The general ideology of *homo faber* has contributed significantly to the assumption that our humanity should be nurtured by work with the understanding that we can manufacture our own identities according to what we fabricate and produce as a functional being in the work world. Consequently, a culture which praises and considers work to be a necessity will regard play to be problematic. For example, "when a work ideology reigns what we fear the most of all is leisure's promise of play" because play basically produces nothing which in essence is in direct contrast to the functional aspects of work; hence, play is often described as a waste of time that could rather be well applied towards some end (Neale, 1969, p. 15). Since play lacks practical application in the work sense it is perceived to be worthless, wasteful and to be a non-serious activity which often gives rise to feelings of guilt and embarrassment that need to be rectified through work. According to Hyland (1977), the reasons why play continues to be relegated to a relatively low status in the "serious business" of life has more to do with two competing ideas which have achieved dominance and which, in turn, have discouraged play and reduced it to the "subordinate status of aid". These two competing ideas he calls the "stance of mastery" and the "stance of submission". He goes on to add that the "stance of mastery" is the more dominant of the two stances because it attempts to "master nature", and this is perhaps best exhibited in the literature of science and technology. The converse of the stance of mastery for those who have been unsuccessful at mastery is the "stance of submission", which is articulated by the view that we must simply accept our place in the "movement of history" in which we "unwittingly participate". Hyland goes on to make the point that the stance of submission functions in a kind of dialectic with the stance of mastery so that they simultaneously hold a "virtual hegemony" over our cultural experience. The dominance of these two stances has been significant in keeping play on the periphery of our culture, primarily because the climate has not been present for play to be taken seriously or even accorded significance by us.

To Fink (1960, 1979), there is a current and rather "vulgar interpretation" of play which states that it is nothing more than a phenomenon on the margins of human life that is used as an occasional break, a pause from the serious aspects of life in a legitimate but quite restricted sense that exists to keep individuals from succumbing to the rigours of the modern world of work by taking on a type of "therapeutic value against the ills of the soul". To Meier (1980) there are three instances that provide support for the claim that play is treated as an instrumental service in the attainment of external ends. First, there are restricted features of play to be found in the approaches of many departments of recreation that seem to reinforce the dominant view of play. For instance, it is not uncommon to have departments charged with the task of making the child or labourer more productive in the school or work environment by providing play forms as a temporary diversion or a form of relaxation. Second, even faculties and departments of physical education, human movement studies and so on are guilty of reducing the body to a biomechanical entity that needs to be disciplined through exercise and only valued because bodies increase labour production through the absence of fatigue. Finally, contemporary professional and elite sport does much to destroy the "play spirit" that can be found in sports, with its obsession with efficiency, reification and productivity in the pursuit of excellence to the detriment of the body, which is seen as a utensil to be appropriately directed and used. Consequently, all three occurrences produce outcomes that are mostly negative and detrimental in coming to a comprehensive view of our embodied dimension and the possibilities inherent in play. Both the remnants of the Protestant ethic of work and the ideology of *homo faber* in contemporary Western culture have reduced play to a form of recreation which either is work free and used to reinvigorate the labourer so they can go back to work or as a type of reward for work accomplished. Furthermore, *homo faber's* obsession with the production of physical labour and his attempts to free him or herself from the bondage of nature have led to a renunciation of the lived body, repression of our sensuous corporeal dimension, quantifiable interpretations of the body to the exclusion of qualitative questions and desensitised movement experiences which have alienated the individual from his own body and made meaningful play impossible. This is further confirmed by Keen (1969) who fears that humanity seems to be moving toward a "machine culture", which appears to be a subtle means of "dehumanizing man" because we are becoming increasingly more like "his products" by making ourselves over in the image of the machine (p. 126). As a result individuals have become isolated and alienated because they no longer feel connected with mystery, wonder and a sense of the intrinsic significance of being lost. He goes on to state:

> For traditional man, leisure was bound up with the holy and the wonderful. On holy days he remembered and celebrated his kinship in an eternal order with the gods, and on ordinary days he paused to contemplate the mystery of meaning and order that pervaded the cosmos. For *homo faber*, leisure has ceased to mean the opportunity to celebrate or contemplate and has become time to be filled with games centering on copulation, consumption, and competition.
>
> (Keen, 1969, pp. 145–146)

Subsequently, *homo faber* in his pursuit of mastery and objectivity reveals a conception of human nature that basically rejects his unique subjectivity, is unreceptive and closed off to different modes of perceiving and relating to the world and subsequently majors in "moulding and manipulation and neglects accepting and welcoming" (Keen, 1969, p. 146). My thesis is that contemporary Western culture has failed to acknowledge an appropriate philosophical foundation surrounding the phenomenon of play because we have misunderstood its nature and at the same time failed to recognise that each form of play in essence is a human activity which has transcendental possibilities derived from experiences that are not possible elsewhere. The argument is developed as follows.

The ontological dimension of play phenomena: play deepens our experience of the world and is a distinct mode of being-in-the-world

The approach adopted by physical education discourse has commonly dealt with play and game playing from a distinctly sociological or psychological developmental point of view and says nothing specifically about the ontological dimension of play that is founded in human nature itself. According to Hyland (1980), the play phenomena through the class of games and sports brings to light a heightened sense of our finitude in an especially striking way. For instance, it brings to our attention that we are limited in our embodied capacities and yet on the other hand provides an avenue in which we can express our embodiment in a physical way. To Fink (1960, 1979), human play is always a process that has a "meaning" primarily because it is present in our daily experiences due to our lived experience. The facticity of our embodiment is present throughout our lives because we are literally situated and cannot be in different places at once. Likewise our bodily limitations become even more evident in play occurrences like sport because our height, our strength, our speed, our skill and so on will be tested and thereby our bodies limit our possibilities. For instance, a person who is of average height may not consider themselves to be small, yet as soon as they step on a basketball court and come up against much taller opponents they discover and recognise that their height is a limitation. But part of what is revealed about our finitude is not just mere limitations. The reverse of finitude is possibility. Rules grant finite meaning to games, and even though in this case the player of average height may have limited possibilities in certain ways, his height may open up other possibilities to his advantage in basketball such as agility, speed and so on compared to his taller opponents. My point here is that we experience bodily possibility in various play forms and also experience in a direct way our embodiment as a limitation, as finitude, which also presents various opportunities to rise above our physical limitations. According to Fink (1979, p. 78), even though play may be a peripheral manifestation of human life it is not a phenomenon that emerges occasionally, but in essence comes under the "ontological disposition of human existence". In his words:

> To oppose play to any other phenomenon is to risk misunderstanding it ... we must recognize that the fundamental phenomena which are decisive in human existence are all interlaced and intertwined. They never appear isolated or juxtaposed against one another. They interpenetrate, interinfluence. Each has a hold over the whole of man.
>
> (Fink, 1979, p. 78)

Since play is universally known and understood in its various forms our experience derived as player possesses a meaning and exclusive uniqueness of its own that is linked in some way to the other fundamental phenomena of existence, just as basic as death, work, domination, love and play. Fink cautions us that even though play may be in essence an ontological disposition of human existence he does acknowledge that at times this disposition is perhaps less known in play than other fundamental phenomena of human life. He states:

> For in all action other than play – whether it be the simple "praxis" which has its ends in itself or the production of the artist (*poiesis*) where the end is the work – there is essentially implied a tendency toward the end of man, toward beatitude, toward *Eudaimonia*.
>
> (Fink, 1979, p. 79)

Even though we may be driven to attain *eudaimonia* we are not in agreement as to what it is. Likewise, it is one of the paradoxes of life that we never fully attain it and so we cannot be truly happy in the sense of complete achievement in this life; however, at the same time this desire carries us forward and is bound up with our fundamental character to find meaning in our existence. This is a deep-seated desire to better understand our source of beatitude as well as our misery. The place of play fits into this case in quite a different way compared to the other fundamental human activities and cannot be expressed in terms of its "architectonic complex" of ends. If we compare play to the rest of our life it takes on an "impetuous dynamism" which carries us forward and has its own "presence" with its own unique meaning in itself and is like an "oasis of happiness found in the desert of our questing … momentarily freed from the daily grind and … magically transported to another planet where life seems more light, more carefree, more happy" (Fink, 1979, p. 79). Fink goes on to add that play is known perhaps less easily than in the other fundamental phenomena of human existence. Since we pursue play to be momentarily freed from the confines of the real world as a type of refreshment it is commonly associated with a gratuitous activity for the sake of our wellbeing, an activity in view of an end other than its own which never appears to end. Consequently, as a whole, the value of play is not easy to see in terms of ends extraneous to its nature. In a sense this is precisely why we play, because it represents and possesses a meaning to those who initiate it and take part in it. The value of play has more to do with understanding the creative quality of the experience, which is also accompanied by a pleasure that is difficult to equate with other joyous experiences. To Fink (1979, p. 81) the pleasure in play is not only grounded in its creative and spontaneous features, it is also an "ecstasy which accompanies our entry into any 'universe'…" that is not only the pleasure of the play experience, but more a joyous attitude towards play. He goes on to add that the fundamental characteristic of play is its creation "through the medium of pleasure" that takes on an "appearance" of joy. In his words:

> Play is always characterized by an element of representation. This element determines its meaning. It then effects transfiguration; life becomes peaceful. We are freed little by little, and we eventually discover that we have been redeemed from the weight of real life. Play lifts us from a situation of fact, from an imprisonment depressing by nature, and by means of fantasy helps us enjoy passing through a multitude of "possibilities" without imposing on us the necessity of making a choice.
>
> (Fink, 1979, p. 83)

Play is one of those phenomena where we again and again can achieve the possibility of our embodiment that is grounded in play itself. Kretchmar (1995) makes the point that physical education is in a unique position to provide, promote and give students the freedom to explore, freedom to discover, freedom to express thoughts or ideas, freedom to invent and the freedom to create. This view would suggest that the ideal of freedom has no limits and is present all the time. Such an account would appear to be problematic at first because when we think of play, we normally associate it with the spontaneous, relatively ungoverned free forms of play that children engage in. The irony is that in adulthood we try to recapture this spontaneity, albeit arbitrarily through game playing. For instance, most of us are eager to find free time in our daily schedules to participate in structured play, such as organised games like tennis, basketball and so on to provide a momentary break from our ordinary lives and at the same times reinvigorate ourselves. But is this not a paradox? We leave the relatively structured place of work to enter a rigorously structured, rule-governed sphere of games and sports that is both policed stringently and arbitrary in the sense that we would never tolerate the inherent restrictions such rules bring in our ordinary lives. Despite first appearances, it is not a paradox but an illustration of the deep complexity surrounding play and in particular the concept of freedom. Although it may be the case that too much limitation restricts freedom, it is also true that a moderate amount of finitude in the form of games and sports provides those occurrences in which we come to know the possibilities of our bodily limitations.

Two of the most obvious dimensions of this bodily limitation are the finitude of space and the finitude of time. The finitude of space is probably the most apparent in those play activities in which there is a clearly delineated space such as a tennis court, soccer field and so on, in which the spatial limitations are rigorously rule governed. For example, a soccer player who is in possession of the ball cannot move outside the confines of the playing area in order to avoid being tackled by his direct opponent. Likewise, temporal limitations are most obvious in highly structured games and sports such as basketball, rugby league and so on. For instance, in a rugby league game of eighty minutes (two halves of forty minutes) the limitations of time are most felt when a team is a few points behind and is attempting to catch up in the last few minutes of the game. The significance of the finitude of space and time in all the previous cases is made obvious in play by view of the fact that rules give our actions in games and sports meaning because the rules force our bodies to confront our embodied dimension and our limitations, and in a sense enhance our embodied freedom. Consequently, highly structured games and sports are clearly the most obvious means by which to engage in those instances that focus our consciousness and our bodies in such a way to pursue to the end a set of possibilities; they are also a place to encounter freedom because in play there is an almost unlimited opportunity to be creative, establish freedom that is impossible in reality, explore in safety and learn from experience without the consequences of real life.

According to Schmitz (1979), the spirit of play with its own arbitrary objectives and formalities may be said to transcend the natural world and the world of everyday concerns by breaking "open a new totality". This does not mean that the natural laws of the world are suspended, because players get tired, get injured and so on, and in some forms of play such as surfing and mountain climbing these natural forces are deliberately pursued because of these natural challenges (see, for example, Meier, 1976). He goes on to add that what is common in these and all forms of play is that the natural processes do not determine the significance of the play. For instance, this is highlighted by the player who may intentionally ignore tiredness, injury, time, hunger and so on as far as possible in the pursuit of play, whereas a worker would most likely acknowledge these and respond in different ways. To Schmitz (1979) the sign of the transcendent qualities of play is most apparent when a player makes a conscious decision to maintain the "play spirit", because play like religion and art shares similarities in the sense that religion celebrates the physicality of our embodiment in the world and art brings to attention the beauty of our embodiment through aesthetic experience. In his words:

> Like art and religion, play is not far from the feast, for art celebrates beauty and religion celebrates glory, but play celebrates the emergence of the finite world that lies outside and beyond the world of nature while at the same time resting upon it.
>
> (Schmitz, 1979, p. 25)

Play has its own unique in-built finality and is an autotelic activity that, like art and religion, is not easily grasped; yet play exemplifies a significant mode of being-in-the-world. Its significance comes from the distinctive way our embodied action breaks open distinctive possibilities of our existence, meaning and freedom of the world, which can be accessed through the phenomena of play. According to Roochnik (1975), there is a basic error in the current discourse surrounding play that equates the play world with an illusion. He goes on to add that play is the antithesis of illusion because it deepens our experience of the world and is a distinct mode of encountering the world, not a pleasurable divergence away from it. This is further confirmed by Roochnik (1975, p. 40), who states:

> If play is grounded upon illusion and the suspension of the natural world, then it is precluded from becoming a mode of being toward the world. At best it could be a thing that happens once in a while and might even be magnificent and beneficial, but it could never be a stance to be cultivated or pursued.

He goes on to explain that the unusual quality of secludedness that can be found in play is more a consequence of the player's immersion that gives rise to its own distinctive temporality and spatiality. For instance, to the tennis player's environment, the tennis court, the net, the ball, the opponents and so on have become intensified and the environment has meaning within itself. Therefore, immersion is more about a commitment of the body to the activity that is grounded in the here and now, that "does justice to the powers of man to encounter the world" (Roochnik, 1975, p. 40). It is this so-called self-contained meaning that is commonly equated with play which is significant because play seems to stand in complete contrast to what we would consider to be non-play in the world or what we would normally refer to as the "real", the "ordinary" or the "serious" side of life.

Even though play is a phenomenon that has an indeterminate mode of being, many prominent philosophers like Plato have insisted on the importance of play (see, for example, Plato, 1961c, *The Laws*). Hyland (1977) develops the Platonic understanding of play as a primordial human phenomenon because it is a way of being in the world and so, most fundamentally, "being a player" is a specific mode of being. He goes on to set out a certain conception of human nature, expressed in its broadest sense in the view that human beings are relational, have a heightened sense of incompleteness and strive for completeness in order to overcome our sense of incompleteness. For instance, if I am a philosopher, teacher, husband, father and so on, this confirms and makes clear the ways in which I have experienced my "partiality" and tried to overcome it because I choose how I shall relate and the objects with which I relate; subsequently, we are literally by nature relational.

Furthermore, when we play we have a certain orientation toward those with whom we play, toward time, toward space, toward the world and so on. According to Hyland (1980), this "orientation" toward things is a distinct mode of "comportment" which can best be described as a mode of being-in-the-world which is not necessarily strange or odd but noticeably unique from our everyday mode of comportment when we consider ourselves not to be playing. It is this "orientation", "mode of comportment" or "mode of being" that he refers to as the "stance of play", in which the play situation brings about a heightened sense of openness toward my environment. Take the example of a volleyball player: they need to be constantly aware of their environment and take into consideration crucial variables such as the location of the ball, whether the team is employing an offensive or defensive pattern of play according to the situational circumstance, the positioning of the other players and most importantly the ability to adapt to whatever possibilities open up in the game and so on. It is play situations like these, which require an ability to be open to and aware of the environment not present in non-play situations, that are a notable feature of play that Hyland refers to as "openness".

The other nuanced feature of play is the ability to adapt and respond quickly to what is happening in the environment, which Hyland refers to as "responsiveness". Responsiveness, in a way, is a second feature in Hyland's stance of play; and when the two are combined this brings about the well-known experience of a being totally involved and immersed in our activity. In his words:

> … play is one of those phenomena where we again and again achieve that sense of totality, that intimation of completeness, and that the possibility of its doing so is grounded in the very stance of play itself, which I have called responsive openness.
>
> (Hyland, 1980, p. 90)

The interpretation of play as the stance of responsive openness does not imply a strict dichotomy between play and non-play activities but places them on a continuum.[9] For instance, anyone who is conscious could be argued to be open and responsive to their environment. The point is that there are various times in our lives when we experience situations that are more open and responsive than normal. In this case, play is one of those situations where we are mostly responsively open.

In addition, it needs to be reiterated that Hyland is not arguing that activities A, B and C are always play, whereas X, Y and Z are not play along a continuum, but rather it is a unique stance, comportment or orientation of the player toward play which enables us to better understand the phenomenon. For example, two people may be exhibiting the same type of behaviour in hitting the ball to each other in a game of tennis and in a sense they are both playing tennis according to the constitutive rules of the game, but after awhile we come to realise the intentions of the two players, which leads us to conclude that only one of them is actually playing tennis, while the other is engaged in the sport of tennis, to win, to compete, to better his opponent and so on. Therefore, play in this sense has more to do with the specific ways in which players look toward those with whom we play, toward time, toward space, toward the world.[10]

In the school curriculum, the stance of play may function more like a device in which individuals can make sense of their world through play, games and sports in a way that is radically different and perhaps not readily available elsewhere in other curriculum areas. As mentioned earlier, the relationship of the tricky triad to physical education is unique because when viewed in isolation the three are distinctly different, yet they can overlap in a unique way. The diverse array of movement activities found in physical education highlights its multifarious nature, but what appears to be missing from this account is physical education's explicit educative intent that has shown that knowing in movement can have a distinct epistemological claim.[11] This last point is significant to my thesis because knowing in movement is a unique synthesis of knowledge types, which is founded on the experimental process of movement in a diverse array of environments that is particularly important in relation to education.[12] Therefore, what makes movement education significant is that it provides the opportunity for students to experience themselves in a sub-set of bodily orientated environments and thereby allows students to learn more about themselves and the world in which they live.

Before going on to say something about the educational significance of play, games and sports in physical education in the next section, it needs to be restated that education involves the development of the whole person. As a result, it involves becoming acquainted with a diverse array of activities in an educational process that aims to nurture and promote the physical, intellectual, social, spiritual and emotional dimensions of a growing person through experiences that have an educational end.

This is further reinforced by van Manen (1977), who argues that the practical understanding of educational experiences finds its theoretical roots in the interpretative practices of the hermeneutic–phenomenological method, which attempts to make meaningful the curriculum as a subjective and interpersonal process. Freedom to create and act are possible only when we are open to these notions, and to neglect either is to accept the limits of our facticity and destroy our freedom, wonder and hope because "future possibility is not to be defined by already known limits; the past does not exercise an absolute tyranny over the future" (Keen, 1969, p. 174). Meier (1980, p. 31) makes the pertinent point that our being-in-the-world is an "indeterminate, open question, a 'not-yet' " in which we have the capacity to transcend present modes of being by constructing our own choices and actions, and to commit to personal projects outside our everyday concerns and contexts – a capacity which is relatively unconstrained by external interventions. Play presents unique opportunities to perceive freshly, to experience novelty and to immerse oneself wholly. This is further reinforced by Keen (1970) who pointedly remarks that this ability is one of the defining features of our humanity. In his words:

> In those moments when I am able to rise above compulsion, need, and expectation and allow some novelty to refresh me, I am most certain of my freedom and my potency. I become gracefully free when I become convinced that I have the power to do a new thing.
>
> (Keen, 1970, p. 30)

Such a passage highlights the unrealistic demands which *homo faber* imposes upon all of us and at the same time illustrates how play can break open those moments that can accentuate our innocence and the spontaneous impulses, movements or actions that can be found in *homo ludens*.

It is also noteworthy to mention at this juncture what Merleau-Ponty calls the "phenomenal body" and refers to what "I" experience as a natural system of one's own body, which takes place in the domain of the phenomena (Merleau-Ponty, 1945/1962, Part I, section 3). For instance, when my hand moves around the object it touches, anticipating the stimuli and tracing out a form which I am about to perceive visually. Our perception ends in objects because our own body as experienced by us "from the inside" makes contact with the object through touch, stimuli and tracing out its form from the first-person point of view. Simply put, we cannot come to understand our embodiment if we do not engage in the world as a being-in-the-world. The phenomenal body is what we experience as a first-person subject of experience and as a result we can only exist in connection with a lived body. We cannot make contact with the world just by thinking about it, but only through experiencing it with our senses and acting in it, in ways that range from the most complex to the most primitive unreflective movements. The student experiences and apprehends his body neither as an abstract object nor as an instrument, but as a "lived-body" subject that senses and does the sensing in a meaningful way.

As argued in earlier chapters, a body portrayed as a biomechanical object that must be managed, maintained, conditioned and repaired for instrumental reasons, such as improving performance or physical appearance, is drained of its humanity, devoid of ecstatic, aesthetic, autotelic, sensuous and holistic experiences. According to Meier (1980), play liberates us from our confines, from the subordination to the impersonal demands and constraints of circumstance, from utilitarian demands and from objective-achievement oriented Western culture, because play, games and sport in general heighten and bring into focus the interplay between possibility and actuality only when we immerse ourselves wholly into the activity to bring into "focus [our] subjectivity and to "luxuriate in the intense, full, lived experience of play" (Meier, 1980, p. 32). This approach gives the play phenomena meaning in the hermeneutic–phenomenological sense because it seeks to provide an understanding of the ways in which human beings subjectively experience the world and make sense of it. As a result not much has been specifically mentioned about the educational significance of play, games and sport in physical education from a philosophical perspective.[13]

The educational significance of play, games and sport in physical education: learning through the physical as a paradigm case for understanding our "phenomenological body"

The trend in attitudes surrounding the place of play in education in the twentieth century has been one of increasing acceptance that is important for cognitive, social and emotional development, particularly for children's learning (see for example Briggs and Hansen, 2012; Broadhead and Burt, 2012; Saracho, 2012; Smith, 1986). As physical education as a profession underwent significant reform during the first half of the twentieth century this also coincided with the development of play theory in education, which in turn had a profound influence in the debate about what methods would be appropriate for imparting educational goals in physical education.[14] According to Mechikoff (2010), the conscious decision to promote and utilise play, games and sport as a means for transmitting educational ends in physical education is significant because it reflected a growing interest in the phenomenon of play which was also popular with the public at large and amongst the ranks of physical education professionals. The idea of play serving as a means of cultivating cognitive, social and emotional development reflected the significant influence of the general trends in education that came to be accepted with fervour in the physical education profession because they provided the theoretical foundations for physical education and a level of legitimacy that had previously been missing. These trends blended the instinctive and natural interest that young people have with play, games and sports with educationally designed environments providing learning experiences that produced specific changes in the physical, social and psychological aspects of individuals. These theoretical elements were expressed in physical education through the following three ways: first, physical activity was considered to contribute to the health of the individual in a positive way; second, playing games and sports, particularly team-orientated ones, was considered to be a major feature in the development of character and the inculcation of moral and ethical values; third, it focused on the integration of the mind and body through physical means.

Generally speaking it is commonly accepted that when we educate a child he or she will transition smoothly from a being that plays into an adult that works. For instance, we present work to a child under the guise of play in which the workload increases little by little in preparation for the serious affairs of the adult world. This well-accepted pedagogical practice is based on the idea that play is an instinctive and natural part of our existence. The belief that children develop and learn best through play forms is a well-established educational position that is expressed in highly subtle and sophisticated ways in secondary schooling as students mature. If we take our idea of play from the world of a child in isolation we will be trapped by ambiguity. As a result if play is to have significance in maturity or adulthood it must have another dimension that is meaningful to the agent, particularly in a secondary school context. For instance, in the play of a child there are usually authentic elements of joy, happiness, fulfilment and excitement and so on which seem to get lost in the transition into adulthood. Take for example the following excerpt from Bannister's (1955, pp. 11–12) book, *The First Four Minutes*:

> In this supreme moment I leapt for joy. I was startled and frightened by the tremendous excitement that so few steps could create. I glanced around uneasily to see if anyone was watching. A few more steps – self consciously now and firmly gripping the original excitement. The earth seemed almost to move with me. I was running now, and a fresh rhythm entered my body. No longer conscious of my movement I discovered a new unity with nature. I had found a new source of power and beauty, a source I never dreamt existed. From intense moments like this, love of running can grow.... This attempt at explanation is of course inadequate, just like any analysis of the things we enjoy – the description of a rose to someone who has never seen one.

Such an example is a paradigm case of the pleasure derived from kinaesthetic flow or patterns of feelings which are constituted as meaningful by the performer and emphasises that tacit knowing is important to my thesis for two reasons: (1) knowledge is personal because the knower relies on certain implied or inferred elements of human knowledge that is subjectively experienced as a being-in-the-world from an experimental perspective; and (2) because we come to know that we have a body.

Within the context of the hermeneutic–phenomenological framework, physical education represents the study of practical educational experiences that attempt to make the subjective and interpersonal process meaningful. As a result it should be treated as a necessary and vital part of education primarily because the diversity of these experiences offer opportunities to explore alternative modes of awareness and to develop insights into and new modes of being and possibilities perhaps not readily available elsewhere in the curriculum. This is further reinforced by Thorburn (2008) and Stolz (2013a) who argue that physical education has lost its connection with practical learning environments and in the process has lost a way of grasping subject knowledge that is significant for the students' learning in question in that it is not purely intellectual or cognitive. Thorburn (2008) goes on to argue that by using a phenomenological framework, physical education could improve the methodological basis for linking students' lived-body experiences with the acquisition of increasingly complex subject knowledge within the curriculum. The emphasis is that learning environments that actively engage students in practical learning, where the integration of performance and subject matter is presented in a natural and feasible way that cultivates feelings and seeks to provide for an understanding of the ways in which we can come to know from subjective experiences, have substantially improved many of the authenticity issues surrounding learning experiences in physical education.

Dewey (1916/1966) reinforces this point further when he argues that one important feature of the educative process is the establishment of special environments intentionally set up to consciously influence how students act and hence think and feel; however, at the same time he acknowledges that the educative process is rich with meaning and at times the direct method may be ineffective because we learn best "indirectly by means of the environment". He goes on to argue that any environment is a "chance" environment in terms of its educative influence unless it has been consciously regulated with reference to its educative effect, which is one of the main features of the school as a special environment. It is not until Dewey broadens his ideas concerning the nature of experience that we come to get a clearer picture of its value in education. According to Dewey (1916/1966, p. 139), the nature of the experience can be understood by an "active and passive element peculiarly combined". In the former phase this involves the experience of "trying" in the concrete sense and in the latter phase "undergoing" refers to a more reflective type of thinking of the interaction being considered in the trial and error problem. For instance, when we do something and it fails, we do something else until it works as a result of undergoing the consequences of thinking reflectively about that something failing. To Dewey, it is this connection of the two phases of experience that "measures" the value of the experience.[15] He goes on to add that mere activity does not automatically equate to a meaningful experience unless it involves change in a meaningful and sustained way. In Dewey's (1916/1966, p. 139) words:

> Experience as trying involves change, but change is meaningless transition unless it is consciously connected with the return wave of consequences which flow from it. When an activity is continued *into* the undergoing of consequences, when the change made by action is reflected back into a change made in us, the mere flux is loaded with significance.

It this meaningful change "made in us" which is "loaded with significance" that is important in this case, as physical education activities are significant in the educative sense because they have respect for the person as an embodied consciousness and, most importantly, all three facets of a person (thinking, feeling and acting) are combined to give a person an experience of what it is to be a moving being which is radically different from traditional forms of education that have a particular focus on propositional forms of knowledge.

It is interesting to note that part of the issue with educational concepts of educational experience seem to reflect an empirical–analytical orientation that is dominant in Anglo–American educational systems in contrast to more hermeneutic–phenomenological methods of the continental school of thought. In the latter context, experience refers to how we make sense of the world as an embodied subject, which we cannot do through simply thinking about it in an abstract way but only through experiencing it with our senses and acting in it, in ways that range from complex forms of movement to the most primitive of unreflective movements; most importantly, we must also have a feeling about it. This is further reinforced by Schrag (1962, 1988) who argues that a person lives through the mass of psycho-physical occurrences as an embodied individual and it is only by reflection that it is possible to distinguish between the four major modes the individual experienced at the time as a synthetic totality of oneness.[16] Although the lived body can be experienced in a multitude of different ways in everyday life, it is only through and in the movement experiences that physical education programmes provide that its various forms can be and are most often intensely felt.

Even though human movement is a fundamental feature of our existence it has significant educational implications in that it provides a rich source of experience of our embodiment; this also has ramifications for self-development and the formation of identity because both are affected by the way we experience and react to our lived body. This is further reinforced by Arnold (1979a), who argues that our experiences become meaningful as a result of being grasped reflectively, particularly those "peak experiences"[17] that are felt more intensely and remembered as moments of significant meaning in an agent's life and which stand out in the memory because they are far from being mundane, but are extraordinary past experiences associated with strong positive and dynamic feelings of joy, happiness, fulfilment and so on. He goes on to add that meaning in movement from the point of view of the agent is not limited to being passive or private but, on the contrary, very much concerned with meaning that is intended to be public and shareable through three categories: (1) primordial meanings; (2) contextual meanings; (3) existential meanings (Arnold, 1979a). Consequently, play, games and sport within physical education programmes are important in education because these activities offer opportunities to explore alternative modes of awareness and to develop insights into and new modes of being and possibilities perhaps not readily available elsewhere in the curriculum.

To Dewey (1916/1966), learning from experience is to make a "backward and forward" connection between "doing" and engaging in "what we enjoy" to the point where "doing becomes a trying", like an "experiment with the world to find out what it is like" and in which the undergoing becomes "instruction-discovery" of the relationship between things.[18] It is noteworthy to mention that

Dewey considered dualism of mind and body to be an "evil" and argued that students have a body which serves as a conductor of experience and meaning to the point where we should never forget that the student brings their body to school along with their mind. He goes on to outline how education has failed to recognise that connecting and making relationships cannot occur without experience to the point where an "ounce of experience is better than a ton of theory because it is only in experience that any theory has vital and verifiable significance" (Dewey, 1916/1966, p. 144). Experience is capable of generating and communicating theory, but theory in isolation from experience without application ceases to be fully grasped in the sense of meaningful significance. No experience that has a meaning is possible without some component of thought. For instance, when we do A and it fails, we try B and so on until we find a method that works, in which case we quickly apply it in subsequent procedures. There is a certain element in experience that can be difficult to articulate fully and as a result we can come to see that a certain way of acting is connected in some way to a consequence. Subsequently, in discovering the detailed connection of our activities and what happens in consequence, the idea of the two phases is meant to make the experience more explicit to the point where the quality of the experience is so significant that it causes a change.

Furthermore, to Dewey the making of these connections constitutes thinking "*par excellence*" as a distinctive experience which can be cultivated in a positive way by securing conditions that engage in situations where activities "generate support and clinch ideas" that are full of meanings or connections. Educational institutions have a diverse array of places in which positive measures have been taken to develop reflective-type experiences (thinking) of a diverse nature that could range from the science and computer (ICT) laboratories, to music and drama studios, to sporting fields, the gymnasium and so on. The intent of different curriculum areas is to provide a well-balanced education in the development of the whole person; physical education does this by offering a radically different opportunity to experience our embodiment not readily available elsewhere in the curriculum. Play, games and sporting activities in physical education programmes are central to its practice and utilised as an educational mechanism because they bring about a heightened awareness, a special meaning and significance to the participating agent that by no means is confined to physical activity but is more completely experienced in such movement forms and activities where the embodied person is most likely to become aware of their lived body in a meaningful way. This is further reinforced by Dewey (1916/1966, p. 237) who states that:

> The educative value of manual activities and of laboratory exercises, as well as of play, depends upon the extent in which they aid in bringing about a sensing of the *meaning* of what is going on.... Were it not for the accompanying play of imagination, there would be no road from a direct activity to representative knowledge; for it is by imagination that symbols are translated over into direct meaning and integrated with a narrow activity so as to expand and enrich it.

Consequently, these activities are not just the exclusive domain for enhancing qualities which make ordinary experiences appealing in education, but they serve a purpose beyond themselves to reveal a depth and range of meaning in experiences which otherwise might be trivial if not seriously reflected upon.

According to Arnold (1979a), the concept of a "meaningful lived experience" is based on the reflective process that can only occur after the action is over and the reflection draws conscious attention to my lived experience even after a considerable lapse of time. It is important to note that lived experiences simply do not become meaningful as a result of merely having been lived through. He goes on to add that it is incorrect to say that experiences have meaning because meaning does not lie in the experience as such, but experiences only become meaningful as a result of being interpreted by the agent as meaningful. Take, for example, the earlier case of Bannister running on the beach. To Bannister, running means more to him perhaps because of the sheer joy derived from the experience. As such, it has individual meaning. It is not just efficient movement for the sake of moving from point A to B, but a specific experience which he emotionally values as a significant part of his life. It is important to note that an experience can take on many different meanings at the same time. Some of these meanings may be personal, as in the case of Bannister, but in general these same experiences can be shared with others even if not necessarily expressible in words. Even though movement is one of the most fundamental features of a human being's existence, it is only in, by and through movement experiences that it can be and often is meaningfully felt. Consequently, within the context of the hermeneutic–phenomenological framework, physical education should be treated as a necessary and vital part of education primarily because the diversity of these experiences offer opportunities to explore alternative modes of awareness and to develop insights into and new modes of being and possibilities perhaps not readily available elsewhere in the curriculum.

Furthermore, the educative value of practical subjects like physical education has more to do with coming to know in movement that arises through direct participation in its diverse array of forms. It is founded on an experimental process that in no way should be equated with knowledge gained about movement in the academic study of movement. This is confirmed by Dewey (1916/1966, p. 238), who argues that practical experience gained from "manual activities" represents the concentration and consummation of "elements of good" which are otherwise incomplete, and as a result they are not "luxuries" of education but "emphatic expressions" of that which makes any education worthwhile. He goes on to argue with respect to educational value that as long as any topic makes an "immediate appeal" it is not necessary to ask what it is good for because some "goods are not good for anything: they are just goods" in which the proof of "goods" can be found in the fact that students genuinely respond and want to learn in the material, which is thus proof of value. Therefore, to value in a sense is to appreciate the experiences gained from the various opportunities found in the created environment.

It is interesting at this juncture to note that to Dewey the issue of educational value is more about the unity or integrity of the experience, and may have more to do with the organisation of schools, materials and methods which function to achieve richness of experience – an experience in which play, games and sport in physical education has a special value representing a heightened realisation of meaning or a particular mode of knowing by means of sensations that cannot be found elsewhere. According to Williams (1951), we misunderstand the nature of experience and tend to break experience into categories such as spiritual, social, moral, intellectual, physical and so on and rank these experiences, which usually results in the spiritual and mental being placed at the top and the physical at the bottom, especially in education. He goes on to argue that because every experience embodies reaction and interaction of the whole organism to and with its environment, the experience cannot be "purely physical" or "purely mental". As a result, when we attempt to classify experiences we continue to perpetuate unaltered views and prejudices that are detrimental to the place of physical education in education. These distortions of experience, whether they are of the spiritual, the mental or the physical, should not mislead us as a profession because we are advocates of the physical and should insist upon its universal and timeless essence in the sense that our human existence is intimately intertwined in play. We should never forget that we have a physical body wherein our whole understanding of the world is grounded in our corporeal nature to the point where we do not have to locate our hands in space before moving them because we posses certain potentialities of movement in us that have significant meaning because we are in the world (Merleau-Ponty, 1945/1962). The claim Polanyi (1958, 1961, 1962, 1966a, 1966b, 1967; Polanyi and Prosch 1975) makes that all knowledge is founded on tacit knowledge is a powerful one and knowing from being on the inside in movement is basically a form of practical knowledge through which the person becomes aware of knowledge through the physical experience.

It will serve the purpose of this chapter to reiterate and make clear that movement forms become educationally significant in physical education not by studying knowledge about the body in some abstract way, but it is rather through doing and being on the "inside" that we become aware of and rediscover our most fundamental ontological existence and bodily facticity, which in turn brings to light a heightened sense of our finitude and presents a diverse array of opportunities to have peak experiences that are unique to human movement, and to develop insights into and knowledge of new modes of being in a safe environment without the consequences of the "real world". As a result, one of the primary roles of physical education is to make this movement experience as meaningful as possible. This is further confirmed by Williams (1951, p. 465) who states:

> The physical can never be understood from an easy chair, and only the person whose physical experiences are superior can ever really know what excellence in the physical means. Man has always played. The forms vary,

the penalties change, but the great athletic festivals of ancient Greece leave a bit of themselves here and there....

He goes on to argue that the "whole man" goes to school and should be educated, not just the "speaking, seeing, writing and reciting person, but also the feeling, believing, doing and behaving person", and he sets out four arguments to counter the traditional view of education which places a significant onus on propositional forms of knowledge in the development of the mind at the expense of the physical. These are as follows. First, every experience, particularly the physical, cannot ignore our bodily facticity. Therefore, life has a tremendous qualitative range in which there will be an enormously diverse array of experiences too diverse to "pigeon-hole". Second, the physical experience will be judged by the purposes to which it is applied. Consequently, when we use physical education for instrumental ends we have failed to recognise the profound educational possibilities that can be posited in physical experience. Third, the physical experience in its broadest expression is one way of reconnecting those individuals with the place of the senses and restores a balance in our life that has been missing in our pursuit of the good life. Fourth, those who are seriously interested in education ought to be interested in physical education, not because of its claimed instrumental promises of development and so on in the lives of young people, but for the extension and enrichment it has in education.

According to Smith (2007), the essential features of movement education in its various derivations have lost sight of physical education's "experiential register" and need to be revitalised and guided towards what the body can do, where and how it comports itself and what it moves in relation to, in a structured way by providing pedagogical direction in sport, physical education, dance and other movement experiences that explore and bring about the phenomenon of the "first rush of movement". To Smith (2007, pp. 66–67) the educational value of physical education is the "delineation of specific motions that can be cultivated and that comprise a developmental movement education". Therefore, such curriculum considerations should accord with this phenomenology of movement consciousness that is rooted in experiential knowledge of the body, because it turns our attention back to the communicative and expressive significances of our human experiences, which in turn contributes to the curriculum in a significant way by addressing our vital ontological and phenomenological connections to the world and to others. The profound connection between "vitality affects" and the "tactile-kinesthetic body" found in Smith's conceptual understanding of the "first rush of movement" owes much to the work of Sheets-Johnstone (1999), who argues that anytime anyone moves, a "vitality" affect is present or a certain "qualitative dynamic" is evident through bursts, surges, swells, risings, undulations, waves and flows.[19] She goes on to caution that we must not make the mistake that, because we all move, movement consciousness is merely an "affect" of movement but the significance of these elemental gestures has more to do with the way we subjectively relate one experience with another and come to appreciate our essentially tactile–kinesthetic body and world in a phenomenological sense and more broadly in the experience of it. It is these hidden dimensions of play, games and sport in physical education in terms of flows, experiences, moments of heightened awareness, transformed states of consciousness, peak experiences, fulfilled presence and so on that are all instances of full, free, joyous play and are all instances of the vital elements essential to open and full human existence.

It has herein been argued in a sustained fashion that in a world dominated by *homo faber* in contemporary achievement-orientated Western culture, the phenomenon of play is alien and the recognition of its educational significance is all but precluded from the pragmatic world of instrumental concerns. According to Meier (1980), play embodies and reflects a radical way of comportment to the world and in a sense functions like a "hammer" that breaks us free from our everyday preoccupations to experience the unquestioned relevance and significance of our extraordinary existence. He goes on to make the salient point that play is an "intrinsically rewarding, purposeless activity" that is characterised by a fluid "letting-be of life and meaning" that is unclear to "real" life. Ultimately, play is a fundamental feature of our humanity – both a distinct mode of encountering the world and an opportunity to experience human possibility.

In conclusion, my thesis has been that contemporary Western culture has failed to acknowledge an appropriate philosophical foundation surrounding the phenomenon of play because we have misunderstood its nature and at the same time failed to recognise the fluidity of play, which can be treated as both serious and non-serious according to the agent's "stance of play", which Hyland (1980) refers to as "responsive openness". In this case, responsive openness is not arguing that activities A, B and C are always play, whereas X, Y and Z are not play along a continuum, but rather it is a unique stance, comportment or orientation of the player toward play which enables us to better understand the phenomenon. For example, two people may be exhibiting the same type of behaviour in hitting the ball to each other in a game of tennis and in a sense they are both playing tennis according to the constitutive rules of the game, but after a while we come to realise the intentions of the two players which leads us to conclude that only one of them is actually playing tennis, while the other is engaged in the sport of tennis, to win, to compete, to better his opponent and so on. Therefore, play in this sense has more to do with the specific ways in which players look toward those with whom we play, toward time, toward space, toward the world.

In addition, it is interesting to note that the standard oppositions of play and work as well as play and seriousness seem contrary to understanding play as responsive openness because we can both play and work with equal seriousness. In fact responsive openness as a stance toward play is not arguing for non-seriousness, or even a lack of work that in turn brings about seriousness and work, because in a sense these are false opposites. Part of the issue surrounding play, games and sport in physical education seems to be a general tendency to assign either a positive or negative valuation based on whether most of its instances are affirmative and fulfilling or not. Of course, this is problematic given that any occasion is thus precarious and can become at a whim either positive or negative. The stance of responsive openness is valuable particularly to those who commit and immerse themselves fully within the activity, because such a stance presents a multitude of opportunities to encounter the lived body through physical education activities that are conducive to intensely felt and meaningful experiences.

Finally, there is a need to explicitly revisit the educational benefits gained from an education in movement in light of what has been discussed in this chapter. Physical education's inherent value is made manifest in movement because it has the capacity to provide an understanding of a unique form of epistemic knowledge (tacit knowing) and in doing so it permits the person to experience him or herself as a holistic and synthesised acting, feeling, thinking being-in-the-world. Arnold (1979a, p. 179) makes the relevant point that to deny "… bodily action and meaning because of prejudice or neglect is to deny the possibility of becoming more fully human". Therefore, those who are serious about education ought to be interested in physical education because the physical experience in its broadest expression is one way of reconnecting those individuals with the place of the senses and restoring a balance in our life that has been missing in education. Greater recognition, then, needs to be given to the role embodiment and corporeal movement play in student learning because the act of knowing is not an end-product stripped bare of experience, but closely connected to the lived body which emphasises that "I" am the absolute source of my knowing because I bring meaning from experiences of the world because the world gives meaning to my experiences. Consequently, physical education should form a necessary part of any educational programme that is concerned with the cultivation of the whole person because it is a body oriented and intimately connected to personal knowledge that is meaningful.

Historically there has been strong educational support for the role of competitive games and sports in the physical education curriculum to the point where it has become synonymous with the development of social and moral virtues, usually under the category of "character development". Much has been written about the educational value of the games ideology and this moral justification for sport and physical education is no stranger to modern society.[20] This view came to dominance in the public schools of Great Britain during the nineteenth century, which in turn had a significant impact on education in Australia, and can be expressed by the well-known analogy that "playing the game", particularly following the constitutive rules of games, is somehow connected to the inculcation of socially desirable virtues and practices, which in turn can lead to success in the "game of life". However, the claims made by such a position have been brought into question; if we accept the argument that participating in sport cultivates character, then at the same time it is reasonable to assume that morally undesirable qualities such as gamesmanship, meanness of spirit, a win at any cost attitude, a tendency to violence and so on that occur in competitive sport are also likely to be transferred into an agent's life. In this case the competitive side of sport may actually be morally miseducative and do more harm than good. As a result, the justification of physical education as an uncritical instrument for "character development" as moral education is problematic. Subsequently in the next chapter, I critically discuss whether sports can provide opportunities to develop moral character in physical education and hence are worthy of inclusion within the school curriculum based on its moral educational potential.

Notes

1 Central to the concept of *homo faber* (man the maker) is the notion that the human mind (or reason) is a "tool" making and using faculty. Subsequently, the problem with *homo ludens* (man the player) is that it interferes with the development of the mind which is the main mechanism for constructing our own identities and the primary means of productivity. A fuller critique of *homo faber* follows in this chapter (see the second section of Chapter 4).

2 Likewise, I would add: Is physical education an education by the physical?

3 For notable literature, see the following: Dearden (1967, 1968); Fink (1960, 1979); Huizinga (1949); Midgley (1974); Miller (1971, 1973); Neale (1969); Riezler (1941); Sutton-Smith (1997).

4 Generally speaking the common characteristics of play can take the following ten forms: (1) universal and cross-culturally prevalent; (2) freely chosen or voluntarily; (3) autotelic activity; (4) has a community element; (5) requires equipment or "play-things"; (6) has its own spacio-temporal parameters; (7) spontaneous and uncertain in the sense of not being planned; (8) unproductive in the sense that there is no commercial exchange; (9) governed by rules and conventions which suspend ordinary laws; (10) make-believe or pretend.

5 For notable literature, see the following: Caillois and Halperin (1955); D'Agostino (1981); Hyland (1977, 1980); Meier (1980, 1988, 1989, 1995); Roochnik (1975); Schmitz (1979); Suits (1967, 1977, 1978, 1988, 2007).

6 The example provided has been taken and adapted from Suits (1988) paper titled "Tricky triad: Games, play, and sport".

7 Meier (1988) utilises aspects of Suits' (1988) "Tricky triad" in producing an outline of the interrelationships among play, game and sport which he considers to be more accurate compared to Suits. Both share similarities surrounding the concepts of play and games; however, the concept of sport is the basis for the greatest difference. See Suits, 1988, 1–9.

8 See Keen, 1969, Part V, Section 2: The Anatomy of Homo Faber. The four forms are as follows: (1) man is the animal who makes and uses tools; (2) the human mind, no less than the hand, is a toolmaking and tool-using faculty; (3) the chief of *homo faber* is man himself; and (4) the image of *homo faber* signifies that man is a worker.

9 Hyland (1980) makes the point that "responsive openness" is not meant to be a definitive definition of play but is meant to function as an "inductive generalization" to highlight those characteristics that we might consider to be playful from non-playful instances of responsive openness.

10 Certain physical activities may have a natural affinity for this stance of responsive openness, such as mountain climbing, whereas others may inhibit it, such as boxing.

11 In some circles the epistemological claim of physical education would be considered to be necessary if an educational value is to be attached to it.

12 In Chapter 3, I presented an extensive exposition outlining how knowledge is personal because the knower relies on certain implied or inferred elements of human knowledge we know but at the same time we usually cannot verbally articulate how we come to know through the tacit dimension. I argue that an understanding of our embodiment, closely connected with the insights brought forward by Merleau-Ponty's phenomenology of embodiment, highlights that the act of knowing is not an

end-product stripped bare of experience but is closely connected to the lived body; which emphasises that "I" am the absolute source of my knowing because I bring meaning from experiences of the world, because the world gives meaning to my experiences.

13 Unfortunately space does not permit it, but the "theology of play" warrants further investigation, particularly when contemporary sports share close similarities with natural religion. For instance, Michael Novak (1976) argues that "sports flows outward from a deep natural impulse that is radically religious"; and, furthermore, that sports create "primal symbols, metaphors, and acts" of cosmic struggle which in turn can be perceived to be "rituals concerning human survival" or "liturgical enactments of animal perfection and the struggles of the human spirit to prevail". In particular, refer to Part One, Section 2: The Natural Religion of Novak's (1976) seminal book titled *The Joy of Sports: End Zones, Bases, Baskets, Balls, and the Consecration of the American Spirit.*

14 Refer to Piaget's three categories of play as an example of a play theory that was influential from this era in physical education. These are as follows: (1) practice play that is characterised by activities pursued for their intrinsic pleasure; (2) symbolic play like make-believe that implies a representation of an absent object; (3) games with rules which are self-evident in highly organised and structured sports. See Piaget, 1951, Chapter VI: Explanation of play.

15 For a detailed analysis of Dewey's work concerning experience, see Quay (2013).

16 Each of the four modes of the lived body that Schrag (1962, 1988) refers to are as follows: (1) the lived body as self-referential; (2) the lived body as reference to others; (3) the lived body and human space; (4) the lived body and human time.

17 The earlier excerpt from Bannister's book is an ideal example of a "peak experience" that can be found in movement and may be regarded as being meaningful because it brilliantly captures a rare moment in the conscious life of a person.

18 Dewey (1916/1966) draws two conclusions about experience important for education. These are: (1) experience is primarily an active–passive affair (not just cognitive); (2) the value of an experience lies in the perception of relationships or continuities it leads up to because the interaction between the trial and error method and reflective thinking provide opportunities to make "new" connections concerning the problem being considered.

19 To Lloyd and Smith (2005) and Smith and Lloyd (2006) "vitality" is an event, a situation, a circumstance that is experienced bodily. As a result, the conceptual term "vital body" basically refers to how we develop the capacity to make meaningful sense of movement as a being-in-the-world.

20 The literature is quite extensive in this area. In Chapter 5 I outline some of these notable contributions in more detail.

5 The moral aspects of sport and physical education

Do sport and physical education provide unique opportunities to develop moral character?

The idea that there is some sort of connection between physical education and moral character development is an ancient and persistent one. For instance, Plato makes it clear in *The Republic* that physical education is a balanced concept taking two forms – physical and intellectual (gymnastics for the body and music for the soul) – that evolved from the application of the "whole man" philosophy of education. The idea is that the harmonious relationship between the physical and mental will produce a citizen who will more likely display a virtuous disposition of temperance and courage as opposed to the polar vices of licentiousness (excess) or insensibility (deficiency) for the former virtue and rashness (excess) or cowardice (deficiency) for the latter virtue. Likewise, Aristotle's lecture on moral goodness in *The Nicomachean Ethics* clearly outlines that moral virtues like "crafts" are acquired by practice and are due to habituation. This was later extended by St Thomas Aquinas in his commentary on Aristotle's *Ethics* (Aquinas, 1271–1272/1993c) and applied to the virtues as these are understood in *On the Virtues in General* (Aquinas, 1269–1272/1993b). Such an idea reoccurs in the educational theory of Rousseau (1762/2003, Book II), who argues that good character development occurs through the inculcation of good habits. Ozolins (2007) continues this debate when he argues that schools are just one of various communities to which human beings belong and in which they live that can have an enormous impact on the formation of character. As a result the practice of virtue is aided by the support of a moral community that is committed to that practice and is crucial in moral education and in the development of moral persons. These are examples that highlight the interwoven nature of the physical life and the development of character. Within this context, both sport and physical education claim that there is a relationship between the playing of games and the formation of character, but if we are to understand this claim more fully it will be important to consider the rise of public school "athleticism"[1] in the middle of the nineteenth century and in state schools during the twentieth century in Britain because this is where the idea of character development was revived as an educational ideology.[2] According to Mangan (1975), athleticism was once a powerful educational ideology that mixed physical exercise (particularly team games), the general aims of education and the formation of character as a highly effective means of inculcating instrumental ends such as physical and moral courage, loyalty and cooperation, and it became firmly established as a valued feature of public school education until the early twentieth century. Within this context, it was believed that team games were an important vehicle in developing "gentlemanly ideals", "moulding the English gentleman" and so on, whereas physical activities for the working class were more likely to be gymnastics and military forms of drill (not team games) because it was believed that the working class had different attitudes, habits and morals to the higher classes (Bamford, 1975). With the introduction of compulsory free schooling towards the end of the nineteenth century[3] it became clear that there existed two very different perceptions of education for children from different social backgrounds and these were to have a profound effect upon the underpinning ideological development of the role of team games in physical education as a mechanism for children's social and moral formation (Theodoulides and Armour, 2001). Although physical education in the public school and state systems initially developed along separate lines at the turn of the century, the importance of team games within physical education had become synonymous with the development of social and moral virtues, usually under the category of "character development". It is this notion of character development through team games in physical education that is of particular interest to me; but I will not pursue this issue immediately, but will return to it in a later section of this chapter.

From the ever-expanding literature concerning this topic there has been quite a diverse array of interest from those who have attempted to respond to the perennial question about whether games and sport can make a serious contribution to the moral education of those who participate.[4] For instance, this can be expressed by the well-known analogy that "playing the game", particularly following the constitutive rules of games, is somehow connected to the inculcation of socially desirable virtues and practices, which in turn can lead to success in the "game of life". As noted in the above analogy, implied in this claim is a causal relationship between the obligation to follow the constitutive rules of games and the inculcation of moral virtues that are considered to be important to "success" in life. Furthermore, the notion that a code of moral rules and concomitant behaviour patterns within the sporting context will be applied blindly within real life in the hope or even expectation that they will be unshakeably followed and lived by the agent is misconceived – not to mention that it neglects the fact that sporting contexts have frequently been arenas for immoral rather than moral behaviour.

The complexity of moral education has been an ongoing issue for philosophers of education for centuries and so it is not surprising that there has also been debate in the physical education literature in which sophisticated arguments and counterarguments have been applied to the problem, but apparently to no avail. Carr (1998) summarises what he sees as the main arguments surrounding the contestable nature of the current debate that serve as a useful starting point for this chapter.[5] They take the following three positions: (1) Physical activities present in physical education programmes such as games and sports have the potential to be morally negative due to the corrupting consequences of competitive practices such as an overemphasis upon winning, commonly referred to as the "win at any cost" attitude. Consequently, the teaching of games and sports can only have a negative moral educational value and act against moral education rather facilitate it. (2) Physical activities present in physical education programmes such as games and sports have the potential to be morally positive and reinforce socially desirable character traits such as cooperation, honesty and so on that are beneficial to society and transferable to one's own moral life, and as a consequence the teaching of sports and games can have a positive educational value. (3) Physical activities present in physical education programmes such as games and sports cannot clearly exhibit internal features of either positive or negative moral significance. As a result physical education from a moral perspective can best be described as morally "neutral" and may or may not make a significant contribution to moral education. These three views represent an inconsistent set because they cannot all be true, but they present a useful starting point for my critical discussion to determine whether any of them is true. Most of the contemporary debate has been quite emotive in character and sustained by an intense love or hatred of sport and physical education. For instance, most debates would seem to take place between supporters of the first claim who argue for the negative moral educational value of games and sports and those of the second who regard games and sports with morally positive educational characteristics and worth. Although such debates and arguments seem to be inconclusive, the reason for this has more to do with the fact that they are moral arguments in themselves, and not so much about whether sport in physical education or even physical education is moral but rather about how sport is practised in physical education. Carr (1998) makes the pertinent point that even though the debate about the moral educational role of sport in physical education seems to be unresolved this does not imply that such debates are a complete waste of time or not worth pursuing, but rather highlights how moral controversies like this debate are perhaps never resolved unequivocally.

In this chapter I will be concerned with the critical discussion of four issues: first, I provide a brief historical overview of how the "games ethic" gained prominence within the education system during the middle of nineteenth-century Britain and subsequently had a profound impact and influence on the development of physical education during the twentieth century. More than ever, it is still prevalent and dominant within educational institutions. Second, I critically explore and challenge a range of complex issues involved in the moral dimensions of sporting participation in order to better understand the claim that there is a special causal relationship between physical education and moral education or that team games contribute to students' moral development. Third, I argue that the kind of environment in which a child is raised will have a significant influence on the kind of moral person they will become and as a result the practice of virtue can be encouraged and supported by a moral community with a commitment to that practice (virtues). Since school communities are moral habitats I argue that they have an important role to play in the development of good persons, as places in which virtues can be practised. In addition, they will have a direct influence on the formation of moral habits needed to become good persons, to have well-rounded characters and to exhibit appropriate virtues according to the context. Lastly, I discuss how the role of sport and physical education provides unique practical opportunities that lend themselves readily to influencing character development, which supports Carr's second position of his trilogy. I argue that sport in physical education along with other learning experiences in the well-balanced education of a student will provide opportunities for him or her to develop habitual modes of conduct in order to know what it means to be part of the that moral community. It is to this I now turn.

A brief historical overview: the enduring influence of the "games ethic" within education and physical education

According to Kirk (1992a), competitive team games and sports have played an exclusive role in the education of upper-class males in British life since the middle of the nineteenth century. However, with the introduction of mass secondary schooling in the late 1940s competitive team games quickly became the core of physical education across all educational sectors to the point where the version of physical education that had been the privileged domain of the public school as traditional became traditional physical education for everyone, state and public schools, albeit with a few changes. The "cult of athleticism" and its accompanying "games ethic" are terms that still serve as the descriptive labels of this once powerful educational ideology in the literature. Mangan (1975) reinforces the point that athleticism was not a mere term signifying a certain liking for physical exercise, outdoor pursuits, games and so on, but an operational educational belief that compulsory physical exercise, particularly team games, was a highly effective means of inculcating valuable goals such as physical and moral courage, loyalty, cooperation and so on that were end products of character development. The games ethic came to express quintessential bourgeois British qualities such cooperation, loyalty, self-control, perseverance, fairness, courage and so on, and also produced a number of clichés like "play the game", "it's just not cricket", "good sport", "bad form", "playing fair" and so on. This ethic had a profound influence on educational systems around the world, particularly British colonies. For instance, in Australia since the 1880s there has been an explicit intent to reconstruct a version of the English public schools games ethic but with a distinctly Australian ethos of games playing (Kirk, 1994a, 1998b). The ethos surrounding games playing became a highly influential educational ideology that continued to reinforce the notion of "manliness" which was one of the central tenets of the games ethic, as well as other more complex moral and civic purposes. While the games ethic was continually reinforcing a system of values its practice came to be underpinned by an increasingly different set of assumptions surrounding what some saw as the true spirit of the games ethic, based on the notion that competitive games and sports reflect inescapable characteristics of life.[6] Despite the obvious tensions that existed, it was generally considered that sport exemplified a system of values, and it was widely held as an ideal, if not always in practice, that sport developed the "best in us" and should govern any decent civilised society and thereby was ideally suited as an educational mechanism.

According to Mangan (1983), there were three significant reasons for the widespread acceptance of games and the games ethic in both public and grammar schools in the Victoria and Edwardian eras. First, games were seen as effective mechanisms of social cohesion and social control that fostered team spirit, provided a break from academic routine and also informalised relationships. Furthermore, games were also considered important catalysts for learning because they provided an outlet in which physical energy could be dissipated and as a result tired students, so they were more manageable in the classroom. Second, games provided a mechanism in which "Englishness", "fair play" and the "British way" could be inculcated in such a way that no other curriculum or classroom environment could do. In addition, it was considered that games players were visible symbols of "moral prophylaxis" and much was made of the relationship between games and being led to moral maturity through games. Third, games playing and the resources required for their practice emphasised the disparate distribution of resources amongst the classes and hence demonstrated superiority. This is further reinforced by Mangan (1983, p. 330) when he states:

> ... playing fields were part of the social and cultural capital to be acquired in the struggle to maintain social position. In this process they served as a means of demonstrating image. They were at one and the same time emblems of similarity and separateness. But above all they were symbols of superiority – not merely social but moral. Schools without them were suspect. They were either inferior institutions of narrow vocationalism or anachronistic institutions of dangerous intellectualism.

Mangan provides a clear indication of the hierarchical nature of British society during the Victorian and Edwardian eras but also highlights how by the twentieth century games were not just attractive or valuable additions, they were *sine qua non* of these educational institutions subsistence. Although physical education in the public school system and the state school system continued to develop along separate lines at the turn of the century the role of games and sport in physical education was starting to be seriously considered in education because of its "educational effect". According to Theodoulides and Armour (2001), the publication of certain key syllabus documents[7] towards the start of the twentieth century was important in reinforcing this "educational effect" because it was claimed that team games were particularly effective in the formation of character and the development of moral qualities. It came to be seen that the pre-eminent place of physical education was as a means of cultivating these virtues. Within this context it was argued that out of all of the school subjects found within the curriculum, team games taught children how their actions had implications for others more effectively when greater emphasis was placed on the concepts of sportsmanship and fair play gained through competitive play. Moreover, this was

considered to have inestimable value later in life and hence it was given prominence as a rationale for physical education in the curriculum. Arguing that the
playing of games and sports was an invaluable means for developing social and
moral character was a pivotal moment in physical education because it provided
an educational rationale that had previously been lacking.

The role of competitive games and sports within the physical education curriculum became consolidated through the late 1940s and early 1950s and quickly
became an established and central part of physical education programmes by the
1960s (Kirk, 1992a).[8] It is important to note that the public school version of the
games ethic that was highly influential as an educational ideology in the nineti-
eth century was modified and adapted simultaneously and reconstructed as "traditional physical education" for the purposes of mass secondary schooling at all
educational levels. Although this transformation of the games ethic took some
time to become a practical reality for the lower-middle and working class children in state schools, mainly due to a lack of resources to accommodate the
masses, this still represented a significant departure from the use of games as a
mechanism for reinforcing class superiority. It moved it towards a greater
emphasis upon team games or sports as a means of developing character through
concepts of sportsmanship and fair play. Even though the games playing ethic of
the public schools (pre-World War I version) was considered to be antiquated
and in decline, its resilience as an educational ideology had not diminished. This
was due in part to sports' universal popularity and the similarities competition
has with some of the most basic themes of life such as success and failure, good
and bad behaviour, ambition and achievement and so on (Hargreaves, 1986).
Furthermore, at a time when physical education was seeking to shift away from
the term "physical training" towards the term "physical education" as a means
of aligning itself with broader educational aims, it was an easy step to reconstruct a new version of physical education based upon the growing influence of
the games ethic that by the mid-1950s had been around almost a century. When
combined with the popularity of sport and symbolic values attached to it, it is
not surprising that this became the central philosophical feature of the new conception of physical education, albeit with some significant changes. This is
further reinforced by Kirk (1992a, pp. 103–104) who states:

> ... reconstructing *a* traditional form of physical education as *the* tradition,
> the interests of the ruling group were selectively chosen and established....
> None of this denies that games and sports have been played by people at all
> levels of the social system for well over one hundred years. The point is that
> it was a santitized version of the bourgeois males' games ethic that formed
> the value structure on which competitive sports and games in the mass sec-
> ondary schools in the 1950s were based and justified....

With the focus in education shifting towards a more child-centred approach to
teaching and learning during the 1960s and 1970s, physical education also
shifted its focus in order to stay relevant by aligning itself with the dominant

educational ideas of the time. Subsequently, we start to see justifications for physical education that claim games and sport are an integral part of the curriculum because they contribute considerably to social, moral and physical development of the whole person more effectively than other curriculum areas.

Historically there was strong educational support for the role of games and sports, particularly team games, in the formation of character and moral growth.[9] The post-World War II reconstructed notion of "traditional" physical education that gained prominence across all educational systems represented a modified version of an educational ideology found in public schools covering competitive team games that had its origins in mid to late nineteenth-century Britain. In Australia, sport was initially the province of males (and some females) of the privileged classes found in the elite public schools; however, over time sport became more established as an extracurricular activity for boys and girls in most government state schools, although the sports played differed significantly depending on the school and the gender of the student. In state schools medical inspection combined with drilling and exercising through physical training was not uncommon in educational policy early in the twentieth century up until the 1940s, albeit with the addition of some other activities like swimming, calisthenics and minor games. The influence of the games ethic that originated in the public school system was to become a significant force in shaping the practices of state schools by the end of World War II in Australia (Kirk, 1998b). For instance, the growing popularity of inter-school sport in Victoria combined with the professed values of the games ethic provided a strong justification for games playing in state schools. As the influence of team games and the ideology that was embedded within it began to be consolidated in schools we start to see a distinct shift away from physical training as a narrowly conceived enterprise, with no educational intent towards the term physical education and its broader educational intent and natural association with the development of the whole person. Consequently, the version of physical education that had until the 1950s only been "traditional" to the public schools of Great Britain and Australia became reconstructed as "traditional" or "new" physical education for everyone, to the point where competitive games and sports became the core philosophical component of and the largest part of physical education programmes (Kirk, 1992a, 2010).[10] Although Hargreaves (1986) and Kirk (1992a) approach this topic from a distinctly sociological perspective and are quite critical of the intent of the games ethic in its overall role in reinforcing and consolidating certain bourgeois values in society, I am more concerned about the part that physical education plays in character development and whether there is enough evidence to support the claims made surrounding the hypothesis that team games are capable of building character.

The critique so far has traced the historical influence of the games ethic as a justification for competitive games and sports in the physical education curriculum from the rise of public school athleticism in the mid-nineteenth century. This provides a background for the analysis of literature in order to identify some of the conceptual and practical complexities surrounding the terms "moral character", "character or moral development" and how these relate to "moral education" in physical education discourse. A quick review of the relevant literature will show a diverse array of contributors from psychology, sociology and philosophy of sport through to educational philosophy and theory. Due to the diversity of these contributions it is not surprising that there is both overlap and confusion in the use of key terms. One of the most significant problems to beset this debate is the sheer diversity of definitions attached to the use of the term "character". In some cases such terms as "socio-moral development" (Thomas, 1979; Miller *et al.*, 1997), "ethical value" (Reid, 1997), "moral values" (Meakin, 1982; Theodoulides, 2003), "moral development" (Dennis and Krebs, 1986; Romance *et al.*, 1986), "personal and social education" (Meakin, 1990) and "psycho-social development" (Lee, 1996) have been used at various times to describe a range of personal, social and moral characteristics claimed to be developed through physical education. Furthermore, it is important to note that over the last twenty or so years there has been a growing trend in social scientific/psychological research to use empirical data to draw conclusions about the role sport can play in moral development and hence its educational value.[11] I am in agreement with Barrow (2000, p. 320), who argues that empirical–scientific research in moral education is quite limiting in its capacity to provide a "richer, more imaginative, more subtle and more discriminate" account of complex human interactions, situations, relationships and so on, whereas philosophy and the humanities should be revered because they can provide us with an "incommensurably greater insight than the crudely hammered-out generalisation of the average academic surveyor" can hope to achieve. What is clear is that the interrelationship between personal, social and moral development is complex and not easily distinguishable. For example, to Shields and Bredemeier (1995), who are firmly located in the cognitivist tradition of moral development, character is constructed around a complex model of moral action (rule-based moral theory),[12] whereas a focus on character and virtue leads to further questions about how the self and identity are integrated in a person's sense of who she or he is, what they aspire to be and so on (Jones and McNamee, 2003). Space does not permit an extended critique of Shields and Bredemeier's model of moral action because I wish to offer an alternative that is less reductive of moral character, unscientific in the sense that it not based on collated data but firmly located in the neo-Aristotelian tradition of virtues, to provide a framework in which to consider character development in and through sport. Although I am in agreement on the idea of character development, I argue for a virtue-based account that provides a richer picture of moral character and emphasises the agent who performs actions, instead of a deontological approach where the rational moral agent is disposed to follow rules that govern right action. A virtues-based approach of moral character and moral education will differ significantly from a deontologist approach, which focuses on the development of rationally autonomous moral agents who dutifully live according to the requirements of rules and principles. For instance, a person of good character is not defined in relation to a system of rules or principles, but rather in relation to actions that correspond to particular virtues and by examining what a virtuous person would do according to institutional expectations and standards of practice. It is in this context of social practices that sport has the capacity to cultivate certain virtues like any practice that is neither synonymous with the rest of society nor separate from it.

Following MacIntyre's (2007) seminal work many philosophers of sport have come to view sport as paradigmatic examples of "practices", and hence the emphasis on the quality of initiation into sports practices and the balance between dispositions and internal and external goods of practices. Consequently, my account of moral education will be based on a general account of moral virtue, one that promotes those attitudes and dispositions I call virtues that establish long-lasting habits in young children or in this case develops character. I do not begin to assume that schools are the only means available in the community or the State by which children can learn to be good persons and be initiated into a certain way of life (Ozolins, 2010a, 2010b). To do this we need to consider the importance of moral habitat in character development; this is sometimes neglected or overlooked but is crucial in moral education and in the development of moral persons, because the kind of environment in which a child is raised will have a significant influence on the kind of moral person they will become and subsequently the practice of virtue can be encouraged and supported by a moral community with a commitment to that practice (Ozolins, 2007). However, before I go on to set out my alternative account of character development and moral education, I wish to challenge some of the influential arguments found in the literature surrounding sporting participation and the moral nature of sport itself.

Do sport and physical education provide unique opportunities to develop moral character?

The relationship between morality and sport in physical education is complex. The notion that game playing in physical education can function as an important instrument of moral education in the curriculum has a long history, as noted earlier in this chapter. According to this view, if you had learned courageous behaviour in rugby or developed the discipline to adhere to a strict training regime while training for a marathon, then these qualities, which the game or sport helped you to show and develop, would somehow be developed in your life, in your professional life, in your family relations or even in how you dealt with moral dilemmas. In summary, physical education was considered a good thing because it "... helped you later on and at the same time – but mostly later on – to lead the good life" (Longland, 1955, p. 7).

The problem with the theory of "transference" is that it implies a causal relationship between participation in a physical activity and that certain qualities will be inevitably developed and necessarily available in other aspects of life. It is a mistake to expect the inculcation of certain qualities to directly accompany the practice of certain competitive games and sports in physical education. Although physical education may provide a multitude of opportunities for stimulating virtuous qualities considered important for engagement in sport, it must be remembered that we cannot directly cultivate specific qualities like courage, either in physical education or out of it. Courage may be developed, but we must realise that it is not a necessary condition that courage will be developed, nor expect it to accompany the practice of specific physical activities. Too much reliance has been placed on transference, and to suggest that transference is the case is misleading because it is based on a fallacy. The kind of opportunities afforded or the number of them evoked in sport and physical education may well lead to the expression of certain desirable qualities; however, it may also be the case that they provide opportunity for the attainment of undesirable qualities as well. I am not saying anything new here (as outlined earlier in the chapter) because advocates against sport and physical education have previously used this same line of argument to highlight the alleged morally negative features as the reason why sport and physical education should be excluded from the curriculum. This certainly may well be the case if there is no guidance, because without guidance an agent will act in accordance with their nature, which may lead to vice. If we continue with the argument, that certain sports help bring out (assuming that they are latent) positive or negative qualities would seem strange because they cannot be good nor bad in themselves, but the way they are practised may be good or bad or positive or negative. To use an example, it could be argued the Hermann Goering was a courageous fighter pilot during World War I; this may well be the case, but this is more a question about what courage is used for. Certainly, the habitat in which he found himself may have not encouraged the exhibition of good character but this does not mean that the qualities that he displayed during war-time as a fighter pilot did not exist, it is just that they did not necessarily ensure that he became a person of good character. Courage and goodness of character are independent of each other because a person of good character will be motivated to act rightly, which may lead them to deliberately decide to disregard certain moral conventions they consider to be wrong according to the situational context, whereas descriptions of courage are usually normative descriptions of behaviour. This is why educational institutions are important to the development of moral character because we are social beings who thrive on belonging. Since schools are part of the various moral habitats and communities in which young people belong, it is advantageous in the sense that the environment will be able to encourage and support the practice of those qualities we would like to see in adult life. I will return to this line of thought in greater detail in the next section, as more needs to be said about the theory of transference.

Longland (1955) is right when he argues that we confuse things we regard as qualities of character with moral behaviour and then somehow feel disappointed and let down when the people we admire on the sporting field don't display the same qualities in the rest of their lives. Normally when we talk of character we use fairly descriptive terms like "conscientious", "courageous", being a "bit of a character", being of "strong or weak character" and so on to tell us how a person pursues certain goals. Of course there are different ways of talking about character and there is a close relationship with cognate fields, but in this case I wish to draw attention to how the notion of character plays a critical function in a person's life because the moral virtues are not innate but acquired through practice and habituation (see Part II of Aristotle's *Ethics*). This is why a person's character is usually judged by his or her disposition to act in a certain way against some wider range of ascriptions for people's moral and immoral action. For example, it would be inconceivable to describe or praise someone for being honest, or to say that they had a mature understanding of honesty and yet could not act honestly. The same applies to the sporting context. We are usually distrustful of the player who claims that they play fairly, yet continues to break the rules or has an atrocious tribunal record.

According to Carr (1998), the debate surrounding the issue of transference is something of a "red herring" about the moral aspects of sport and would appear to be based on the dubious assumption that there is some sort of gap to be bridged between sport and reality. For instance, the conceptual support for this distinction between sport and "real life" would appear to originate in the highly influential work of Huizinga (1949), but the problem is that such an extreme dichotomy does not really exist in this way, because when we participate in sport we do not leave the so-called real world and enter into another world. In a way Huizinga's ideas surrounding play have been misrepresented. As mentioned in Chapter 4, the interrelationship of play, games and sport is complex and although play may share some qualities with games and sports, sport is never just play. There has been a general tendency to view each in isolation, which in turn has propagated a misunderstanding that play is set apart from the everyday world and hence reinforced a fallacy that sport is also set apart from ordinary life. Although we may play sport with a playful (lusory) attitude this does not mean that games and sports are play. To think as such is to misinterpret the interrelationship of play, games and sport. Sport is simply part of life and just another form of human interaction. Although such a position can be easily confused by the vast array of sporting practices that seem at odds with the ethos of sport,[13] not to mention the sheer diversity of behaviour – much of which seems morally questionable – found in sport. We cannot avoid the vexed issue about the moral aspects of sport, not because it is all-pervasive in modern contemporary society and culture, but because the moral evaluation of sport as separate or continuous with the rest of human life has serious implications for determining whether sport and physical education can provide opportunities to develop moral character and hence qualify for inclusion within the school curriculum based on its moral educational potential.

Although I am sympathetic to the debate surrounding both the nature of sport and how it is practised, my aim in this section will be to look closely at these arguments so as to disentangle and challenge some of these views that have misconceived not only sport and morality but also the relationship between them. In particular, I wish to challenge the notion that sport is somehow separate or discontinuous with other human interests and concerns. An excellent starting point is Simon's (2000) influential analysis of "internalist" accounts of sport. According to Simon (2000, pp. 1–2), "... internalists ... hold that sport has a significant degree of autonomy from the wider society and supports, stands for, or expresses a set of values of its own ...", in contrast to "externalism", which denies that sport is a special source of values and simply mirrors, reflects or reinforces values that already exist in society found outside of sport itself. He goes on to set out his own version of internalism called "broad internalism"[14] which, in addition to the rules of sports, proposes that there are certain norms or moral principles that are "neither social conventions nor moral principles" of sport, but which have a kind of internal ethic or what he refers to as an "internal morality of sport". These can be used to determine what to do in situations where the constitutive rules cannot be easily applied, as illustrated in the case of "racquetless Josie" as outlined in Butcher and Schneider (1998). Butcher and Schneider use this case to highlight how we sometimes want certain important principles important to sport like "fair play" to be applied outside the rules of sport, particularly when the constitutive rules of play are not clear.[15] They argue that rather than present ready-made solutions to issues surrounding fair play like rules, the player needs to be guided by the norms, values and traditions that are in the best interests of the game concerned. For instance, if a sportsperson is committed to the highest standards of play (individually and for his or her opponents) they will ask themselves the following questions: Do practices X, Y and Z enhance the playing of the game? Do they make for better sport? Do they test game-related skills? If not, on the grounds of the fair play framework presented by Butcher and Schneider they should be avoided. Although Annaka acts altruistically if she lends Josie her racquet this is a supererogatory act, and hence morality does not dictate that she loans the racquet and this needs to be taken into consideration in such a case.

On the face of it, the internal morality of sport and what Russell (2007) calls the "separation thesis"[16] seem consistent with each other; however, in the same discussion about the applications of broad internalism, Simon (2000), on the one hand, wants to preserve the notion that sport has its own unique autonomous moral values and, on the other hand, acknowledges that there are important moral principles that can be found outside of sport that may in fact contradict well-established rules to the point where "we would be right to at least question the ethics of sport, not the traditional ethical theories" (p. 13). He goes on to add that it may appear that internalism brings about its own set of moral principles that are unique to sport but only highlights important "ethical principles" that seem exclusive and inherent to sport. Simon's sophisticated arguments for broad internalism seem convincing when he outlines how rules (formalism) and the ethos of the game (conventionalism) seem inadequate in dealing with difficult cases like racquetless Josie that are sports issues. The issues raised by internalism in general provide an interesting starting point between sport and what we traditionally think of as morality because if we argue that there are moral values inherent within the nature of sport it is only logical to enquire whether they are unique to sport or not. Interestingly, Russell (1999, 2007) argues that Simon's broad internalism should be interpreted as embracing a "continuity thesis"[17] that has an interpretative element as a means of maintaining and fostering the "lusory goal" of the game.

Much of the current literature in philosophy of sport seems to support an internalist approach to understanding the nature of sport. It presupposes certain moral duties that demand that the competitors pursue genuine competition and in turn assume a competitive duty to strive to win. Indeed, a preoccupation with the conditions of competition so that they are fair and the importance assigned to winning in competitive games and sport have been used as arguments for an internalist position. Even though these moral ideals may seem unique to games and sports, there does not seem to be anything that is distinctive about sport that can support the claim for an internal morality of sport and, further, how sport may be supportive of moral education. For instance, the moral values associated with the context of competition are not merely limited to sport but are present, perhaps arguably, in most institutions that are seriously committed to the promotion and pursuit of human excellence. Likewise, the aim to win is certainly not just found in sport but seems part of framing a competitive context in which excellence can be measured. Pawlenka's (2005) work complements this discussion because she questions the notion that fairness in sports has a set of morals all its own that cannot be transferred to other areas of life. Yet again we see the misguided notion of transference playing its part as a justification for why the sports-specific concept of fairness is not applicable to life in general. I agree with Pawlenka that fairness in sports should be positioned within the sphere of moral philosophy, because certain general moral principles found in everyday life are applicable in sport, albeit with a few contextual alterations (*mutatis mutandis*). To achieve this she sets out four arguments.

First, she argues that the idea that we have an obligation to follow rules is a "weak kind of obligation" because play can be deferred or suspended at any time, whereas morality demands that we acknowledge that there are certain absolutes that cannot be easily broken, like the intentional killing of innocent human beings (Pawlenka, 2005). She goes on to argue that within the context of sports a diverse array of situations can arise in which there is a moral duty to disregard the obligation to follow the rules in order to fulfil other duties like protecting oneself or others from serious injury. This is further reinforced by Kolnai (1966), who makes the pertinent point that only a restricted analogy can be established between the rules of a game and the moral rules that guide an agent's life. Kolnai (1966, p. 121) goes on to state:

> ... moral rules, however relevant they are to the conduct of life, do not define life, which can be carried on with more or less success and enjoyment in occasional or systematic defiance of some or many moral rules; what they define is the person's moral status in life which has no analogue in game. The concern of "being moral" or "being good", no doubt intimately conjoined with many standard and focal purposes of life, itself constitutes one such paramount purpose whose service demands a great deal of thematic attention, thought, strategy and effort; whereas to abide by the rules of the game is not a thematic part of the *game* but merely a self-evident presupposition of playing it.

A second reason for the misguided notion that sport has its own unique set of morals revolves around the connection between the structural features of sports competition and the concept of fairness (Pawlenka, 2005). For instance, it is often misunderstood that the agonal attitude to win allows or even expects competitors to refrain from behaving altruistically during sporting competitions. Therefore, the antagonist's pursuit to strive to defeat the other has something to do with morals insofar as there is a conflict in balancing the idea of playing fairly on the one hand and the determination to win on the other. For instance, on the face of it would appear that the concept of fair play seems only limited to the sporting context, but as a concept it cannot be made comprehensible without considering aspects of justice.[18] Consequently, fairness should not just be limited to the sporting sphere as it is commonly understood in competitive sports, but also should extend beyond the playing field because it shares similarities with aspects of justice and respect in ordinary life, albeit modified to fit the context.

A third particularity of competitive sport is the impression that it appears to be governed by special morals because there is a relatively high tolerance for physical aggression and what counts as acceptable forms of aggression (Pawlenka, 2005). Certain sports accept different levels of physical aggression and violence. Understandably, one might gain the impression, as an outsider looking in, that sports have their own unique set of moral values. After all, who can intentionally punch someone in the face in everyday life without being punished? For instance, ice hockey is infamous for tolerating certain levels of violence that would not be tolerated in other sports. It is interesting to note, however, that both the McSorely and Bertuzzi incidents[19] were clear examples of acts of violence against an opponent that were clearly condemned and, understandably, led to criminal convictions.[20]

I will now consider Pawlenka's last argument against the notion that fairness in sports is a concept that is exclusive to sports. One must be cautious not to buy into the fallacious argument that playing fair in sports as constituted as an obligation to rule following is somehow transferable to other areas of life such as driving on the road. As argued earlier, the theory of transference is altogether too easy and deeply questionable in how it is applied to different contextual situations. There simply is no comparison between, say, the illegal passing of another car in a risky situation, with giving away a free kick to an opposition player in soccer. In this case, we would tend to describe the driver's behaviour as reckless, rather than unfair. Likewise, there is a certain level of ultimacy with breaking the road rules in such a reckless way that could have serious consequences in life, whereas giving away a free kick in soccer has a certain level of non-ultimacy attached. There is no question that when we speak of fairness in our ordinary lives, we equate this with a kind of equal opportunity and impartiality amongst other things that justice can give us.[21] My position differs somewhat from Pawlenka's because I would argue that sport borrows from our everyday understanding of fairness that has its origins within justice, not the other way around.[22] To me, equal opportunity and impartiality share similarities with the logic of what competitive sports calls for, and what the umpire attempts to guarantee. I am the first to acknowledge that, despite the best endeavours of rules to achieve equality, the reality is that these efforts are not always totally successful due to unrealistic expectations, and disproportionate advantages like superior organisations, resources and even individual skill. This is further reinforced by Ingham and Loy (1973), who argue that we generally want sporting contests to have the semblance of equality but at the same time have a "structural tension" so the outcomes are uncertain and problematic.

Russell (2004) presents two key moral principles that are continuous with and represent, reflect, extend and reinforce basic moral values found outside of sport in everyday life which he refers to as the "internal principle of games" and the "external principle of games". It is important to note that Russell's (2004) use of the term "internal principle" of sport is in no way the same as Simon's (2000) use of the term "internal morality" of sport. The latter functions as a normative principle that governs participants' behaviours in games that are derivative from and continuous with certain moral ideals for promoting human flourishing, whereas the "external principles of games" to Russell reflects the idea that games are institutions grounded in a principle of consent. He goes on to defend the continuity thesis by arguing that virtually all moral theories recognise either direct or indirect duties related to the promotion of respect for persons and of human flourishing, and these duties are also fundamental to the nature of sport (Russell, 2007).[23] Russell makes a strong case for sport being continuous with basic moral ideals found outside sport; however, this still does not resolve once and for all the issue of how games and sport can be morally practised (positively or negatively) and hence qualify or exclude physical education from being included within the school curriculum.

Carr (1998) makes the pertinent point that if we want games and sports to be part of the curriculum, physical education needs to fulfil two conditions: (1) be widely endorsed in society as morally beneficial; and (2) be amenable to contexts of formal institutional school. I am in agreement that some sporting practices will be automatically ruled out as being morally questionable within the context of formal schooling, such as the mixed martial arts that can be seen in the Ultimate Fighting Championship (UFC). In most societies such practices will be quite rightly condemned as barbaric and, of course, excluded from the formal school context. In a sense, the same applies to other activities taught within the curriculum that are considered to be contestable. For instance, there are many who would be eager and ready to insist that religious education within the context of formal schooling, particularly to young children, is a sinister form of indoctrination within schooling, or who disagree with certain aspects of how science is taught because it is at odds with certain religious beliefs and values.

Education has a variety of aims that may be legitimately sought and that can range across habituation, attitude formation, knowledge and skill development, character development and so on. Normally we anticipate certain positive benefits associated with the teaching of certain sorts of subjects or activities to young people that we would not anticipate for others, which may mean "ruling in" science, religion, physical education and so on, and "ruling out" witchcraft, pornography, gambling and so on (Carr, 1998). This does not mean that science, religion, physical education and so on can be regarded as moral pursuits in themselves or even that the way they are taught is beyond criticism. The point is that some things like games and sports, science and religious education within the context of formal schooling are not only continuous with the wider concerns of human life but are considered valuable because of their connection to truth, knowledge and human flourishing. Whether such features as competition or certain physical activities are conducive to the promotion of character development is both heterogeneous and complex.

This is further reinforced by Putman (1995) who argues that we may disagree about which virtues or qualities may be important or desirable but the goal of character development either at home or at school is to establish deeply ingrained habits in young people so they become moral and upright citizens. For instance, if an adult does not possess justice as a character trait, it is doubtful whether they will be able to recognise rights or duties when they arise irrespective of the context. It is, therefore, the cultivation of good habits in general that I am seeking, particularly in sport. The moral educational potential of physical education rests on sport functioning as a place in which the virtues can be practised in a supportive environment. This possibility is not unique to sport and the physical education profession should not overstate its role, but in saying this, games and sport in physical education provide opportunities for practising habitual modes of conduct. In order to do this, greater consideration needs to be given to how the moral habitat plays an important role in moral character development because the kind of environment in which a child is raised will have a significant influence on the kind of moral person they will become. Hence, if this line of argument is right the cultivation of character can be encouraged in physical education and provide an arena for practising moral behaviour that is supported by a moral community with a commitment to that practice (virtues).

In addition, to ask whether certain physical activities like soccer in physical education are positive, negative or neutral seems disingenuous because the development of moral character is dependent upon imitation and initiation into the conventions, norms, standards and traditions of the practice amongst other things. The role of the teacher in this process should not be underestimated, because I take the view that a teacher, either directly or indirectly, does have a moral influence upon the students with whom they come in contact. This is why all teachers are moral educators, whether they like it or not, in the sense that as part of their role within the school community they will continually tell students what to do, make evaluations regarding appropriate and inappropriate behaviours, apply suitable consequences in response to correct (reinforcement) or incorrect acts (punishment), monitor social interactions within the classroom and so on.[24] In support of this Pring (2001) argues that teaching is a moral practice, because teaching reflects the very moral divisions of the wider community; teachers are thus inevitably caught in a moral debate that they cannot avoid, because decisions about what is worth learning and the best ways of pursuing it are essentially moral judgements. I do not assume that schools are the only place in which children can learn to be good persons, but I would argue that due to the amount of time young people spend in educational institutions over their life-span, such institutions can have a significant part to play in the kind of people children will become, and hence the moral habitat to which they belong, can influence moral character.

Since games and sports represent a large proportion of physical education programmes much of our action, particularly in sport, is habitual, and often precludes the kind of rational reflection typified by cognitivist accounts of moral development and methodology used by social scientific/psychological research into the relationship between sports participation and character. Becoming a good person is a complex and multifaceted process and not exclusively about following certain kinds of rules unconditionally or even being concerned about consequences of particular actions.[25] I turn now to consider the crucial role of the school community as a moral habitat in which the virtues can be practised, which in turn can influence the formation of moral habits.

The importance of moral habitat in the development of moral persons: the practice of virtue is aided by the support of moral communities

When Ryle (1975) asks the self-imposed question "Can virtue be taught?" he makes the point that moral standards are not inborn but have to be learned by example, practice and critically supervised practice. He goes on to add that we learn to do by doing, with the added support from wiser people whom young people are likely to look up to. For instance, we remember the difference in gravity between the occasions when we were seriously punished and the occasions when we were routinely punished for minor offenses at school or by our parents. It is in this sense of "taught" that we are taught to treat certain things as important and hence taught to care more, say, about whether we cheated or not than whether we won the game or lost it. Likewise, we come to acquire the virtues through habituation. For example, when a father gives his son his first bike as a present, the child of course cannot ride it at first. He has to learn to balance, steer and brake when it is necessary. Neither can he learn to ride his bike didactically. He needs to be told what to do, to be shown what to do and most importantly allowed to practise what to do until he can ride the bike. These skills are inculcated in him by example and by doing, and not just due to mere talk. According to Ryle (1975), we know from our own experience that the same "holds true of conduct". He goes on to add that if virtue is to be learnt we first need to learn from others, then by being trained by others and lastly by being trained by ourselves. Initially instinctive imitation is a *sine qua non* part of learning when a child is young, but as the child grows this does not suffice to get the child to the higher stages of mastery. To do this the agent has to think for themselves and decide to reproduce the right acts, for the right reason, at the right times while feeling appropriately about them (Ryle, 1975).

The best way for young people to develop character is by imitation of those who exemplify good habits as opposed to bad habits. Character development does not occur in isolation but in social conditions that enhance or frustrate that development. As a result sport just so happens to be one place in which our moral character can be inculcated by example, by practice and by critical supervision. If we accept that moral education is about the inculcation of children to be good persons, well-rounded characters who exhibit virtuous dispositions and habits that are appropriate acts according to the particular context and situation, then sport is an excellent tool of moral education. According to McNamee *et al.* (2003) sport can play a more robust role in moral character development and therefore moral education if we consider more seriously the "tri-partite account" of moral action offered by Aristotle, which requires a greater emphasis on the importance of childhood learning, imitation, emulation and so on that is more powerful than commonly acknowledged. They go on to add that this means examining more closely patterns of normalcy as a "complex of perception, emotion and deliberation" which are more a product of a habituation into modes of perception and feeling that are not "precursors to, but rather constitutive of, mature moral action and reflection" (McNamee *et al.*, 2003, p. 71). Therefore, it is the acquisition of virtuous dispositions and habits that I am seeking in general, particularly in sport.

The notion of moral "habitat" owes much to Aristotle's lecture on how we come to acquire moral goodness. According to Aristotle (2004, p. 31; 1103a), moral virtues, like crafts, are acquired by practice and habituation and in his words:

> Virtue, then, is of two kinds, intellectual and moral. Intellectual virtue owes both its inceptions and its growth chiefly to instruction and for this very reason needs time and experience. Moral goodness, on the other hand, is the result of habit from which it has actually got its name, being a slight modification of the word *ethos*.

Much can be learnt from Aristotle's teaching on moral virtues, particularly upon the process of how we should learn by doing. For example, a builder learns how to become a builder by building and to become a good builder is a result of building well as opposed to building badly. By analogy this applies to performing "just acts" and to self-control (temperance) – by practising to be in control of ourselves and to perform other virtuous acts we learn to be good. Therefore, the type of environment in which a child is raised will have a significant impact on the kind of moral agent they will become. The opportunity to exercise how to be virtuous can only be sustained by moral communities or habitats that have a commitment to that practice of virtue (Ozolins, 2007). The importance of community in the moral development of young people cannot be underestimated because we are social beings who need community in order to be fulfilled and to flourish. The need for community can have both a positive and negative influence on the practice of virtue. For instance, a moral community can provide a safe place in which to learn and practise good acts. Alternatively, a moral community can reinforce vice, such as learning to lie to deflect and avoid personal responsibility for a wrong act, for instance, this is evident by an agent choosing to thieve as a way of life.

According to Ozolins (2007), the practice of virtue on this perspective can be aided by both active and passive support from the moral community in which the agent belongs. He goes on to add that belonging to a moral community provides passive support for the practice of virtue by providing the background beliefs and values that are taken as unquestioned influence and also provided by certain structural features like class distinctions that perpetuate and reinforce these; whereas, active support can best be understood as the approval and disapproval given to certain actions and a conscious effort to create a just and good society. Since we belong to multiple communities, the extent to which the virtues flourish or are undermined will depend on the reinforcement of the other moral communities to which the agent belongs, because they are all interconnected and dependent upon each other in quite explicit and implicit ways.

Rather than referring to a "community" as an abstract concept, it is clearer to talk about the notion of community through concrete examples to which human beings belong and by which they are normally influenced like: (1) the family; (2) the extended family and friends; (3) for children, a child-care centre; (4) primary school; (5) secondary school (Ozolins, 2007). Furthermore, a sporting club, and more generally the neighbourhood in which people live, followed by regions and so on, are other communities.[26] Just as human beings belong to many diverse communities, neither are such communities separate entities functioning in isolation. Rather, they are part of a much larger community, and dependent upon each other in various ways.

Ozolins (2007) expertly uses the analogy of an ecosystem to explain the notion of moral communities, emphasising the interconnectedness that each community has with each other as a whole. For example, a tropical rainforest environment develops microhabitats within it and these in turn will be adapted to the general environment. Conversely, desert environments will be different from tropical ones and arctic environments as well. Certain species (such as polar bears) will struggle to survive in desert environments. This analogy when applied to moral environments shows how there will be a variety of different moral habitats, such as a Judaeo-Christian environment that will differ from a Hindu environment and so on. This is, of course, an analogy, and so serves only a limited purpose of emphasising how it is possible for human beings to belong and adapt to different moral habitats. The analogy should not be taken too far.

I agree with MacIntyre (MacIntyre and Dunne, 2002) that the aim of education is to develop children to become reflective and independent members of their families and the political communities to which they belong; the aim also is the inculcation of those virtues needed to direct us towards the attainment of common and individual goods, which can only be achieved by learning how to act in situations in a virtuous manner or with practical wisdom. As argued earlier by Aristotle and Ryle, virtue, like skills, crafts, arts and so on, can be taught, not by didactic instruction alone, but by example, exercise and critically supervised practice that can only happen within a community with certain traditions, values and practices. For instance, it is not possible to practice the virtues without the presence of others because one cannot be courageous, generous, prudent and so on without being in a community.

A school community, like any other community, provides a moral habitat in which the values of a particular community can be acted out and reinforced. For example, the values that young people learn from membership of a school community can be acquired through the creation of a safe environment. Schools are nurturing environments that provide various opportunities for the young to practise the virtues by reinforcing good moral habits acquired through performing virtuous acts and, conversely, using disciplinary measures for correcting acts of vice that do not reflect the values of the moral habitat. Undoubtedly, teachers have a significant role within this whole process in the school setting due to the influence they can have on young people. Teachers in their own training learn how to use pedagogical methods that reinforce good behaviours and punish bad actions. These are important means for forming virtuous dispositions, so that the young come to value right things and deprecate wrong things. This is why a central feature of virtue requires the development of an agent's disposition to act in a certain way. Hence, the best way for young people to learn how to become moral agents is by imitation and acting like people who exemplify good habits as opposed to bad habits because the development of character occurs not in isolation but in social conditions that enhance or frustrate that development.

Applying these ideas to sport, it is evident that sport is a practice like farming, physics or architecture, because it is has certain goods internal to that activity that are realised in the course of trying to achieve the standards of excellence that characterise it.[27] Although there is considerable divergence between sports, MacIntyrean practice highlights the importance of belonging to communities because it is both from current examplars and from the tradition of the practice that one must learn appropriate conduct. Acknowledging that sports are practices in this sense, then, is to recognise the essentially "social character of the activities in and through which goods definitive of the activity ... are required and developed" (Jones and McNamee, 2003, p. 42). Subsequently, the cultivation of virtue is both a necessary condition and consequence of proper engagement in sport. For instance, in sport a player is not called a "cheat" because they have broken some formal universal principle familiar from moral theories. Rather, this usually occurs as a result of the player's undermining the commitment to that sport as a practice and disregarding the pursuit of excellence and what it means to play sport in the first place, and instead trying to win through unfair means. The point here is that such a judgement is made by reference to the ethos of a game and its current exemplars of the relevant traditions of sporting practice upon which it is based. Consequently, in this case it cannot be said that the cheat has been properly initiated into sport or is even playing the game in its true sense as they haven't learnt the interlocking processes of judging, caring and acting (basis for moral education) for successful practice.

It has been argued that educational institutions are important to the development of moral character because we are social beings that thrive on belonging. Schools are nurturing environments that provide various opportunities for the young to practise the virtues by reinforcing good moral habits acquired through performing virtuous acts and conversely using disciplinary measures for correcting acts of vice that do not reflect the values of the moral habitat. In this sense, games and sports in physical education can provide unique opportunities to develop habitual modes of conduct.

The role of sport and physical education in cultivating character: an opportunity for practising moral behaviour

Earlier in the chapter I provided a brief historical overview of how the cult of athleticism and its accompanying games ethic gained prominence within the English education system during the middle of the nineteenth century and subsequently had a profound impact and influence on the development of physical education during the twentieth century. I have argued that it still exerts a powerful influence in physical education today. This is evident by the fact that competitive games and sport still represent a large proportion of most physical education programmes in schools. The main reason why this has occurred is due to apologists of physical education being quick to capitalise on the popularity of sport within society in general and claim that there is a causal relationship between certain physical activities and character development as moral education. For instance, the argument that competitive games and sports have moral educational potential and hence qualify for inclusion within the curriculum is misleading because they are often taught and practised in a wide range of morally suspect ways. I argue that much of this confusion has been due to a misunderstanding of the role sport can play in the development of moral character in physical education, particularly within educational institutions.

The role of sport and physical education in cultivating character is really no different from any other realm of human practice. Since the virtues are not innate, my point is that the virtues can be learnt by example, practice and critical supervision. According to Putman (1995), the development of character is one of the major goals of child-raising, in which schools play a vital role by providing moral exemplars for children to see and emulate. He goes on to add that even though it may be desirable to reason with students about rights or duties, the purpose of teaching children to control impulses or care about others in their behaviour is to build a foundation upon which later in life, the adult is ready, willing and able to apply this behaviour. This is why character formation is crucial in children's development because without a good character, he or she will not be able to recognise rights or duties when they arise in adulthood. This is further reinforced by Ozolins (2010b, p. 11) who argues that the effects of belonging to good moral habitats will eventually reinforce good moral habits and vice versa; however, it is not just good habits that we wish young people to have but also an "... ability to make reasoned, autonomous moral choices which result in virtuous action". He goes on to add that routine and habit exert a powerful influence over our actions; they should not be ignored in moral education because the inculcation of good moral habits is an important initial step in bringing young people to knowledge of virtue and hatred of vice. Becoming a good person embodies a wide range of virtues, which will determine both what an agent should do and be motivated to do according to the situational context. In the case of physical education, when we use games and sport what we are trying to teach children to do is to play fairly, be gracious winners, accept losing and respect their opponent. This is further elaborated by Carr, who argues that when it comes to acquiring those dispositions we call virtues it is not about reasoning what is the morally right thing to do in some abstract sense but more about a child's training in honesty, fairness and so on until he or she is old enough to make independent decisions (Carr, 1991, Chapter 12: Education and the virtues: Objectivity, subjectivity and teaching). This can only be achieved when children have strong characters to exercise these virtues in concrete situations, and are not tempted by, say, cheating, lying, meanness and so on. Maraj (1965, p. 107) makes the point that the claim of sport in physical education in the development of moral character lies rather in the fact that there are not many activities in life that provide either the "kind of opportunities or the number of them for evoking the qualities which are considered desirable".

I argue that moral education aims to inculcate habits of virtue that enable us to see, in a more general way, the goods that are served by our activities that direct our actions that both transform and build up just communities (Ozolins, 2007). Although Ozolins (2007) makes no specific reference to sporting communities as a moral habitat, however, I consider it to be consistent with the idea that human beings belong to a range of different communities that are interconnected and dependent on one another and are ideal places in which to practise the virtues in a supportive environment. To take this idea further, sporting communities or habitats are just one part of the many moral habitats to which we belong, having their own particular moral values, traditions, practices and so on; as a result the moral virtues that participants will learn and the practices to which they will become habituated will be those that are practised in their community. Acting rightly in sport (as elsewhere in life) is much a matter of habituation, practice and the support of morally committed communities in which the activity belongs. Arnold (1994) reinforces this point when he argues that to have a moral character in the context of sport entails both proper habit formation through initiation and a commitment to sports' internal goods and standards. Such goods and standards presuppose a set of ideals of what people within the sporting fraternity are meant to strive for and hold up as moral exemplars. For example, when we say that someone is a "good sport", we are saying that not only do they act according to the rules of the game, but also more importantly that they exercise such virtues as honesty, courage, fairness and so on which "not only characterise sport as a practice, but which are indispensable elements that allow it to flourish" (Arnold, 1994, p. 85).

Although there continues to be doubt within the literature[28] surrounding the role games and sports can play in developing moral character in physical education, this work is ill-informed, as it attempts to turn the general normativity of education into a kind of quasi-science-based technology that fails to appreciate that education and teaching is essentially a moral practice that is not conducive to conventional empirical–scientific research methods (Carr, 2001). Jones (2008) makes the point that our expectations of moral character through sport seem unrealistic in what we want it to deliver because it cannot deliver "athlete-saints". Such an idea of sport functioning in this way is problematic because the idea that a person of good character must possess all the virtues is flawed. Hence, it follows that a range of virtues needs to be cultivated, celebrated and rewarded through practice. Moral character development is not just about teaching children to know that X, Y and Z are right or wrong in some abstract sense, but more about teaching children to be good persons of moral character by learning to do, by performing good actions (Ryle, 1975). It is important to note that an Aristotelian scheme of moral character development does not expect perfection; only that we strive toward being good, which can be accomplished by belonging to a moral habitat in which good moral habits can be practised or supported. Since human beings belong to a diverse array of moral habitats or communities that overlap and intersect, some of these will be more important than others in the cultivation of moral virtues. One such habitat in which young people spend considerable time in their formative years is the school or educational institution. Hence it seems reasonable to argue that sport and physical education are also important moral habitats to which human beings belong and that can also influence moral character. I have argued that good moral habits will be reinforced by good moral habitats and vice versa. Sport and physical education complement other moral habitats by providing the unique possibility to practise the moral virtues in concrete situations. Abstract moral principles such as fair play or sportsmanship, which are central to sporting practice, are meaningless without these concepts being connected with those virtues practised in our daily encounters with others in moral habitats, albeit with a few contextual alterations.

In this chapter, I provided a brief historical overview of how athleticism and its accompanying games ethic exerted a powerful influence on the development of physical education in the 1950s. For instance, at a time when physical education was seeking to shift away from the term "physical training" towards the term "physical education" as a means of aligning itself with broader educational aims, the games ethic provided a ready-made justification for its inclusion within the school curriculum based on serious moral grounds – although its inclusion within the curriculum was based on an overstated and misleading claim that physical activities have moral educational potential and hence are necessarily available in other aspects of life. I argued that the moral educational potential of physical education rests on competitive games and sport functioning as a place in which the virtues can be practised in a supportive environment. This possibility is not unique to sport and the physical education profession should not overstate its role, but in saying this, games and sport in physical education provide opportunities for practising habitual modes of conduct or developing moral habits. In order to bring this about we need to consider how the moral habitat plays an important role in moral character development because the kind of environment in which a child is raised will have a significant influence on the kind of moral person they will become. One such habitat in which young people spend considerable time in their formative years is the school or educational institution. Thus it seems logical to argue that sport and physical education are also important moral habitats to which human beings belong and at the same time influence moral character. Subsequently, the cultivation of character can be encouraged in physical education, and physical education provides an arena for practising moral behaviour that is supported by a moral community with a commitment to that practice.

Much has been written about physical education being in crisis and consequently in need of reform. In fact it seems *de rigueur* in the literature to argue that physical education is in crisis due to rival and competing traditions of physical education vying to be the dominant set of practices. Indeed, a precursory survey of the various traditions outlined in Chapter 1 highlights the highly contested terrain in which physical education is located. Understandably, this has led many theorists and scholars of physical education within, and many "outside", the profession to conclude that the field is divided within itself, particularly regarding the lack of consensus surrounding its nature. That physical education is located within a historical tradition and constantly changing makes it particularly predisposed to contestability. Indeed, a significant feature that a tradition is in good working order is the constant debate about its particular point and purpose. Consequently in the next chapter, I outline how MacIntyre's work is particularly apt for understanding why and how rival and competing traditions of physical education can be rationally resolved in some cases through the integration of rival traditions into a new tradition.

Notes

1 It is crucial to recognise that the "cult of athleticism" was not an exclusive ideology during this era; other ideologies existed, albeit explicitly or implicitly, such as the "English gentleman", "manliness" or "muscular Christianity", "intellectual excellence and endeavour" and so on. These may have coexisted, openly competed and overlapped with athleticism; however, for the present critique highlights athleticism's influence during this era for the purposes of this chapter and should not be considered to be an exclusive ideology.

2 In the British tradition it is the elite non-government or independent schools that are sometimes referred to as "public schools". The term "public school" (or "grammar school") over time came to mean a school with certain characteristics, such as having a very old foundation, a boarding facility, its own system of rituals, customs, traditions, terminology, prejudices and an accompanying ethos that favoured the strong, solely with the aim of better equipping men for the highest offices of the church, military and the state. The terminology can be confusing, particularly as the words have changed over the years. For example, today the terminology most commonly used by Australians in this context is to refer to public or government schools being managed and funded by State governments with the purpose of free education for all unconditionally, whereas in the alternative case, private or independent schools are autonomously funded and are available to certain sections of the community who are prepared to pay tuition fees. In this chapter, the term "public school" (or "grammar school") is intentionally used in its historical context.

3 Between 1872 and 1895, all of the Australian colonies passed education laws that established a system of government primary schools, but it wasn't until 1939 that schooling was compulsory in most states for children between the ages of six and fifteen. In England, the Education Act in 1870 brought about compulsory schooling between the ages of five and twelve.

4 For some of the more notable contributions in this area refer to the following literature: Arnold (1984a, 1984b, 1988a, 1989a, 1992, 1994, 1997, 2001, 2003); Bergmann-Drewe (2000); Caine and Krebs (1986); Carr (1998); Dennis and Krebs (1986); Feezell (2007); Fernandez-Balboa (1993); Figley (1984); Jones (2005, 2008); Jones and McNamee (2000, 2003); Keating (2003); Kirk (2002); Kretchmar (2005a, 2005b, 2007a); Laker (2000); Longland (1955); Maraj (1965); McFee (2004a, 2004b); McNamee (1995a, 1995b, 1998a, 2008); McNamee *et al.* (2003); Meakin (1981, 1982, 1986, 1990); Miller *et al.* (1997); Morgan (1976, 1987, 1994, 2006, 2007a, 2007b, 2007c); Osterhoudt (1973, 1976); Pawlenka (2005); Romance (1988); Romance *et al.* (1986); Russell (1999, 2004, 2007); Simon (1991, 2000); Shields and Bredemeier (1995); Theodoulides (2003); Theodoulides and Armour (2001); Thomas (1979); Wandzilak (1985); Wandzilak *et al.* (1988); Wright (1987); and Zaner (1979).

5 The background of this paper is important as it puts into perspective Carr's objections to the dominance of empirical–scientific research that claims to test the moral atmosphere of sport to determine whether it has important implications in moral (character) development. Refer to Carr (1998).

6 An expression of this notion is best understood by the adage: "The strong and dominant are destined to win and the weak and inferior are meant to lose."

7 The key documents referred to are mainly syllabus documents that were produced by the Board of Education (England) in this case.

8 The reconstruction of the games ethic for use in Australian schools can be seen to take effect around the same period (post-World War II) and was predicated on the same three reasons for their inclusion within the curriculum as in Great Britain. First, games came to express the attitudes and ideas of the large majority of males infiltrating the physical education profession after World War II who enthusiastically embraced competitive games and sports in general. Second, by adopting and championing competitive team games, male physical educators inadvertently emulated the public school tradition of athleticism, which had enormous benefits for their status. Third, the application of new scientific knowledge from the fields of physiology, biomechanics and skill acquisition in their teaching about competitive games and sports had a profound impact on establishing the newly arrived male physical educators with a ready-made educational "tradition" that was at least a century old.

9 Competitive team games have played a significant part in Australian schools since the 1880s, albeit through a reconstructed version of the English public schools games ethic that had a uniquely Australian flavour, particularly in the Australian public (private) school system. Although most of this section has focused on the significant factors that led to games and sport gaining an increased status within the school curriculum, it is still applicable in this case due to the close historical relationship Australia shares with English life and the obvious imitation of English educational life in Australian public schools in the late nineteenth to the twentieth centuries. It is important to note that in Australia there was no formal time allocated to teaching games in schools until around the 1940s and 1950s, in which we start to see the subject of physical education being formally part of the school curriculum thanks to the nexus between specialist teachers' roles in the timetable, a move away from physical training to physical education and competitive sport in schools.

10 Kirk (1992a, 2010) argues that physical education from the 1950s has taken on the form of "physical education-as-sport-techniques" to the point where it has become the dominant ideology for so long that it has become the way of thinking about and doing physical education that has strong historical links to the practices that preceded it.

11 Shields and Bredemeier (1995) dominate this area of literature. Most of their research findings can be found in their book *Character Development and Physical Activity*. For examples of their other work, refer to: Bredemeier (1994); Bredemeier and Shields (1984, 1985, 1986a, 1986b); Bredemeier *et al.* (1987); Bredemeier *et al.* (1986). For other examples, refer to: Guivernau and Duda (2002); Kavussanu *et al.* (2002); Lee and Cockman (1995).

12 According to this model, moral action involves four processes: (1) interpretation; (2) judgement; (3) choice; (4) acting.

13 A case in point is strategic fouling in basketball. This usually occurs when a competitor deliberately breaks the rules willingly (expecting to be penalised) in the hope of obtaining a strategic advantage. For instance, in a close basketball game the losing team that is not in possession of the ball will strategically foul an opposing player in the dying minutes of a game in an attempt to regain possession of the ball either after a free-throw or from a passing error when the ball re-enters play.

14 Simon (2000) provides three approaches to "broad internalism". These are: (1) hypothetical social contract; (2) respect for and striving for the good of the game; (3) presupposed elements of the ethos of particular sports.

15 Central to Butcher and Schneider's (1998) paper is the case study of "racquetless Josie". Josie is a top amateur squash player who arrives at a national squash championship without her racquet, not because she was careless or intentionally lost it, but due to the airline which misplaced it. Josie's main opposition for the tournament is Annaka, who just happens to have a back-up set of racquets that are the same as those lost by Josie. What should Annaka do? Should she lend Josie her spare racquet so she can compete in the tournament? Can we discern an internal ethic of sport to assist us in finding a suitable solution for Annaka's dilemma? At first glance it would appear obvious that the fair thing to do is to lend Josie the back-up racquet so she can compete. In this case there are no rules that can be used to provide a solution and it would appear that an appeal to constitutive rules does not help because Annaka breaks no rules in declining to lend Josie her racquets. The concept of fair play prescribes that you should let your opponents play and that you will only use legal means to frustrate their intended goals. This is all well and good; however, one must be cognisant that there is no obligation that you must be nice or even care for your opponent. In the case of the case of "racquetless Josie" Annaka's contractual agreement is to play fairly, to keep the rules of the game. If Annaka decided not to lend her spare racquet, she breaks no rule, and consequently, breaks no promise, yet we want to say that fair play dictates that she ought to lend her racquet. But this move raises the question of how we are to understand the notion of the "spirit of the rules" and their central theme. The reality is that strict adherence to rule-following would appear to be quite limiting in this case because problems in sport that do not clearly fall under the domain of rules cannot provide a plausible account of how to proceed in certain situations arising in competition. Playing fair as a respect for the rules is understood as respecting the "spirit of the rules"; however, if there are no rules to apply it is unclear what to say about the matter and, consequently, we are left in a state of uncertainty. Fair play as respect for rules cannot account for actions we take to be required by fair play but which are not directly covered by any rule.

16 The "separation thesis" claims that sport supports, stands for or expresses a set of values that are uniquely its own.

17 The "continuity thesis" claims that moral values found in sport are expressions or reflections of the more basic moral values found outside of sport.

18 The concept of fairness within the context of the sporting sphere usually manifests itself in the following three forms: (1) consistent adherence to the rules; (2) accepting disproportionate advantages or disadvantages of the opponent during the competition; (3) respecting one's opponent as a person or a partner. See, for example, Pawlenka (2005, pp. 50–52).

19 The McSorley incident of 2000 and the Bertuzzi incident of 2004 are well-known ice hockey cases because they involved serious assaults to an opponent that led to criminal law proceedings. In the first case McSorley intentionally targeted the head of another player with his stick whilst the latter was unaware. The second case involved an intentional and premeditated punch to the head of another player from behind.

20 Just as in most sports there are formal and informal rules. In the case of ice hockey, certain levels of violence are tolerated and even expected, but the McSorely and Bertuzzi incidents clearly fell outside the boundaries of the game because vulnerable participants either cannot, or could not, consent to such dangerous actions as being part of the game; as such, they are simply examples of everyday criminal assault.

21 Justice is a complex concept that can range from a particular distribution of benefits and burdens in an equitable manner to retributive and rectificatory justice.

22 Pawlenka (2005) argues that our everyday notion of fairness is borrowed from sports.

23 Russell (2007) cites Kantian deontology, utilitarianism and a version of neo-Aristotelian theories to highlight that they all recognise the moral importance of developing and actualising our human potentiality.

24 From a pedagogical perspective, schools do provide an environmental habitat in which moral development can take place through the process of initiation and imitation. Consequently, Arnold (2001) is right to argue that teachers can have an influence on what it means to acquire virtues in at least four ways. These being: (1) the teacher initiates the student into and is a guardian of sport and physical education for the student; (2) the teacher is a stimulator and leader of discussion about value-related questions in sport; (3) the teacher is a provider of pastoral care in relation to sport; (4) the teacher is a good exemplar of the best sport can be.

25 Theories of moral philosophy can be generally divided into three broad categories: (1) deontological; (2) consequentialism; (3) teleological. Most of the social scientific/psychological research clearly falls into the deontological and consequentialist categories of moral philosophy because they focus on "doing", whereas I am interested in accounts of moral philosophical thinking and practice that celebrate the situated nature of character and of virtue that focuses on "being" a certain type of person.

26 I would also like to add religious communities.

27 I use the word "practice" in a MacIntyrean sense to highlight how the goods internal to a practice can only be identified by first-hand experience in the relevant practice; it demands from the participant who is engaged in the practice in a strong and important way to conduct themselves in a moral way (uphold and pursue the internal goods and standards of excellence that characterise the practice) that advances the whole community of practitioners and makes possible the cooperative pursuit of the practice's goals. When MacIntyre uses the examples of W. G. Grace and Turner, he is attempting to highlight those goods internal to the practice that, first, personifies the standards of excellence such as goals, skills, styles, products and so on; and, second, exemplifies a certain kind of life that has advanced and enriched the relevant community in such a way as to justify the pursuit of a single calling to such a practice in question. Refer to MacIntyre (2007, Chapter 14: The nature of virtues).

28 The physical education literature continues to call for empirical–scientific evidence to determine whether to support or refute these claims by investigating what we are attempting to teach and why, what are the appropriate methods for teaching morality and testing whether they have been successful or not. Two notable examples of this trend are Theodoulides and Armour (2001) and Theodoulides (2003).

6 MacIntyre, rival traditions and physical education

In Chapter 1, I briefly outlined what I consider to be some of the influential traditions of physical education.[1] In fact, the narrative of physical education has undergone significant historical change due to rival and competing traditions vying to be the dominant set of practices. Indeed, Kirk (1990, 1992a, 2009, 2010) has written extensively on this topic concerning how the once dominant practice of physical education in schools was gymnastics ("physical education-as-gymnastics") from around the middle to late nineteenth century until around the middle of the twentieth century, but due to a number of significant factors, such as a shift from authoritarian to child-centred pedagogical approaches and philosophies, the hegemonic influence of sport, a discourse of scientific measurement, and an increase in male physical education teachers all contributed in various ways to bring about the demise of what was considered to be "old" physical education and ushered in physical education-as-sport-technique as the "new" tradition. Certainly, the rhetoric in the physical education literature contributes significantly to the view that the various traditions are in conflict with each other.[2] In a sense, the narrative presents competing viewpoints of what the practice of physical education necessarily involves, and hence why interpretative debates between each tradition concerning the meaning and rationale of its constituted practice is in continual conflict. An obvious example to highlight how rival traditions of physical education are in competition can be found in my characterisation of the academic and health tradition in physical education (see Chapter 1). The academic tradition as it exists in most senior school physical education subjects has a clear focus upon theoretical knowledge for certification purposes, whereas the health tradition is concerned with the open-ended notion of behaviour modification, informed decision-making, and the construction of active and healthy lifestyles as a form of health prevention and promotion. Clearly these two traditions are logically incompatible with each other. Likewise, another example is the subtle yet ongoing debate that exists between advocates of various "models" of teaching advocated for in physical education, as if model A is better than model B and so on (Kirk, 2013). In addition, what I find to be particularly disconcerting about the discourse of models-based teaching is the inference that teaching in physical education involves the teaching of discrete bodies of knowledge in a rigidly non-negotiable specific way which can be followed like a "blueprint" (see, for example, Metzler, 2011). As a result, the notion of "models" creates unnecessary artificial boundaries that are logically problematic – not to mention raises other serious issues – however, the point I wish to raise here is that teaching is a fluid and constantly changing multifarious activity and not fixed.[3]

Part of the problem why there exists an "either/or" proposition between rival and competing accounts of physical education is due to an inability to recognise that the primacy of an educated public requires a "narrative unity" that encompasses a community's cultural development in the form of a tradition (MacIntyre, 1987; MacIntyre and Dunne, 2002). Since the concept of physical education is located within a historical tradition and is constantly changing makes it particularly apt to contestability due to its essential incompleteness (MacIntyre, 1973). Undeniably, this has led to the situation where scholars, teachers, students and so on have been thrown into what MacIntyre (1977, p. 453) describes as an "epistemological crisis" because what was initially considered to be unambiguous truth now appears to be "susceptible to rival interpretations". Consequently, for the purposes of this chapter I will be concerned with the critical discussion of three issues. First, I provide a brief critique of MacIntyre's work surrounding rival and competing traditions of enquiry in order to highlight that when a tradition is in good working order it is partially constituted by an argument about the goods which gives the tradition its particular point and purpose. It is argued that much can be gained when rival and competing traditions are prepared to engage in open dialogue, not only within traditions, but also between traditions. Second, I explore what conditions are necessary for rival and competing traditions to be rationally resolved. Lastly, I argue for a new tradition of physical education that extends Merleau-Ponty phenomenological project by providing an account of the role of embodiment in learning, which I refer to as embodied learning.

MacIntyre on rival and competing traditions of enquiry[4]

The claim advanced and defended by MacIntyre (1988, 1990, 2007) in his key texts is that all traditions experience from time to time their own internal conflicts and tensions. In fact, confrontation may be necessary to overcome and resolve the tensions within, and also between traditions. What MacIntyre means by his conceptual account of "tradition" is crucial to understanding how every tradition can be distinguished by a rational form of enquiry that is unique to the tradition, but more importantly how we can go about deciding between rival and competing accounts when there is no neutral standpoint. In MacIntyre's (2007, p. 222) words, a tradition "... is an historically extended, socially embodied argument, and an argument precisely in part about the goods which constitute that tradition". It is important to note that to MacIntyre, traditions are dynamic because historically traditions change, develop over time, some on occasion are destroyed, some divide into two or more warring traditions, some become extinct altogether, and some emerge in response to the circumstances. Indeed, my argument is that when traditions are in good working order, continuous conflict *about* its particular point and purpose is a normal part of what it means to be a tradition of practices. This is further reinforced by MacIntyre (1988, p. 12) who states:

> The history of any society is thus in key part the history of an extended conflict or set of conflicts. And as it is with societies, so too it is with traditions ... in which fundamental agreements are defined and redefined in terms of two kinds of conflicts: those with critics and enemies external to the tradition who reject all or at least key parts of those fundamental agreements, and those internal, interpretative debates through which the meaning and rationale of the fundamental agreements come to be expressed and by whose progress a tradition is constituted. Such internal debates may on occasion destroy what had been the basis of common fundamental agreement, so that either a tradition divides into two or more warring components, whose adherents are transformed into external critics of each other's positions, or else the tradition loses all coherence and fails to survive.

In order to highlight the distinguishing features of conflict that exist within a tradition, MacIntyre provides a range of views which are not only logically incompatible with each other, but also invoke concerns of incommensurability. One such example put forward by MacIntyre in *After Virtue* is the discussion of Rawl's and Nozick's conceptions of justice, later extended upon in more detail in *Whose Justice? Which Rationality?*.[5] The reason why MacIntyre uses Rawl's (1971) and Nozick's (1974) arguments concerning principles of justice is to demonstrate both how these disputes originate within a tradition, and at the same time resist rational resolution due to incompatibility and incommensurability. What he means by incompatibility and incommensurability in a general sense relates to theories that do not all share the same standards of assessment by which they are compared. In a more specific sense, the failure of theories to share the same standards of assessment may be due to the following reasons: they start from different premises; they use different conceptions of rationality; and/or, different theories may be untranslatable from one to the other (Mason, 1994). I will consider each briefly in turn.

In MacIntyre's view, the reason why disputes exist between Rawl's and Nozick's theories of justice is in part due to each starting from different premises. MacIntyre (2007, p. 248) makes this evident when he writes:

> Rawls makes primary what is in effect a principle of equality with respect to needs.... Nozick makes primary what is a principle of equality with respect to entitlement. For Rawls how those who are in grave need come to be in grave need is irrelevant; justice is made into a matter of present patterns of distribution to which the past is irrelevant. [Whereas, for] Nozick only evidence about what has been legitimately acquired in the past is relevant....

It follows that if each antagonist starts from different premises they will not share enough common ground to resolve these disputes via rational means. For instance, how do you rationally weigh the claim by Rawl that "needs" ought to be given priority versus Nozick's claim that "entitlement" ought to be given priority in justice, or vice versa? Clearly belief has a role to play here, but of course, a person must have reasons for believing something that coheres with others. In saying all of this, MacIntyre (1988, 1990) is right to highlight that when two rival points of view are incompatible and incommensurable they both cannot be true. Understandably belief in one over the other will be based upon certain "… first metaphysical or practical principles … justified within a particular body of theory …" as a whole theory according to the problems it resolves, and judged by the tradition's own standards (MacIntyre, 1988, p. 360).

This leads to the second reason – which shares some similarities with the first reason already discussed – why two rival points of view are incommensurable is by applying different conceptions of rationality. To MacIntyre (1988, p. 4), rationality is more than following the laws of logic, because it is "… only a necessary and not sufficient condition for rationality …". He goes on to add, it is "… what has been added to … the laws of logic to justify ascriptions of rationality … that disagreement arises concerning the … nature of rationality …" (MacIntyre, 1988, p. 4). In most cases, rationality is clearly a necessary feature of arguments; however, intractable disputes that arise would appear to revolve around a lack of shared standards of rational evaluation, and what weighting is given to them.

The third reason which MacIntyre (1988, Chapter XIX) attributes to incommensurability concerns partial untranslatability. He argues that certain theories or conceptual frameworks may be untranslatable from one to another, particularly in the "languages of modernity". Suppose I was to translate a rival's concept, say from language A into language B. From the perspective of those that inhabit the language tradition from which they are taken (language A) there will be some form of distortion because every translation (language B) is an interpretation of the original text. Compounding the issue further, when rival traditions do not share much in common with each other, of course, translation can occur by what MacIntyre refers to as "same-saying", but the less each has is in common with each other the greater the likelihood of untranslatability.

The arguments so far have briefly outlined what MacIntyre means by incommensurability. In the next section, I explore how rival and competing traditions can be rationally resolved.

Can rival and competing traditions of physical education ever be rationally resolved?

When two or more rival, incompatible and apparently incommensurable traditions of enquiry confront each other two central problems emerge. These being: (1) How do we decide between rival or competing accounts when there is no neutral standpoint? (2) By what standards are these rival or competing accounts to be evaluated?

According to MacIntyre (1988, Chapter X) the resolving of disputes characteristically takes place in two stages. In the first stage, each typically describes the conflict of their rivals in their own terms by making explicit the reasons why they disagree according to their own central theses. It is interesting to note that sometimes allowances are made concerning standards of judgement just in case something can be learnt from their rival. In the second stage, if the protagonists of each party are incapable of reaching consensus the onus is put on their rival to explain in detail the flaws of their own tradition using the theses of that tradition.

What I find particularly attractive about MacIntyre's (1988) discussion of rival and competing traditions of enquiry is the argument that to pass from the first to the second stage "... requires a rare gift of empathy as well as ... intellectual insight ...", so that the protagonists of one tradition can come to understand the theses of their rival in such a "... way that they are able to view themselves from such an alien ..." point of view and come to "... recharacterize their own beliefs in an appropriate manner from the alien perspective of the rival tradition" (p. 167). MacIntyre is right to argue that it is not easy to come to understand an "alien perspective" because it requires a "rare gift" of "empathy" and "intellectual insight", not to mention risk. In the latter case, coming to understand an alien tradition has the potential to lead to an "epistemological crisis" as the rival tradition may be able to provide cogent and illuminating explanations for what was unable to be understood by the standards of its own tradition and why this incoherence had arisen. A central tenet of MacIntyre's "Enlightenment" conception of rational resolvability is the notion that if an argument is a good one it must be convincing for any reasonable person to accept, irrespective of the tradition to which they give their allegiance. In MacIntyre's (1990, p. 172) words:

> ... it was a tenet of Enlightenment cultures that every point of view, whatever its source, could be brought into rational debate with every other, this tenet had as its counterpoint a belief that such rational debate could always, if adequately conducted, have a conclusive outcome. The point and purpose of rational debate was to establish truths and only those methods were acceptable which led to the conclusive refutation of error and vindication of truth.

Indeed, MacIntyre's (2007, p. 71) position has shifted somewhat from *After Virtue*, where he states that the "... facts of incommensurability ensure that protest can never win an *argument* ...", to a position in *Whose Justice? Which Rationality?*, where disputes between traditions can be rationally resolvable in some cases, if the norms of rational enquiry are adhered to by both parties. But, in saying all of this, if conflict cannot be settled by rational methods of enquiry, and progress ceases to be made because the "... trusted methods of enquiry have become sterile ...", are all the tell-tale signs of an epistemological crisis? MacIntyre (1988, p. 362) believes that the solution to a "genuine epistemological crisis" requires the development of new concepts and frameworks which "... meet three exacting requirements". First, in order to put an end to the epistemological crisis, a solution needs to be found to what caused the insoluble problems. Second, an explanation needs to be given surrounding what rendered the tradition's methods of enquiry sterile and unresolvable. Lastly, there needs to be some form of continuity in which the "defeated" tradition is "compelled" to give up its allegiance to the tradition in crisis to the newly developed theory or theories. Understandably, MacIntyre (1988) cautions us that not all epistemological crises are resolved so successfully, and hence, why some traditions are either dissolved into two or more warring parties in which each become critics of each other's positions, or else the tradition loses all coherence and becomes extinct.

It is not until MacIntyre (1990) expands on his theme of immensurability and untranslatability in *Three Rival Versions of Moral Enquiry* do we get a sense of how "… one party can emerge as undoubtedly rationally superior …" through the tradition of rational debate (p. 5). The "three rival versions of moral enquiry" which he refers to in his title are encyclopaedia, genealogy and Thomist. The thesis MacIntyre wishes to advance and defend in both *Whose Justice? Which Rationality?* and *Three Rival Versions of Moral Enquiry* is the notion that rationality is not something independent of social practice, but rationality or rationalities are immanent in social practices (Mason, 1994), since every tradition when vital will experience from time to time conflict and tension or an epistemological crisis. When these become serious, and when devotees of these same traditions recognise a crisis, progress is possible between rival traditions. The example given by MacIntyre (1990, p. 123) is the conflict between Augustinianism and Aristotelianism in thirteenth-century Paris that came to be resolved by the emergent Thomist tradition because Aquinas:

> … integrated both rival schemes of concepts and beliefs in such a way as both to correct in each that which he took by its own standards could be shown to be defective or unsound and to remove from each, in a way justified by that correction, that which barred from reconciliation.

In this section I have explored what conditions are necessary for rival and competing traditions to be rationally resolved. Since conceptions of physical education are essentially contested, what is of interest in the next section is to critically discuss how a new tradition of physical education is possible. Just like Aquinas, who integrated the rival traditions of Augustianism and Aristotelianism into a new Thomist tradition in the thirteenth century, in a broad sense I would like to argue for a new tradition of physical education.

A new tradition of physical education: embodied learning[6]

The idea of promoting learning would appear to be a central intent of educationalists. Indeed, well-known and seminal accounts by Oakeshott (1967), Hirst (1967, 1971), Hirst and Peters (1970) and Passmore (1980) discussing the relationship between teaching and learning make it clear that the intent to bring about learning is a consistent characteristic of teaching. Understandably, due to the diverse array of things we want students to learn it is not surprising that how we come to learn is equally varied and diverse. So the questions then become: How then does learning take place? What does it mean to learn something? Why do some students learn better than others? Are there different ways in which we come to learn? These questions posed so far are meant to highlight the complexities involved in any discussion concerning learning, as they are a long way from being resolved. Since much of what we understand about learning in education owes much to the enormous influence of twentieth-century psychology it needs to be noted from the outset that learning can take a great many different forms and that sometimes people come to understand in surprising ways that do not fit neatly within empirical or rationalist explanations of learning. According to Carr (1994, p. 39) the basic problem of psychological discourse is that it is "held completely captive" by a description of mental or behavioural processes that are identifiable and analysable in "natural scientific terms", as if they are events in a "causal relationship" that can be explained somehow with "laws established on the basis of observation and experiment". This is why Hamlyn (1967, (p. 24), in discussing the logical and psychological aspects of learning, makes the pertinent point that certain questions about learning, such as "what learning is" and what is implied "when someone has learnt something" are not so "much a matter for the psychologist as for the philosopher".

In light of what has just been mentioned, Merleau-Ponty's philosophy seems particularly apt for explaining the significant role perceptual experience and embodiment plays in understanding what has been learned, and understanding that has been grasped meaningfully. The importance of embodiment and its role in how we think and learn can be seen in the new research programme or movement known as "embodied cognition" that draws on a number of distinct traditions in philosophy, psychology and cognitive science. It is often presented as an alternative or challenger to traditional cognitive science due to its reluctance to conceive of cognition as computational (Shapiro, 2004, 2007, 2011). Although the research themes in embodied cognition are various, proponents of embodied cognition "take as their starting point not a [disembodied] mind working on abstract problems, but a body that requires the mind to make it function" (Wilson, 2002, p. 625).[7] The similarities with Merleau-Ponty's understanding of embodiment are striking, and hence why I mention it here because his work has been the catalyst in the writing of others like Lakoff and Johnson's (1999), *Philosophy in the Flesh: The Embodied Mind and its Challenge to Western Thought*, Noë's (2004), *Action in Perception*, and Varela *et al.*'s (1993), *The Embodied Mind: Cognitive Science and Human Experience*. In saying all of this, Shapiro (2004, 2007, 2011) quite rightly cautions that it is too early and premature to determine whether to abandon cognitive science in favour of embodied cognition altogether, because each assigns to the body a different role in cognition that often results in two competing viewpoints from which to understand who we are, and what we are, resulting in significant ramifications concerning how we come to think and learn. Indeed, what is of interest in this book is the role of embodiment within education, particularly its role in learning.[8] In fact, the new interdisciplinary research paradigm between phenomenology and the cognitive sciences known as embodied cognition has shown that cognition is embodied and involves a deep connection between perception and action (see for example, Varela *et al.*, 1993; Clark, 1997, 2008). Merleau-Ponty (1945/1963, p. 3) recognised that psychology distorts how we come to learn because it remains "faithful to realism and to casual thinking" and only provides atomistic accounts of learning. In a sense, this is why Merleau-Ponty (1945/1962, p. 266) wanted to emphasise how "scientific knowledge shifts the centre of gravity of experience" to the point where we unlearn how to see, hear, feel and speak "in order to deduce, from our bodily organization" the world as the scientist conceives it and "what we are to see, hear and feel". Consequently, by criticising empirical psychology, cognitivist approaches or related constructivist accounts of learning highlight what I see as age-old debates between rationalists and empiricists,[9] but more importantly highlight the failure in so called "learning theories" to provide an account of meaning and the role of embodiment in learning.[10]

The educational implications of Merleau-Ponty's phenomenological account of human experiences connect strongly with the notion that learning involves the exploration of the world from where one is and a clear understanding of how things relate to each other and to oneself in the world. It is an ongoing process. The key here is that we "come to" understand something (if successful) from our own point of view as a result of experiencing it (Stolz, 2013a). The concept of "experience" to Merleau-Ponty is a central theme of his philosophy and implies that since human beings are "embodied subjects" we do not think about the world from some position beyond the body or outside it, but something we "inhabit" because our being is necessarily present in it and involved with it.

Merleau-Ponty (1947/1964, p. 13) recognised the importance of ordinary pre-reflective experience as always the "presupposed foundation of all rationality, all value and all existence". The experience of "perception" or the world perceived is "primary" for Merleau-Ponty and is not about reducing understanding to sensation but of "assisting at the birth of this knowledge" in order to make sense of it. In Merleau-Ponty's (1947/1964, p. 25) words:

> ... the experience of perception is our presence at the moment when things, truths, values are constituted for us; that perception is a nascent *logos*; that it teaches us, outside all dogmatism, the true conditions of objectivity itself; that it summons us to the tasks of knowledge and action. It is not a question of reducing human knowledge to sensation, but of assisting at the birth of this knowledge, to make it as sensible as the sensible, to recover the consciousness of rationality.

As human beings we seem to take the experience of perception for granted because we either assume that our senses are "self-evident" or overestimate that we know these the "best of all", but it is only when we "re-learn to look at the world" that we come to knowledge and understanding of the world, which

Merleau-Ponty refers to as the "experience of rationality". What Merleau-Ponty (1945/1962) is opposed to here is the influence of empiricism and what he refers to as "intellectualism", particularly how psychology attempts to be a natural science by providing causal explanations of perception from an objectifying viewpoint of science. But Merleau-Ponty (1945/1962, p. 33) is quite right to argue that neither of these two can "grasp consciousness in the act of learning". Since "real" human experience is subjective and full of meaning the ramification for how we come to learn is significant, particularly how we learn through our embodiment. Take for instance Wittgenstein's (1953/2009) ambiguous "duck-rabbit" figure used to high-light the complexities of perception. The fact that I can distinguish between a duck's head or a rabbit's is more a matter of education than it is of physiology. Merleau-Ponty (1942/1963), in the *Structure of Behavior*, goes to great lengths to highlight how human perception takes into consideration structural characteristics of our embodiment that give "signification" to our "dialectical" relationship between "man and the world". He goes on to talk about a "third dialectic" between "use-objects" like tables, gardens and so on, and "cultural objects" like musical instruments, language and so on that play a significant role in human understand-ing. Part of the reason why Piaget's conservation experiments of young children could not explain conceptual transitions that are alleged to occur from one stage or phase to another was in part due to the uncertain grasp children of a certain age had with familiar concepts and what certain words mean (Carr, 1988, 2003). Con-sequently, a central tenet of any educational learning involves helping others to refine their concepts and to be taught to perceive.

Wittgenstein makes a pertinent point that when I say that I see a duck or rabbit head I am describing my experiences of perception. As long as my physi-ological structures are not defective in some capacity I should see something. Whether I come to see the duck and not the rabbit (or vice versa) may be due to cultural factors such as not knowing what a rabbit (or duck) looks like as a frame of reference to the point required to successfully prosecute the task in question. Although, initially, I may be quite blind in coming to see either the duck or rabbit it seems reasonable within the contexts of teaching that I may come to perceive or refine my concepts in such a way that duck or rabbit identification is possible. In a similar vein, take for example the analogy offered by Merleau-Ponty (1945/1962, p. x) concerning how we come to know "what a forest, a prairie or a river is", because we have already experienced the countryside as a place we have explored, not because of the abstract symbols of the geographer's map. In a sense we come to knowledge and understanding through human experience first before coming to understand abstract or intellectual concepts. As Merleau-Ponty (1947/1964, p. 17) reveals, perceptual capacities underpin all abstract or intellectual capacities, for as he says:

> … we can only think the world because we have already experienced it; it is through this experience that we have the idea of being, and it is through experience that the words "rational" and "real" receive a meaning simultaneously.

The world is not something which "I think, but what I live through" because I am in "communication with it" and so human experience is a kind of never ending or open dialogue with the world we inhabit (Merleau-Ponty, 1945/1962, pp. xvii–xix). The use of the term "communication" is particularly apt in this case because when we interact with others, say about a personal issue, we can, if we are fortunate, come to some understanding of what the other is saying. However, this is not something that automatically occurs from the beginning, mainly because we tend to perceive things from our own point of view first. Since part of what it means to be a being-in-the-world necessarily involves a dialogue with others within the world we share, the process of coming to understand others is something that needs to be learnt, but at the same time can never be complete. Consequently, coming to understand other human beings' perspectives necessarily involves appreciating other perspectives better which is inextricably connected to our own experiences. In Merleau-Ponty's (1945/1962, p. xxii) words:

> The phenomenological world is not pure being, but the sense which is revealed where the paths of my various experiences intersect, and also where my own and other people's intersect and engage each other like gears. It is thus inseparable from subjectivity and intersubjectivity, which find their unity when I either take up my past experiences in those of the present, or other people's in my own.

Take, for instance, the case offered by Merleau-Ponty (1948/2004, Lecture 5) in the *World of Perception* concerning how we come to know that someone "is extremely annoyed with me". We don't come to know that the "interlocutor" is angry in "some otherworldly realm" that is "beyond the body of the angry man". We come to know that someone is angry only when we step out of our own viewpoint as an "external observer of this anger" and consider what it is like when I am angry. By doing this it forces me to acknowledge that "anger" is not an abstract concept that is located outside me, but in some sense an inexplicable part of me. In this description we start to see the relationship between "intersubjective" (public world) and "subjective" (individual world) aspects of our experience in which we derive meaning from being-in-the-world.

My conceptual account of embodied learning owes much to Merleau-Ponty's (1942/1963, p. 96) positive description of learning that involves "adapted responses to the situation by different means" so that we learn from our mistakes, rather than repeat them over and over again. The educational implications being that learning involves the exploration of the world from where one is and a clear understanding of how things relate to each other and to ourselves in the world. In a sense, this is a heuristic approach to learning that can be nurtured and guided by teachers so that students come to a greater understanding of embodied experience developed in the educational context.

The idea that the body has no role to play in learning follows the tradition of Plato to Descartes in assuming that the body gets in the way of cognition, rather than being an indispensible part of it. Merleau-Ponty is right that the body has presented significant problems for traditional philosophies which always seem inclined to conceive of our "corporeal schema" from an intellectual perspective that reduces movement to an "act of understanding" or discovery by analysis. Compounding the issue further is the general tendency to take the experience of perception for granted, primarily because we tend to take activities with which we are familiar, such as opening doors, walking, talking and driving cars for granted over time. Indeed, Dreyfus (1991, Chapter 4) – borrowing heavily from Heidegger's (1927/2010) *Being and Time* – argues that "mindless" everyday coping skills, such as walking and talking, are taken for granted because we spend the majority of our lives in this state; whereas "deliberate" and "effortful" acts of volition tend to be the times we remember the most, and hence, become meaningful to us because we spend the least amount of time in this mode. Taking a step further, Holst (2013, p. 964) argues that we need to "insist upon re-educating ... students primarily in the aspects of being in the body" by finding ways of "re-educating the body" in education so that students can learn to both reconnect with having a body and being embodied. Consequently, embodied learning from inside educational systems not only acts as a counter balance to the strong pedagogical tendency to favour abstract and conceptual thinking, but more importantly it provides students with experiences of the phenomenal body that are meaningful.

What I mean by the "phenomenal body" draws from those embodied experiences of the world that arise naturally through bodily movement which Merleau-Ponty (1945/1962, p. 121) calls the "phenomenal body" and refers to what "I" experience as a natural system of one's own body taking place in the domain of the phenomenal. An example of this occurs when my hand moves around the object it touches, anticipating the stimuli and tracing out its form for which I am about to perceive. Our perception ends in objects because our own body as experienced by us "from the inside" makes contact with the object through touch, stimuli and tracing out its form from the first-person point of view. Simply put, we cannot come to understand our embodiment if we do not engage in the world as a being-in-the-world. The phenomenal body is what we experience as a first person subject of experience and as a result we can only exist in connection with a lived body. We cannot make contact with the world just by thinking about it, but through experiencing it with senses, acting in it, in ways that range from the most complex to the most primitive unreflective movements. Hence, the idea of embodied learning within the educational sense involves coming to know ourselves and the world around us better neither as an abstract object nor as an instrument, but as a "lived body" subject that senses and does the sensing in a meaningful way.

Take, for instance, the example offered by Merleau-Ponty in the *Phenomenology of Perception* concerning how we come to learn and understand a new dance routine. To learn a new dance is not discovered by analysing dance from some objective perspective or even reconstructed upon already acquired movements like walking and running. Just as we have to learn to become aware of the body's role in taste, touch, smell, and so on, the same applies to learning any new skill (or habit)[11] like dancing, driving, batting in cricket, for example, because the body "... 'catches' (kapiert) and 'comprehends movement' ... [so that the] habit is indeed grasping of significance, but it is the motor grasping of a motor significance" that needs to be learnt, and in a sense, is its own form of unique knowledge (Merleau-Ponty, 1945/1962, p. 165). As Dreyfus (2002a, 2002b) has highlighted in his critique of his five stages of skill acquisition,[12] when we finally become an expert "our everyday dealing with things and people switches over from the planning and goal directedness" of the first four stages to what is "experienced as a spontaneous response to the demands of the whole situation" or the learnt muscular gestalt which gives our behaviour intelligent automaticity. This is why the expert dancer knows how to dance without being able to describe where his or her limbs are or even consciously think about what to do next because they are attending to the future horizon. When the dancer performs the necessary movements in space, these movements are governed by intention, but this intention does not lay down the position of the limbs as objective locations. As Merleau-Ponty would say, the subject who has acquired the motor habit of dancing incorporates the movement of their limbs into their bodily space in all the things one just skilfully does. In a sense, the dance routine has become an extension of the dancer like the stick to the blind man. This is further reinforced by Dreyfus (2002a) who makes the pertinent point that skilful action has a "world-to-mind" direction, and thus we do not "experience our intentions as causing our bodily movements; rather, in skilful coping we experience the situation as drawing the movements out of us". This means that we make sense of the world as the perceiver through physical movement and interaction due to our embodiment encompassing both the "... body as a lived, experiential structure and the body as the context or milieu of cognitive mechanism" (Varela *et al.*, 1993, xvi). As Merleau-Ponty's example shows, our embodiment both initiates and is shaped by the environment. Consequently, one of the primary roles of education is provide and explore different learning environments from the students' perspective so students gradually come to understand how things relate to each other and to themselves. To do this we need to locate the body as the focal point in the production of the lived experience, and also recognise the role corporeal movement and embodiment plays in learning in, by and through education (Stolz, 2013a).

In this chapter I have extended upon MacIntyre's argument that the conception of physical education is essentially a contested concept because it is located within a historical tradition. Since every tradition when vital will experience from time to time what MacIntyre refers to as "epistemological crises", when these become serious, and when devotees of these same traditions recognise a crisis, progress is possible. As a means to demonstrate how disputes can originate within a tradition, and at the same time resist rational resolution due to incommensurability, MacIntyre in *After Virtue* and *Whose Justice? Which Rationality?* features the disputes between Rawl's and Nozick's theories of justice. Although MacIntyre cautions us that not all epistemological crises are resolved so successfully, disputes between traditions can be rationally resolved in some cases, particularly if the norms of rational enquiry are adhered to by both parties. Just like Aquinas who integrated the rival traditions of Augustianism and Aristotelianism into a new Thomist tradition in the thirteenth century, in a broad sense I have argued for a new tradition of physical education.

In the last section of this chapter, I argued that learning theorists have failed to provide an account of learning that can explain how humans come to understand, particularly understanding that is grasped meaningfully. Indeed by criticising empirical psychology, cognitivism or constructivism it was my intent to highlight what I see as age-old debates between rationalists and empiricists, and a crucial failure in learning theory to provide an account of meaning and the role of embodiment in learning. To some extent the former philosophical debates have either privileged the mind over the body (rationalism) or viewed the body as a type of sensorial instrument where knowledge is verified (empiricism). What is clear though is that neither viewpoint recognises the role of embodiment in how we come to understand and understand in a meaningful way. Compounding the issue further to some extent have been the different philosophies of mind that have influenced psychology, which in turn have been highly prominent in education. Hamlyn (1967) was right when he commented that some questions concerning learning are simply not meant for the psychologist, but should be for the philosopher. This is why Merleau-Ponty's phenomenological account of perceptual experience is particularly apt for explaining the significant role embodiment plays in understanding and/or explaining understanding that is meaningful, because it connects strongly with Oakeshott's (1967, p. 156) notion that learning involves coming to "know ourselves and the world around us" which can range from merely "being aware" to "understanding and being able to explain".

What makes my conceptual account of embodied learning educationally significant is that the whole person is treated as a whole being, permitting the person to experience himself or herself as a holistic and synthesised acting, feeling, thinking being-in-the-world, rather than as separate physical and mental qualities that bear no relation to each other. More importantly Merleau-Ponty's phenomenological account connects strongly with the notion of learning to "rediscover" for ourselves the world by "relearning" the way we look at the world, so that we may come to a clearer understanding of how things relate to each other and to ourselves in the world. This is an ongoing process and never ends because as beings-in-the-world we are in an open dialogue with the world we inhabit; the key concept being that we "come to" an understanding of something from our own point of view as a result of experiencing it. Since our engagement with the world is not just cognitive or theoretical, but involves the emotional, practical, aesthetic and so on, we need to recognise that these various meanings are united by an "act of intellectual synthesis" in which I am engaged and their interrelated meanings give coherence to my world.

Notes

1 These being physical education: as health prevention and promotion, as character development and moral education, as art and beauty, as a mechanism for finding meaning through movement, as sport education, as preparation for leisure and as academic study.

2 It is often argued by various scholars that Bunker and Thorpe's (1982, 1983) teaching of games for understanding (TGfU) model and its subsequent developments (Butler and Griffin, 2010; Griffin and Butler, 2005) have been particularly advocated as a superior alternative (Kirk, 2010; Metzler, 2011; Tinning, 2010) to what has been referred to as a "traditional method" (Hoffman, 1971; Kirk, 2010; Metzler, 2011; Tinning, 2010). However, internationally the critical literature has shown that many physical education teachers have not changed the way that they teach (see for example Capel, 2005; Capel and Blair, 2013; Kirk, 1992a, 2010), for a variety of complicated reasons. For papers that discuss this topic, see Stolz and Pill's (2013) paper that was presented at the 2013 Australian Council for Health, Physical Education and Recreation (ACHPER) International Conference, an extended version of this paper titled "A narrative approach to exploring TGfU-GS" can be found in *Sport, Education and Society* (Stolz and Pill, in press), and Stolz and Pill's (2014) paper published in *European Physical Education Review*. Other literature that contributes to this confusion are, for example, Sport Education (Siedentop, 1994), Physical Literacy (Whitehead, 2010), Cooperative Learning (Dyson and Casey, 2012) and Personal and Social Responsibility (Hellison, 2011).

3 It goes without saying that some systematic ordering for pedagogic purposes of what is to be taught may assist the learning process. Indeed, a teacher could not hope to teach something effectively by exclusively using just one method or model all the time. To argue otherwise would be absurd, and so the statement that there is no "one best way" to teach physical education or any subject is stating a self-evident truth that contributes nothing to the debate about teaching (see, for example, Metzler, 2011). However, in saying this, some approaches to teaching are more suitable to teaching certain kinds of things than others. After all, how many different ways can you teach a forward role safely, say in gymnastics?

4 The first two sections of Chapter 6 have been adapted from my unpublished manuscript titled "MacIntyre, rival traditions and education" specifically for the purposes of this book. My intention is to have this published soon in an academic journal.

5 Another notable example worth mentioning found in *After Virtue* is the "disquieting suggestion" that the nature of modern moral disagreement today is incapable of being resolved because "... we have ... lost comprehension, both theoretical and practical, [of] morality" (MacIntyre, 2007, p. 2). In order to highlight the poverty of modern moral theory MacIntyre contrasts modern conceptions of morality, such as emotivism, with Aristotelian conceptions of morality to demonstrate how our understanding of morality has changed to a set of incoherent rules or principles that are constantly changing. Likewise, in *Three Rival Versions of Moral Enquiry*, MacIntyre (1990) sets out three rival traditions of moral enquiry which he identifies as encyclopaedia, genealogy and the Thomist tradition to demonstrate incompatibility, incommensurability and untranslatability.

6 Parts of the section that follow have been taken from my paper accepted for publication in *Educational Philosophy and Theory* (EPAT) titled "Embodied Learning". I would like to thank the executive editor Michael Peters for permission to reproduce material soon to be published in this journal.

7 Wilson (2002) outlines six claims involved in embodied cognition. These are as follows: (1) cognition is situated; (2) cognition is time pressured; (3) we off-load cognitive work onto the environment; (4) the environment is part of the cognitive system; (5) cognition is for action; and (6) off-line cognition is body based. Whereas it is

interesting to note that Shapiro (2004, 2007, 2011) outlines three themes in embodied cognition: (1) conceptualisation; (2) replacement; and (3) constitution.

8 I am cognisant that there exists considerable literature concerning the body and embodiment in education, particularly from a distinctly sociological point of view. I have intentionally not engaged with this literature for three reasons: first, such an approach would distract from the central thesis of this chapter which is to draw on the work of Merleau-Ponty and make new connections with my conceptual understanding of embodied learning; second, due to space restrictions an extensive critique of the socio-cultural influences of the "embodied learner" within schools and/or education – although interesting – is not possible, and arguably not relevant; and, lastly, my intention in this study is to explain learning from a distinctly philosophical point of view, and not from a psychological or sociological perspective.

9 Hamlyn (1973) refers to "rationalism" and "empiricism" as the "two great theories of knowledge" that bring with them not only different conceptions of knowledge, but different conceptions of acquiring knowledge, primarily because these conceptions are based on different philosophies of mind.

10 Educationalists should heed more closely Wittgenstein's (1953/2009, Part II, section xiv; §371) criticism of psychology and maybe question its influence on educational theory taking into consideration that psychology is all "experimental methods and *conceptual confusion*" and should not be exempt from condemnation because it is a "young science".

11 Although the term "habit" has negative connotations in its English usage surrounding a lack of volition, this is not how Merleau-Ponty intended it to be used in this context. Others, like Dreyfus, use the term "skill" instead of "habit", but one needs to be cognisant that Merleau-Ponty ascribed "habit" as an *in situ* ability to act in a flexible way.

12 The five stages are as follows: (1) Novice; (2) Advanced beginner; (3) Competence; (4) Proficient; (5) Expert. For a detailed account refer to Chapter 1 from Dreyfus and Dreyfus (1986). A shorter version of this earlier account can be found in Dreyfus (2002a). It is the fifth level that is of interest in this case because the expert performer acts without conscious deliberation and becomes one with what he or she is doing. For instance, the expert batsman in cricket becomes one with his batting and experiences himself batting, rather than consciously deliberating about how to play certain shots as a batsman whilst playing.

References

Ainsworth, B. E. (2005). Movement, mobility and public health. *Quest, 57*(1), 12–23.

Almond, L. (1983). A rationale for health related fitness in schools. *Bulletin of Physical Education, 19*(2), 5–10.

Anderson, D. (2001). Recovering humanity: Movement, sport, and nature. *Journal of the Philosophy of Sport, 28*(2), 140–150.

Anderson, D. (2002). The humanity of movement or 'It's not just a gym class'. *Quest, 54*(2), 87–96.

Aquinas, T. (1265–1274/1993a). *Summa theologica* (English Dominican Fathers, Trans.; electronic edn). Charlottesville, VA: InteLex Corporation. (Original work published *c.*1265–1274).

Aquinas, T. (1269–1272/1993b). On the virtues in general. In *The Collected Works of St Thomas Aquinas* (J. P. Reid, Trans.; electronic edn). Charlottesville, VA: InteLex Corporation. (Original work published *c.*1269–1272).

Aquinas, T. (1271–1272/1993c). Commentary on the Nicomachean Ethics. In *The Collected Works of St Thomas Aquinas* (C. I. Litzinger, Trans.; electronic edn). Charlottesville, VA: InteLex Corporation. (Original work published *c.*1271–1272).

Aquinas, T. (1994). *Commentary on Aristotle's De Anima* (K. Foster and S. Humphries, Trans.; R. McInerny, Intro.). Notre Dame, IN: Dumb Ox Books.

Armitage, J. (1977). *Man at Play: Nine Centuries of Pleasure Making*. London, UK: F. Warne.

Armour, K. (1999). The case for a body-focus in education and physical education. *Sport, Education and Society, 4*(1), 5–15.

Aristotle (1986). *De Anima* (H. Lawson-Tancred, Trans. and Intro.). London, UK: Penguin Books.

Aristotle (1995). *Aristotle: Politics.* (E. Barker, Trans.; R. F. Stalley, Rev. and Intro). Oxford, UK: Oxford University Press.

Aristotle (2004). *Aristotle: The Nicomachean Ethics.* (Further revised edn). (J. A. K. Thomson, Trans; H. Tredennick, Rev.; J. Barnes, Intro). London, UK: Penguin Books.

Arnold, P. (1979a). *Meaning in Movement, Sport and Physical Education*. London, UK: Heinemann.

Arnold, P. (1979b). Intellectualism, physical education, and self-actualization. *Quest, 31*(1), 87–96.

Arnold, P. (1979c). Agency, action and meaning 'in' movement: An introduction to three new terms. *Journal of the Philosophy of Sport, 6*(1), 49–57.

Arnold, P. (1984a). Sport, moral education and the development of character. *Journal of Philosophy of Education, 18*(2), 275–281.

Arnold, P. (1984b). Three approaches towards an understanding of sportsmanship. *Journal of the Philosophy of Sport, 10*(1), 61–70.

Arnold, P. (1988a). *Education, Movement and the Curriculum*. London: Falmer Press.

Arnold, P. (1988b). Education, movement, and the rationality of practical knowledge. *Quest, 40*(2), 115–125.

Arnold, P. (1989a). Competitive sport, winning and education. *Journal of Moral Education, 18*(1), 15–25.

Arnold, P. (1989b). Democracy, education and sport. *Journal of the Philosophy of Sport, XVI*, 100–110.

Arnold, P. (1990). Sport, the aesthetic and art: Further thoughts. *British Journal of Educational Studies, 38*(2), 160–179.

Arnold, P. (1991). The preeminence of skill as an educational value in the movement curriculum. *Quest, 43*(1), 66–77.

Arnold, P. (1992). Sport as a valued human practice: A basis for the consideration of some moral issues in sport. *Journal of Philosophy of Education, 26*(2), 237–255.

Arnold, P. (1994). Sport and moral education. *Journal of Moral Education, 23*(1), 75–89.

Arnold, P. (1997). *Sport, Ethics and Education*. London: Cassell.

Arnold, P. (2001). Sport, moral development, and the role of the teacher: Implications for research and moral education. *Quest, 53*, 135–150.

Arnold, P. (2003). Three approaches toward an understanding of sportsmanship. In J. Boxall (Ed.), *Sports Ethics: An Anthology* (pp. 72–80). Oxford, UK: Blackwell Publishing.

Aspin, D. (1975). Ethical aspects of sport and games and physical education. *Journal of Philosophy of Education, 19*(1), 49–71.

Ayer, A. J. (1957). *The Problem of Knowledge*. London: Penguin Books.

Australian Bureau of Statistics (2011). *Sports and Recreation: A Statistical Overview, Australia*. Retrieved from www.abs.gov.au/ausstats/abs@.nsf/Products/5A4BFF9E0C9 B2C8ECA25796B00151513?opendocument.

Australian Government (2009). *The Future of Sport in Australia*. Canberra, ACT: Commonwealth of Australia.

Bamford, T. W. (1975). Thomas Arnold and the Victorian idea of a public school. In B. Simon and I. Bradley (Eds), *The Victorian Public School: Studies in the Development of an Educational Institution* (pp. 58–71). London: Gill and Macmillan.

Bannister, R. (1955). *The First Four Minutes*. London: Putnam.

Barrow, R. (2000). The poverty of empirical research in moral education: Beyond John Wilson. *Journal of Moral Education, 29*(3), 313–321.

Belaief, L. (1977). Meanings of the body. *The Journal of the Philosophy of Sport, 4*, 50–68.

Bergmann-Drewe, S. (1999). Acquiring practical knowledge: A justification for physical education. *Paideusis, 12*(2), 33–44.

Bergmann-Drewe, S. (2000). The logical connection between moral education and physical education. *Journal of Curriculum Studies, 32*(4), 561–573.

Best, D. (1974). The aesthetic in sport. *British Journal of Aesthetics, 14*(3), 197–213.

Best, D. (1978). *Philosophy and Human Movement*. London: George Allen & Unwin.

Bredemeier, B. (1994). Children's moral reasoning and their assertive, aggressive, and submissive tendencies in sport and daily life. *Journal of Sport and Exercise Psychology, 16*, 1–14.

Bredemeier, B. and Shields, D. (1984). Divergence in moral reasoning about sports and everyday life. *Sociology of Sport Journal, 1*, 348–357.

Bredemeier, B. and Shields, D. (1985). Values and violence in sports today. *Psychology Today, 19*, 23–32.

Bredemeier, B. and Shields, D. (1986a). Athletic aggression: An issue of contextual morality. *Sociology of Sport Journal, 3*, 15–28.

Bredemeier, B. and Shields, D. (1986b). Moral growth among athletes and nonathletes: A comparative analysis. *Journal of Genetic Psychology, 147*, 7–18.

Bredemeier, B., Shields, D., Weiss, M. and Cooper, B. (1987). The relationship between children's legitimacy judgements and their moral reasoning, aggression tendencies, and sport involvement. *Sociology of Sport Journal, 4*, 48–60.

Bredemeier, B., Weiss, M., Shields, D. and Shewchuk, R. (1986). Promoting moral growth in a summer sport camp: The implementation of theoretically grounded instructional strategies. *Journal of Moral Education, 15*(3), 212–220.

Briggs, M. and Hansen, A. (2012). *Play-based Learning in the Primary School*. London: SAGE.

Broadhead, P. and Burt, A. (2012). *Understanding Young Children's Learning through Play: Building Playful Pedagogies*. London and New York: Routledge.

Brooker, R. and Macdonald, D. (1995). Mapping physical education in the reform agenda for Australian education: Tensions and contradictions. *European Physical Education Review, 1*(2), 101–110.

Bunker, D. and Thorpe, R. (1982). A model for the teaching of games in secondary schools. *Bulletin of Physical Education, 18*(1), 5–8.

Bunker, D. and Thorpe, R. (Eds) (1983). Games teaching revisited [Special issue]. *Bulletin of Physical Education, 19*(1).

Butcher, R. and Schneider, A. (1998). Fair play as a respect for the game. *Journal of the Philosophy of Sport, XXV*, 1–22.

Butler, J. and Griffin, L. (Eds) (2010). *More Teaching Games for Understanding: Moving Globally*. Champaign, IL: Human Kinetics.

Caillois, R. and Halperin, E. (1955). The structure and classification of games. *Diogenes, 3*(12), 62–75.

Caine, D. and Krebs, E. (1986). The moral development objective in physical education: A renewed quest?. *Contemporary Education, 57*(4), 197–201.

Carlisle, R. (1969). The concept of physical education. *Journal of Philosophy of Education, 3*(1), 5–22.

Carr, D. (1978a). Practical pursuits and the curriculum. *Journal of Philosophy of Education, 12*, 69–80.

Carr, D. (1978b). Practical reasoning and knowing how. *Journal of Human Movement Studies, 4*(1), 3–20.

Carr, D. (1979a). Aims of physical education. *Physical Education Review, 2*(2), 91–100.

Carr, D. (1979b). The logic of knowing how and ability. *Mind, 88*, 394–409.

Carr, D. (1980a). The language of action, ability and skill: Part I – The language of action. *Journal of Human Movement Studies, 6*, 75–94.

Carr, D. (1980b). The language of action, ability and skill: Part II – The language of ability and skill. *Journal of Human Movement Studies, 6*, 111–126.

Carr, D. (1981a). On mastering a skill. *Journal of Philosophy of Education, 15*(1), 87–96.

Carr, D. (1981b). Knowledge in practice. *American Philosophical Quarterly, 18*(1), 53–61.

Carr, D. (1983a). On physical education and educational significance. *Momentum, 8*(3), 2–9.

Carr, D. (1983b). The place of physical education in the school curriculum. *Momentum, 8*(1), 9–12.

Carr, D. (1988). Knowledge and curriculum: four dogmas of child-centred education. *Journal of Philosophy of Education, 22*(2), 151–162.

Carr, D. (1991). *Educating the Virtues*. London and New York: Routledge.

Carr, D. (1994). Educational enquiry and professional knowledge: towards a Copernican revolution. *Educational Studies, 20*(1), 33–52.

Carr, D. (1997). Physical education and value diversity: A response to Andrew Reid. *European Physical Education Review, 3*(2), 195–205.

Carr, D. (1998). What moral educational significance has physical education? A question in need of disambiguation. In M. McNamee and J. Parry (Eds), *Ethics and Sport* (pp. 119–133). London and New York: Routledge.

Carr, D. (1999). Toward a re-evaluation of the role of educational epistemology in the professional education of teachers. In S. Tozer (Ed.), *Philosophy of Education 1998*. Champaign, IL: Philosophy of Education Society.

Carr, D. (2001). Educational philosophy, theory and research: A psychiatric autobiography. *Journal of Philosophy of Education, 35*(3), 461–476.

Carr, D. (2003). *Making Sense of Education: An Introduction to the Philosophy and Theory of Education and Teaching*. London and New York: Routledge.

Carroll, B. (1982). Examinations and curriculum change in physical education. *Physical Education Review, 5*(1), 26–36.

Carroll, B. (1998). The emergence and growth of examinations in physical education. In K. Green and K. Hardman (Eds), *Physical Education: A Reader* (pp. 314–332). Germany: Meyer & Meyer.

Chapel, S. (2000). Physical education and sport. In S. Chapel and S. Piotrowski (Eds), *Issues in physical education* (pp. 131–143). London and New York: Routledge.

Capel, S. (2005). Teachers, teaching and pedagogy in physical education. In K. Green and K. Hardman (Eds), *Physical Education: Essential Issues* (pp. 111–127). London: SAGE.

Capel, S. and Blair, R. (2013). Why do physical education teachers adopt a particular way of teaching? In S. Capel and M. Whitehead (Eds), *Debates in Physical Education* (pp. 120–139). London and New York: Routledge.

Chapel, S. and Whitehead, M. (2013). What is physical education?. In S. Chapel and M. Whitehead (Eds), *Debates in Physical Education* (pp. 3–21). London and New York: Routledge.

Clark, A. (1997). *Being There: Putting Brain, Body and World Together Again*. Cambridge, MA: Massachusetts Institute of Technology (MIT) Press.

Clark, A. (2008). *Supersizing the Mind: Embodiment, Action and Cognitive Extension*. Oxford, UK: Oxford University Press.

Commonwealth of Australia. (2009). *The Future of Sport in Australia*. Canberra, ACT: Commonwealth of Australia.

Connolly, M. (1995). Phenomenology, physical education, and special populations. *Human Studies, 18*(1), 25–40.

Copleston, F. (1993). *A History of Philosophy: Volume I – Greece and Rome*. New York: Doubleday.

D'Agostino, F. (1981). The ethos of games. *Journal of Philosophy of Sport, VIII*, 7–18.

Dearden, R. F. (1967). The concept of play. In R. S. Peters (Ed.), *The Concept of Education* (pp. 73–91). London: Routledge & Kegan Paul.

Dearden, R. F. (1968). *The Philosophy of Primary Education: An Introduction*. London: Routledge & Kegan Paul.

Dennis, C. and Krebs, E. (1986). The moral development objective in physical education: A renewed quest?. *Contemporary Education, 57*(4), 197–201.

Descartes, R. (1641/1986). *Meditations on First Philosophy: With Selections from the Objections and Replies* (J. Cottingham, Trans.; B. Williams, Intro.). Cambridge, UK: Cambridge University Press. (Original work published 1641).

Dewey, J. (1938/1963). *Experience and Education.* New York: Collier Books. (Original work published 1938).

Dewey, J. (1916/1966). *Democracy and Education.* New York: The Free Press. (Original work published 1916).

Donald, M. (1991). *Origins of the Modern Mind.* Cambridge, MA: Harvard University.

Dreyfus, H. (1991). *Being-in-the-world: A commentary on Heidegger's Being and Time.* Cambridge, MA: Massachusetts Institute of Technology (MIT) Press.

Dreyfus, H. (1993). *What Computers Still Can't Do: A Critique of Artificial Reason,* Cambridge, MA: MIT Press.

Dreyfus, H. (1996). The current relevance of Merleau-Ponty's phenomenology of embodiment. *Electronic Journal of Analytic Philosophy, 4.* Retrieved from http://ejap.louisiana.edu/EJAP/1996.spring/dreyfus.1996.spring.html.

Dreyfus, H. (2002a). Intelligence without representation: Merleau-Ponty's critique of mental representation. *Phenomenology and the Cognitive Sciences, 1*(4), 367–383.

Dreyfus, H. (2002b). Refocusing the question: Can there be skilful coping without propositional representations or brain representations?. *Phenomenology and the Cognitive Sciences, 1*(4), 413–425.

Dreyfus, H. (2005). Overcoming the myth of the mental. Paper presented at the American Philosophical Association, Pacific Division Presidential Address, Berkley, California. Retrieved from http://socrates.berkeley.edu/~hdreyfus/pdf/Dreyfus%20APA%20Address%20%2010.22.05%20.pdf.

Dreyfus, H. and Dreyfus, S. (1986). *Mind over Machine: The Power of Human Intuition and Expertise in the Era of the Computer.* Oxford, UK: Basil Blackwell.

Dyson, B. and Casey, A. (Eds) (2012). *Cooperative Learning in Physical Education: International Perspectives.* London: Routledge.

Egan, K. (1997). *The Educated Mind: How Cognitive Tools Shape Our Understanding.* New York: Teachers College Press.

Ennis, C. D. (1999). Creating a culturally relevant curriculum for disengaged girls. *Sport, Education and Society, 4*(1), 31–49.

Evans, J. (1990). Defining a subject: the rise and rise of the new physical education. *British Journal of Sociology of Education, 11,* 155–169.

Evans, J. (2003). Physical education or health: A polemic or "let them eat cake!". *European Physical Education Review, 9*(1), 87–101.

Fairs, J. (1968). The influence of Plato and Platonism on the development of physical education in Western culture. *Quest, 11*(1), 14–23.

Feezell, R. (2007). Sport and the view from nowhere. In W. J. Morgan (Ed.), *Ethics in Sport* (2nd edn) (pp. 67–84). Champaign, IL: Human Kinetics.

Fernandez-Balboa, J. (1993). Sociocultural characteristics of the hidden curriculum in physical education. *Quest, 45*(2), 230–254.

Figley, G. (1984). Moral education through physical education. *Quest, 36*(1), 89–101.

Fink, E. (1960). The ontology of play. *Philosophy Today, 4*(2), 95–109.

Fink, E. (1979). The ontology of play. In E. W. Gerber and W. J. Morgan (Eds), *Sport and the Body: A Philosophical Symposium* (2nd edn) (pp. 73–83). Philadelphia, PA: Lea & Febiger.

Flintoff, A. (2008). Targeting Mr Average: Participation, gender equity and school sport partnerships. *Sport, Education and Society, 13*(4), 393–411.

Flintoff, A. and Scraton, S. (2001). Stepping into active leisure? Young women's perceptions of active lifestyles and their experiences of school physical education. *Sport, Education and Society, 6*(1), 5–22.

Flintoff, A. and Scraton, S. (2010). Chapter 10: Gender and physical education. In K. Green and K. Hardman (Eds), *Physical Education: Essential Issues* (pp. 161–179). London: SAGE.

Franklin, R. L. (1981). Knowledge, belief and understanding. *The Philosophical Quarterly, 31*(124), 193–208.

Freeman, W. (2012). *Physical Education, Exercise and Sport Science in a Changing Society* (7th edn). Massachusetts, MA: Jones & Bartlett Learning.

Gard, M. and Kirk, D. (2007). Obesity discourse and the crisis of faith in disciplinary technology. *Utbildning och Demokrati, 16*, 17–36.

Gard, M. and Wright, J. (2005). *The Obesity Epidemic: Science, Morality and Ideology.* London: Routledge.

Gerber, E. W. and Morgan, W. J. (Eds) (1979). *Sport and the Body: A Philosophical Symposium* (2nd edn). Philadelphia, PA: Lea & Febiger.

Green, K. (1998). Philosophies, ideologies and the practice of physical education. *Sport, Education and Society, 3*(2), 125–143.

Green, K. (2001). Examinations in physical education: A sociological perspective on a 'new orthodoxy'. *British Journal of Sociology of Education, 22*(1), 51–73.

Green, K. (2005). Examinations: A "new orthodoxy" in physical education. In K. Green and K. Hardman (Eds), *Physical Education: Essential Issues* (pp. 143–160). London: SAGE.

Griffin, L. and Butler, J. (Eds) (2005). *Teaching Games for Understanding: Theory, Research and Practice.* Champaign, IL: Human Kinetics.

Guivernau, M. and Duda, J. (2002). Moral atmosphere and athletic aggressive tendencies in young soccer players. *Journal of Moral Education, 31*(1), 67–85.

Hamlyn, D. W. (1967). The logical and psychological aspects of learning. In R. S. Peters (Ed.), *The Concept of Education* (pp. 24–43). London: Routledge & Kegan Paul.

Hamlyn, D. W. (1973). Human learning. In R. S. Peters (Ed.), *The Philosophy of Education* (pp. 178–194). Oxford: Oxford University Press.

Hardman, K. (2006). Promise or reality? Physical education in schools in Europe. *Compare: A Journal of Comparative and International Education, 36*(2), 163–179.

Hargreaves, J. (1986). *Sport, Power and Culture.* Cambridge, UK: Polity Press.

Harris, J. (2005). Health-related exercise and physical education. In K. Green and K. Hardman (Eds), *Physical Education: Essential Issues* (pp. 78–97). London: SAGE Publications Company.

Harris, J. (2009). Health-related exercise and physical education. In R. Bailey and D. Kirk (Eds), *The Routledge Physical Education Reader* (pp. 83–101). London and New York: Routledge.

Harris, J. and Cale, L. (1998). Activity promotion in physical education. In K. Green and K. Hardman (Eds), *Physical Education: A Reader* (pp. 116–131). Germany: Meyer & Meyer.

Hawkins, A. (2008). Pragmatism, purpose and play: Struggle for the soul of physical education. *Quest, 60*(3), 345–356.

Heidegger, M. (1927/201). *Being and Time.* (J. Stambaugh, Trans.; D. Schmidt, Foreword). Albany, NY: State University of New York.

Hellison, D. (2011). Teaching personal and social responsibility through physical activity (3rd edn). Champaign, IL: Human Kinetics.

Hirst, P. H. (1967). The logical and psychological aspects of teaching a subject. In R. S. Peters (Ed.), *The Concept of Education* (pp. 44–60). London: Routledge & Kegan Paul.

Hirst, P. H. (1971). What is teaching? *Journal of Curriculum Studies, 3*(1), 5–18.

Hirst, P. H. (1974). *Knowledge and the Curriculum.* London: Routledge & Kegan Paul.

Hirst, P. H. (1979) 'Human movement, knowledge and education', *Journal of Philosophy of Education, 13*(1), 101–108.

Hirst, P. H. (1993). Education, knowledge and practices. In R. Barrow and P. White (Eds), *Beyond Liberal Education: Essays in Honour of Paul H. Hirst* (pp. 184–199). London: Routledge.

Hirst, P. H. and Peters, R. S. (1970). *The Logic of Education.* London: Routledge & Kegan Paul.

Hobbes, T. (1651/1999). *Leviathan* (electronic edn). Hamilton, Ontario: McMaster University. (Original work published 1651).

Hoffman, S. (1971). Traditional methodology: Prospects for change. *Quest, 23*(1), 51–57.

Holst, J. (2013). Re-educating the body. *Educational Philosophy and Theory, 45*(9), 963–972.

Honderich, T. (Ed.) (2005). *The Oxford Companion to Philosophy* (2nd edn). Oxford, UK: Oxford University Press.

Hughson, J. and Inglis, D. (2002). Inside the beautiful game: Towards a Merleau-Pontian phenomenology of soccer play. *Journal of Philosophy of Sport, 29*(1), 1–15.

Huizinga, J. (1949). *Homo Ludens: A Study of the Play Elements in Culture.* London: Routledge & Kegan Paul.

Hurka, T. (2007). Games and the good. In W. J. Morgan (Ed.), *Ethics in Sport* (2nd edn) (pp. 21–34). Champaign, IL: Human Kinetics.

Hyland, D. A. (1977). "And that is the best of us": Human being and play. *Journal of the Philosophy of Sport, 4*(1), 36–49.

Hyland, D. A. (1980). The stance of play. *Journal of the Philosophy of Sport, VII*, 87–99.

Ingham, A. and Loy, J. (1973). The social system of sport: A humanistic perspective. *Quest, 19*(1), 3–23.

Jones, C. (2005). Character, virtue and physical education. *European Physical Education Review, 11*(2), 139–151.

Jones, C. (2008). Teaching virtue through physical education: Some comments and reflections. *Sport, Education and Society, 13*(3), 337–349.

Jones, C. and McNamee, M. (2000). Moral reasoning, moral action, and the moral atmosphere of sport. *Sport, Education and Society, 5*(2), 131–146.

Jones, C. and McNamee, M. (2003). Moral development and sport: Character and cognitive developmentalism contrasted. In J. Boxall (Ed.), *Sport Ethics: An Anthology* (pp. 40–52). Oxford, UK: Blackwell Publishing.

Kant, I. (1781/2007). *Critique of Pure Reason* (M. Weiglet, Trans. and Intro.). London: Penguin Books. (Original work published 1781).

Kavussanu, M., Roberts, G. and Ntoumanis, N. (2002). Contextual influences on moral functioning of college basketball players. *The Sport Psychologist, 16*, 347–367.

Keating, J. (2003). Sportsmanship as a moral category. In J. Boxall (Ed.), *Sports Ethics: An Anthology* (pp. 63–71). Oxford, UK: Blackwell Publishing.

Keen, S. (1969). *Apology for Wonder.* New York: Harper & Row.

Keen, S. (1970). *To a Dancing God.* New York: Harper & Row.

Kenny, A. (1993). *Aquinas on Mind.* London and New York: Routledge.

Kenny, J. (1966). Practical inference. *Analysis, 26*(3), 65–75.

Kentel, J. A. and Dobson, T. M. (2007). Beyond myopic visions of education: Revisiting movement literacy. *Physical Education and Sport Pedagogy, 12*(2), 145–162.

Kirk, D. (1983). A new term for a vacant peg: Conceptualising physical performance in sport. *Bulletin of Physical Education, 19*(3), 38–44.

Kirk, D. (1988). *Physical Education and Curriculum Study*. London: Croom Helm.

Kirk, D. (1990). Defining the subject: Gymnastics and gender in British physical education. In D. Kirk and R. Tinning (Eds), *Physical Education, Curriculum and Culture: Critical Issues in the Contemporary Crisis* (pp. 43–66). London: Falmer Press.

Kirk, D. (1992a). *Defining Physical Education: The Social Construction of a School Subject in Postwar Britain*. London: Falmer Press.

Kirk, D. (1992b). Physical education, discourse and ideology: Bringing the hidden curriculum into view. *Quest, 44*(1), 35–56.

Kirk, D. (1994a). Making the present strange: Sources of the current crisis in physical education. *Discourse: Studies in the Cultural Politics of Education, 15*(1), 46–63.

Kirk, D. (1994b). Physical education and regimes of the body. *The Australian and New Zealand Journal of Sociology, 30*(2), 165–177.

Kirk, D. (1995). "Thanks for the history lesson": Some thoughts on a pedagogical use of history in educational research and practice. *Australian Educational Research, 22*, 1–20.

Kirk, D. (1998a). Educational reform, physical culture and the crisis of legitimation in physical education. *Discourse: Studies in the Cultural Politics of Education, 19*(1), 101–112.

Kirk, D. (1998b). *Schooling Bodies: School Practice and Public Discourse 1880–1950*. London: Leicester University Press.

Kirk, D. (1999). Physical culture, physical education and relational analysis. *Sport, Education and Society, 4*(1), 63–75.

Kirk, D. (2002). Junior sport as a moral practice. *Journal of Teaching Physical Education, 21*(4), 402–408.

Kirk, D. (2004). Framing quality physical education: The elite sport model or sport education?. *Physical Education and Sport Pedagogy, 9*(2), 185–195.

Kirk, D. (2006a). The "obesity crisis" and school physical education. *Sport, Education and Society, 11*(2), 121–133.

Kirk, D. (2006b, June). The Idea of Physical Education and Its Discontents: An Inaugural Lecture. Paper presented at Leeds Metropolitan University, UK.

Kirk, D. (2009). The idea of the idea of physical education: Between essentialism and relativism in studying the social construction of physical education. *e Journal de la Recherche sur l'Intervention en Éducation Physique et Sport (eJRIEPS), 18*, 24–40.

Kirk, D. (2010). *Physical Education Futures*, London and New York: Routledge.

Kirk, D. (2013). Educational value and models-based practice in physical education. *Educational Philosophy and Theory, 45*(9), 973–986.

Kirk, D. and Colquhoun, D. (1989). Healthism and physical education. *British Journal of Sociology of Education, 10*(4), 417–435.

Kirk, D. and Gorely, T. (2000). Challenging thinking about the relationship between school physical education and sports performance. *European Physical Education Review, 6*(2), 119–133.

Kolnai, A. (1966). Games and aims. *Proceedings of the Aristotelian Society, 66*, 103–128.

Kreeft, P. and Tacelli, R. K. (1994). *Handbook of Christian Apologetics*. Downers Grove, IL: InterVaristy Press.

Kretchmar, R. S. (1972). Ontological possibilities: Sport as play. *Philosophic Exchange, 1*, 113–122.

Kretchmar, R. S. (1990). Values, passion and the expected lifespan of physical education. *Quest, 42*, 95–112.

Kretchmar, R. S. (1995). T. D. Wood: On chairs and education. *The Journal of Physical Education, Recreation and Dance, 66*, 12–15.

Kretchmar, R. S. (1996). Movement and play on higher education's contested terrain. *Quest. 48*(4), 433–441.

Kretchmar, R. S. (1998). Building strong academic programs: The problem of perform-ance. *Quest, 50*(2), 185–190.

Kretchmar, R. S. (2000a). Moving and being moved: Implications for practice. *Quest, 52*, 260–272.

Kretchmar, R. S. (2000b). Movement subcultures: Sites for meaning, *Journal of Physical Education, Recreation and Dance, 71*(5), 19–25.

Kretchmar, R. S. (2005a). *Practical Philosophy of Sport and Physical Education Activity* (2nd edn). Champaign, IL: Human Kinetics.

Kretchmar, R. S. (2005b). Game flaws. *Journal of the Philosophy of Sport, 32*(1), 36–48.

Kretchmar, R. S. (2007a). Dualisms, dichotomies and dead ends: Limitations of analytic thinking about sport. *Sport, Ethics and Philosophy, 1*(3), 266–280.

Kretchmar, R. S. (2007b). What to do with meaning? A research conundrum for the 21st Century. *Quest, 59*, 373–383.

Kretchmar, R. S. (2008a). The increasing utility of elementary school physical education: A mixed blessing and unique challenge. *The Elementary School Journal, 108*(3), 161–170.

Kretchmar, R. S. (2008b). The utility of silos and bunkers in the evolution of kinesiology. *Quest, 60*, 3–12.

Kuntz, P. (1974). Aesthetics applies to sports as well as to the arts. *Journal of Philosophy of Sport, 1*, 6–35.

Laker, A. (2000). *Beyond the Boundaries of Physical Education*. London: Falmer Press.

Lakoff, G. and Johnson, M. (1999). *Philosophy in the Flesh: The Embodied Mind and its Challenge to Western Thought*. New York: Basic Books.

Land, M. and McLeod, P. (2000). From eye movements to actions: How batsmen hit the ball. *Nature Neuroscience, 3*(12), 1340–1345.

Lee, M. (1996). Psycho-social development from 5 to 16 years. In N. Armstrong (Ed.), *New Directions in Physical Education* (pp. 337–347). London: Cassell.

Lee, M. and Cockman, M. (1995). Values in children's sport: Spontaneously expressed values among young athletes. *International Review for the Sociology of Sport, 30*(3), 337–352.

Lloyd, R. and Smith, S. (2005). A "vitality" approach to health-related, physical educa-tion programs. *Avante, 11*(2), 120–136.

Locke, J. (1689/2001). *An Essay Concerning Human Understanding* (electronic edn). Kitchener, Ontario: Batoche. (Original work published 1689, although dated 1690).

Locke, L. (1992). Changing secondary school physical education. *Quest, 44*, 361–372.

Loland, S. (1992). The mechanics and meaning of alpine skiing: Methodological and epistemological notes on the study of sport technique. *Journal of the Philosophy of Sport, 19*(1), 55–77.

Loland, S. (2006). Morality, medicine, and meaning: Toward an integrated justification of physical education. *Quest, 58*, 60–70.

Loland, S. and McNamee, M. (2000). Fair play and the ethos of sports: An eclectic philo-sophical framework. *Journal of the Philosophy of Sport, XXVII*, 63–80.

Longland, J. (1955). Physical recreation and character. *Physical Recreation, 7*, 7–10.

MacAllister, J. (2013). The 'physically educated' person: Physical education in the philosophy of Rcid, Peters and Aristotle. *Educational Philosophy and Theory, 45*(9), 908–920.

Macdonald, D. and Brooker, R. (1997). Moving beyond the crisis in secondary physical education: An Australian initiative. *Journal of Teaching Physical Education, 16*(2), 155–175.

Macdonald, D., Kirk, D. and Braiuka, S. (1999). The social construction of the physical activity field at the school/university interface. *European Physical Education Review, 5*(31), 31–52.

MacIntyre, A. (1973). The essential contestability of some social concepts. *Ethics, 84*(1), 1–9.

MacIntyre, A. (1977). Epistemological crises, dramatic narrative and the philosophy of science. *Monist, 60*(4), 453–472.

MacIntyre, A. (1987). The idea of an educated public. In G. Haydon (Ed.), *Education and the Values: The Richard Peters Lecturers* (pp. 15–36). London: University of London.

MacIntyre, A. (1988). *Whose Justice? Which Rationality?*. London: Duckworth.

MacIntyre, A. (1990). *Three Rival Versions of Moral Enquiry*. Notre Dame, IN: Notre Dame University Press.

MacIntyre, A. (2007). *After Virtue*. (3rd edn). Notre Dame, IN: University of Notre Dame Press. (Original work published 1981).

MacIntyre, A. and Dunne, J. (2002). Alasdair MacIntyre on education: In a dialogue with Joseph Dunne. *Journal of Philosophy of Education, 36*(1), 1–19.

Mangan, J. A. (1975). Athleticism: A case study of the evolution of an educational ideology. In B. Simon and I. Bradley (Eds), *The Victorian Public School: Studies in the Development of an Educational Institution* (pp. 147–167). London: Gill and Macmillan.

Mangan, J. A. (1983). Grammar schools and the games ethic in the Victorian and Edwardian eras. *Albion, 15*(4), 313–335.

Maraj, J.A. (1965). Physical education and character. *Education Review, 17*(2), 103–113.

Maritain, J. (1995). *The Degrees of Knowledge*. Notre Dame, IN: Notre Dame University Press.

Marshall, J. and Hardman, K. (2000). The state and status of physical education in schools in international context. *European Physical Education Review, 6*(3), 203–229.

Maslin, K. T. (2001). *An Introduction to the Philosophy of Mind*. Cambridge: Polity Press.

Mathews, E. (2002). *The Philosophy of Merleau-Ponty*. Chesham, UK: Acumen.

Matthews, E. (2006). *Merleau-Ponty*. London: Continuum.

Mason, A. (1994). MacIntyre on Liberalism and its critics: Tradition, incommensurability and disagreement. In J. Horton and S. Mendus (Eds), *After MacIntyre* (pp. 225–244). Cambridge, UK: Polity Press.

McFee, G. (2004a). Normativity, justification, and (MacIntyrean) practices: Some thoughts on methodology for the philosophy of sport. *Journal of the Philosophy of Sport, 31*(1), 15–33.

McFee, G. (2004b). *Sport, Rules and Values: Philosophical Investigations into the Nature of Sport*. London and New York: Routledge.

McIntosh, P. (1979). *Fair Play: Ethics in Sport and Education*. London: Heinemann.

McKay, J. Gore, J. and Kirk, D. (1990). Beyond the limits of technocratic physical education. *Quest, 42*, 52–76.

McNamee, M. (1988). Health-related fitness and physical education. *British Journal of Physical Education, 19*(2), 83–84.

McNamee, M. (1992). Physical education and the development of personhood. *Physical Education Review, 15*(1), 13–28.

McNamee, M. (1995a). Hubris, humility and humiliation: Vice and virtue in sporting communities. *Journal of the Philosophy of Sport, XXIX*, 38–53.

McNamee, M. (1995b). Sporting practices, institutions and virtues: A critique and restatement. *Journal of the Philosophy of Sport, XXII*, 61–82.

McNamee, M. (1998a). Contractualism and methodological individualism and communitarianism: Situating understanding of moral trust. *Sport, Education and Society, 3*(3), 161–179.

McNamee, M. (1998b). Philosophy and physical education: Analysis, epistemology and axiology. *European Physical Education Review, 4*(1), 75–91.

McNamee, M. (2005). The nature and values of physical education. In K. Green and K. Hardman (Eds), *Physical Education: Essential Issues* (pp. 1–20). London: SAGE.

McNamee, M. (2008). *Sports, Virtues and Vices*. London and New York: Routledge.

McNamee, M., Jones, C. and Duda, J. (2003). Psychology, ethics and sports: Back to an Aristotelian "museum of normalcy". *International Journal of Sport and Health Sciences, 1*(1), 61–75.

Meakin, D. (1981). Physical education: An agency of moral education?. *Journal of Philosophy of Education, 15*(2), 241–253.

Meakin, D. (1982). Moral values and physical education. *Physical Education Review, 5*(1), 62–82.

Meakin, D. (1983). On the justification of physical education. *Momentum, 8*(3), 10–19.

Meakin, D. (1986). The moral status of competition: An issue of concern for physical educators. *The Journal of Philosophy of Education, 20*(1), 59–67.

Meakin, D. (1990). How physical education can contribute to personal and social education. *Physical Education Review, 1*(1), 108–119.

Mechikoff, R. (2010). *History and Philosophy of Sport and Physical Education: From Ancient Civilizations to the Modern World* (5th edn). New York: McGraw-Hill.

Meier, K. V. (1975). Cartesian and phenomenological anthropology: The radical shift and its meaning for sport. *Journal of the Philosophy of Sport, 2*, 51–73.

Meier, K. V. (1976). The kinship of the rope and the loving struggle: A philosophic analysis of communication in mountain climbing. *Journal of the Philosophy of Sport, 3*, 52–64.

Meier, K. V. (1979). Embodiment, sport, and meaning. In E. W. Gerber and W. J. Morgan (Eds), *Sport and the Body: A Philosophical Symposium* (2nd edn) (pp. 192–197). Philadelphia, PA: Lea & Febiger.

Meier, K. V. (1980). An affair of flutes: An appreciation of play. *Journal of the Philosophy of Sport, VII*, 24–45.

Meier, K. V. (1988). Triad trickery: Playing with sport and games. *Journal of the Philosophy of Sport, 15*(1), 11–30.

Meier, K. V. (1989). Performance prestidigitation. *Journal of the Philosophy of Sport, XVI*, 13–33.

Meier, K. V. (1995). Tricky triad: Playing with sport and games. In W. J. Morgan and K. V. Meier (Eds), *Philosophic Inquiry in Sport* (2nd edn) (pp. 23–36). Champaign, IL: Human Kinetics.

Merleau-Ponty, M. (1942/1963). *Structure of Behavior*. (A. L. Fisher, Trans.; J. Wild, Foreword). Pittsburgh, PA: Duquesne University Press. (Original work published 1942).

Merleau-Ponty, M. (1945/1962). *Phenomenology of Perception.* (C. Smith, Trans.). London and New York: Routledge. (Original work published 1945).

Merleau-Ponty, M. (1947/1964). The primacy of perception and its philosophical consequences. In J. M. Edie (Ed.), *The Primacy of Perception and Other Essays* (J. M. Edie, Trans.) (pp. 12–42). Evanston, IL: Northwestern University Press. (Original work published 1947).

Merleau-Ponty, M. (1948/2004). *The World of Perception.* (O. Davis, Trans.; Stéphanie Menasé, Foreword; T. Baldwin, Intro.). London and New York: Routledge. (Original work published 1948).

Metheny, E. (1968). *Movement and Meaning.* New York: McGraw-Hill.

Metzler, M. (2011). *Instructional Models for Physical Education* (3rd edn). Scottsdale, AZ: Holocomb Hathaway.

Midgley, M. (1974). The game game. *Philosophy, 49*(189), 231–253.

Miller, D. (1971). Theology and play studies: An overview. *Journal of the American Academy of Religion, 39*(3), 349–354.

Miller, S. (1973). Ends, means, and galumphing: Some leitmotifs of play. *American Anthropologist, 75*(1), 87–98.

Miller, S., Bredemeier, B. and Shields, D. (1997). Sociomoral education through physical education with at-risk children. *Quest, 49*(1), 114–129.

Moe, V. (2005). A philosophical critique of classical cognitivism in sport: From information processing to bodily background knowledge. *Journal of the Philosophy of Sport, 32*(2), 155–183.

Morgan, W. J. (1976). An analysis of the Sartrean ethic of ambiguity as the moral ground for the conduct of sport. *Journal of the Philosophy of Sport, 3*, 82–96.

Morgan, W. J. (1987). The logical incompatibility thesis and rules: A reconsideration of formalism as an account of games. *Journal of the Philosophy of Sport, XIV*, 1–20.

Morgan, W. J. (1994). *Leftist Theories of Sport.* Chicago, IL: University of Illinois Press.

Morgan, W. J. (2006). *Why Sports Morally Matter.* New York: Routledge.

Morgan, W. J. (2007a). Caring, final ends and sports. *Sport, Ethics and Philosophy, 1*,(1), 7–21.

Morgan, W. J. (2007b). Ethics, ethical inquiry, and sport. In W. J. Morgan (Ed.), *Ethics in Sport* (2nd edn) (pp. xiii–xxxxvii). Champaign, IL: Human Kinetics.

Morgan, W. J. (2007c). Why the "view from nowhere" gets us nowhere in our moral considerations of sport. In W. J. Morgan (ed.), *Ethics in Sport* (2nd edn) (pp. 85–102). Champaign, IL: Human Kinetics.

Morgan W. J. and Meier, K. V. (Eds) (1995). *Philosophical Inquiry in Sport* (2nd edn). Champaign, IL: Human Kinetics.

Mountakis, C. (2001). Differences between physical education and top-level sport. *European Physical Education Review, 7*(1), 92–106.

Neale, R. (1969). *In Praise of Play.* New York: Harper & Row.

Noë, A. (2004). *Action in Perception.* Cambridge, MA: Massachusetts Institute of Technology (MIT) Press.

Novak, M. (1976). *The Joy of Sports: End Zones, Bases, Baskets, Balls, and the Consecration of the American Spirit.* New York: Basic Books.

Nozick, R. (1974). *Anarchy, State and Utopia.* New York: Basic Books.

Oakeshott, M. (1967). Learning and teaching. In R. S. Peters (Ed.), *The Concept of Education* (pp. 156–176). London: Routledge & Kegan Paul.

O'Loughlin, M. (1998). Paying attention to bodies in education: Theoretical resources and practical suggestions. *Educational Philosophy and Theory, 30*(3), 275–297.

O'Loughlin, M. (2006). *Embodiment and Education: Exploring Creatural Existence*. Netherlands: Springer.

O'Neill, J. (1974). The spectacle of the body. *The Journal of the Philosophy of Sport, 1*, 110–122.

Osterhoudt, R. (1973). The Kantian ethic as a principle of moral conduct in sport. *Quest, 19*(1), 118–123.

Osterhoudt, R. (1976). In praise of harmony: The Kantian imperative and Hegelian sittlichkeit as the principle and substance of moral conduct in sport. *Journal of the Philosophy of Sport, 3*(1), 65–81.

Ozolins, J. T. (2007). Avoiding bad company: The importance of moral habits and moral habitat in moral education. In D. Aspin and J. Chapman (Eds), *Values Education and Lifelong Learning: Principles, Policies and Programmes* (pp. 107–126). Heidelberg: Springer.

Ozolins, J. T. (2010a). Creating public values: Schools as moral habitats. *Educational Philosophy and Theory, 42*(4), 410–423.

Ozolins, J. T. (2010b). Popper's third world: Moral habits, moral habitat and their maintenance. *Educational Philosophy and Theory, 42*(7), 742–761.

Ozolins, J. T. and Stolz, S. A. (2013). The place of physical education and sport in education. *Educational Philosophy and Theory*, 45(9), 887–891.

Parry, J. (1987). Physical education under threat. *British Journal of Physical Education, 18*(6), 243–244.

Parry, J. (1998a). Reid on knowledge and justification in physical education. *European Physical Education Review, 4*(1), 70–74.

Parry, J. (1998b). Physical education, justification and the national curriculum. *Physical Education Review, 11*(2), 106–118.

Parry, J. (1998c). Physical education as Olympic education. *European Physical Education Review, 4*(2), 153–167.

Parry, J. (1998d). The justification of physical education. In K. Green and K. Hardman (Eds), *Physical Education: A Reader* (pp. 36–68). Germany: Meyer & Meyer.

Pasnau, R. (2002). *Thomas Aquinas on Human Nature*. Cambridge: Cambridge University Press.

Passmore, J. (1980). *The Philosophy of Teaching*. London: Duckworth.

Paul, J. (1996). Centuries of change: Movement's many faces. *Quest, 48*(4), 531–545.

Pawlenka, C. (2005). The idea of fairness: A general ethical concept or one particular to sports ethics. *Journal of the Philosophy of Sport, 32*(1), 49–64.

Penney, D. (Ed.) (2002). Gender and Physical Education: Contemporary issues and future directions. London and New York: Routledge.

Penney, D. and Chandler, T. (2000). Physical education: What future(s)?. *Sport, Education and Society, 5*(1), 71–89.

Penney, D. and Evans, J. (1999). *Politics, Policy and Practice in Physical Education*. London and New York: E. & F. N. Spon.

Peters, R. S. (1966). *Ethics and Education*. London: Allen & Unwin.

Peters, R. S. (1970). Education and the educated man. *Journal of Philosophy of Education, 4*(1), 5–20; reprinted in R. F. Dearden, P. H. Hirst and R. S. Peters (Eds.), *Education and the Development of Reason* (pp. 3–18). London: Routledge & Kegan Paul.

Peters, R. S. (1973). The justification of education. In R. S. Peters (Ed.), *The Philosophy of Education* (pp. 239–267). Oxford, UK: Oxford University Press.

Piaget, J. (1951). *Play, Dreams and Imitation in Childhood*. New York: Routledge & Kegan Paul.

Plato, (1961a). Phaedo. In E. Hamilton and H. Cairns (Eds), *Plato: The Collected Dialogues* (pp. 40–98). Princeton, NJ: Princeton University Press.

Plato, (1961b). The Republic. In E. Hamilton and H. Cairns (Eds), *Plato: The Collected Dialogues* (pp. 575–844). Princeton, NJ: Princeton University Press.

Plato, (1961c). Laws. In E. Hamilton and H. Cairns (Eds), *Plato: The Collected Dialogues* (pp. 1225–1513). Princeton, NJ: Princeton University Press.

Plato, (2007). *The Republic* (2nd edn). (D. Lee, Trans.; M. Lane, Intro.). London: Penguin.

Polanyi, M. (1958). *Personal Knowledge: Towards a Post-Critical Philosophy*. Chicago, IL: University of Chicago Press.

Polanyi, M. (1961). Knowing and being. *Mind, LXX*(280), 458–470.

Polanyi, M. (1962). Tacit knowing: Its bearing on some problems in philosophy. *Review of Modern Physics, 34*, 601–616.

Polanyi, M. (1966a). *The Tacit Dimension*. Chicago, IL: The University of Chicago Press.

Polanyi, M. (1966b). The logic of tacit inference. *Philosophy, 41*(155), 1–18.

Polanyi, M. (1967). Sense-giving and sense-reading. *Philosophy, 42*(162), 301–325.

Polanyi, M. and Prosch, H. (1975). *Meaning*. Chicago, IL: The University of Chicago Press.

Powell, J. (1968). On learning to be original, witty, flexible, resourceful etc. *Journal of Philosophy of Education, 2*(1), 5–65.

Pring, R. (2001). Education as a moral practice. *Journal of Moral Education, 30*(2), 101–112.

Putman, D. (1995). The primacy of virtue in children's moral development. *Journal of Moral Education, 24*(2), 175–183.

Quay, J. (2013). *Education, Experience and Existence: Engaging Dewey, Peirce and Heidegger*. London and New York: Routledge.

Queensland Studies Authority (2010). *Physical Education Senior Syllabus*. Brisbane, QLD: Queensland Studies Authority.

Rawls, R. (1971). *A Theory of Justice*. Cambridge, MA: Belknap Press of Harvard University Press.

Reid, A. (1996a). Knowledge, practice and theory in physical education. *European Physical Education Review, 2*(2), 94–104.

Reid, A. (1996b). The concept of physical education in current curriculum and assessment policy in Scotland. *European Physical Education Review, 2*(1), 7–18.

Reid, A. (1997). Value pluralism and physical education. *European Physical Education Review, 3*(1), 6–20.

Reid, A. (1998). Knowledge, practice and theory in physical education. In K. Green and K. Hardman (Eds), *Physical Education: A Reader* (pp. 17–35). Germany: Meyer & Meyer.

Reid, L. (1970). Sport, the aesthetic and art. *British Journal of Educational Studies, 18*(3), 245–258.

Riezler, K. (1941). Play and seriousness. *The Journal of Philosophy, 38*(19), 505–517.

Romance, T. (1988). Promoting character development in physical education. *Strategies, 1*(5), 16–17.

Romance, T., Weiss, M. and Bockoven, J. (1986). A program to promote moral development through elementary school physical education. *Journal of Teaching in Physical Education, 5*(2), 126–136.

Roberts, K. (1996a). Youth cultures and sport: The success of school and community sport provisions in Britain. *European Physical Education Review, 2*(2), 105–115.

Roberts, K. (1996b). Young people, schools, sport and government policies. *Sport, Education and Society, 1*(1), 47–57.

Roochnik, D. (1975). Play and sport. *Journal of the Philosophy of Sport, 2*, 36–44.

Rothblatt, S. (1997). *The Modern University and Its Discontents: The Fate of Newman's Legacies in Britain and America*. Cambridge, UK: Cambridge University Press.

Rousseau, J. (1762/2003). *Emile or Treatise on Education* (W. H. Payne, Trans.). New York: Prometheus Books. (Original work published 1762).

Russell, J. (1999). Are rules all an umpire has to work with?. *Journal of the Philosophy of Sport, 26*(1), 27–49.

Russell, J. (2004). Moral realism in sport. *Journal of the Philosophy of Sport, 31*(2), 142–160.

Russell, J. (2007). Broad internalism and the moral foundations of sport. In W. J. Morgan (Ed.), *Ethics in Sport* (2nd edn) (pp. 51–66). Champaign, IL: Human Kinetics.

Ryle, G. (1945). Knowing how and knowing that. *Proceedings of the Aristotelian Society, 46*, 1–16.

Ryle, G. (1949). *The Concept of Mind*. London: Penguin.

Ryle, G. (1975). Can virtue be taught?. In R. F. Dearden, P. H. Hirst and R. S. Peters (Eds), *Education and Reason: Part 3 of Education and the Development of Reason* (pp. 44–57). London: Routledge & Kegan Paul.

Saracho, O. (2012). *An Integrated Play-based Curriculum for Young Children.* London and New York: Routledge.

Scottish Qualifications Authority (2004). *Arrangements Document for Higher Still Physical Education: Higher Level*. Edinburgh: Scottish Qualifications Authority.

Schilling, C. (1993). *The Body in Social Theory*. London: Sage.

Schmitz, K. (1979). Sport and play: Suspension of the ordinary. In E. W. Gerber and W. J. Morgan (Eds), *Sport and the Body: A Philosophical Symposium* (2nd edn) (pp. 22–29). Philadelphia, PA: Lea & Febiger.

Schrag, C. (1962). The lived body as a phenomenological datum. *The Modern Schoolman: A Quarterly Journal of Philosophy, 39*, 203–219.

Schrag, C. (1988). The lived body as a phenomenological datum. In W. J. Morgan and K. V. Meier (Eds), *Philosophic Inquiry in Sport* (pp. 109–118). Champaign, IL: Human Kinetics.

Scraton, S. (1995). "Boys muscle in where angels fear to tread": Girls' sub-cultures and physical activity. In C. Critcher, P. Bramham and A. Tomlinson (Eds), *Sociology of Leisure: A Reader* (pp. 117–129). London: E. & F. N. Spon.

Shaffer, J. (1965). Recent work on the mind-body problem. *American Philosophical Quarterly, 2*(2), 81–104.

Shapiro, L. (2004). *The Mind Incarnate*. Cambridge, MA: Massachusetts Institute of Technology (MIT) Press.

Shapiro, L. (2007). The embodied cognition research programme. *Philosophy Compass, 2*(2), 338–346.

Shapiro, L. (2011). *Embodied Cognition*. London and New York: Routledge.

Sheets-Johnstone, M. (1999). *The Primacy of Movement*. Philadelphia, PA: John Benjamins.

Shields, D. and Bredemeier, B. (1995). *Character Development and Physical Activity*. Champaign, IL: Human Kinetics.

Siedentop, D. (1992). Thinking differently about secondary physical education. *Journal of Physical Education, Recreation and Dance, 63*(7), 69–77.

Siedentop, D. (Ed.) (1994). *Sport Education: Quality Physical Education through Positive Sport Experiences*, Champaign, IL: Human Kinetics.

Simon, R. (1991). *Fair Play: Sports, Values and Society*. Oxford, UK: Westview Press.

Simon, R. (2000). Internalism and internal values in sport. *Journal of the Philosophy of Sport, 27*(1), 1–16.

Smith, A. and Parr, M. (2007). Young people's views on the nature and purposes of physical education: A sociological analysis. *Sport, Education and Society, 12*(1), 37–58.

Smith, P. (1986). Play research and its application: A current perspective. In P. Smith (Ed.), *Children's Play: Research Developments and Practical Applications* (pp. 1–14). London: Gordon and Breach.

Smith, S. (2007). The first rush of movement: A phenomenological preface to movement education. *Phenomenology and Practice, 1*(1), 47–75.

Smith, S. and Lloyd, R. (2006). Promoting vitality in health and physical education. *Qualitative Health Research, 16*(2), 249–267.

Sparkes, A., Templin, T. and Schempp, P. (1993). Exploring dimensions of marginality: Reflecting on the life histories of physical education teachers. *Journal of Teaching in Physical Education, 12*(4), 386–398.

Stanley, J. and Williamson, T. (2001). Knowing how. *Journal of Philosophy, 98*(8), 411–444.

Stevenson, C. (1975). The meaning of movement. *Quest, 23*, 2–9.

Stolz, S. A. (2010). Health, physical education, sport: What's the main game?. *Teacher, January/February*, 24–26.

Stolz, S. A. (2013a). Phenomenology and physical education. *Educational Philosophy and Theory, 45*(9), 949–962.

Stolz, S. A. (2013b). The philosophy of G. Ryle and its significance for physical education: Some thoughts and reflections. *European Physical Education Review, 19*(3), 381–396.

Stolz, S. A. (in press). Embodied learning. *Educational Philosophy and Theory*.

Stolz, S. A. and Pill, S. (2013). TGfU-GS: an imagined dialogue between a teacher and an academic. In J. Quay and A. Mooney (Eds) *A Defining Time in Health and Physical Education: Proceedings of the 28th ACHPER International Conference* (pp. 148–157). Melbourne, 27–29 November 2013.

Stolz, S. A. and Pill, S. (2014). Teaching games and sport for understanding: Exploring and reconsidering its relevance in physical education. *European Physical Education Review, 20*(1), 36–71.

Stolz, S. A., and Pill, S. (in press). A narrative approach to exploring TGfU-GS. *Sport, Education and Society*.

Stone, R. (1975). Human movement forms as meaning-structures: Prolegomenon. *Quest, 23*(1), 10–17.

Stroot, S. (1994). Contemporary crisis or emerging reform? A review of secondary physical education. *Journal of Teaching in Physical Education, 13*(4), 333–341.

Stroot, S., Collier, C., O'Sullivan, M. and England, K. (1994). Contextual hoops and hurdles: Workplace conditions in secondary physical education. *Journal of Teaching in Physical Education, 13*(4), 342–360.

Suits, B. (1967). What is a game?. *Philosophy of Science, 34*(2), 148–156.

Suits, B. (1977). Words on play. *Journal of the Philosophy of Sport, 4*, 117–131.

Suits, B. (1978). *The Grasshopper: Games, Life and Utopia*. Toronto: University of Toronto Press.

Suits, B. (1988). Tricky triad: Games, play, and sport. *Journal of the Philosophy of Sport, 15*(1), 1–9.

Suits, B. (2007). The elements of sport. In W. J. Morgan (Ed.), *Ethics in Sport*, (2nd edn) (pp. 9–20). Champaign, IL: Human Kinetics.

Sutton, J. (2007). Batting, habit and memory: The embodied mind and the nature of skill. *Sport in Society, 10*(5), 763–786.

Sutton-Smith, B. (1997). *The Ambiguity of Play.* Cambridge, MA: Harvard University Press.

Theodoulides, A. (2003). "I would never personally tell anyone to break the rules, but you can bend them": Teaching moral values through team games. *Physical Education and Sport Pedagogy, 8*(2), 141–159.

Theodoulides, A. and Armour, K. (2001). Personal, social and moral development through team games: Some critical questions. *European Physical Education Review, 7*(1), 5–23.

Thomas, D. (1979). A definitional context for some socio-moral characteristics of sport. *Journal of the Philosophy of Sport, 6*(1), 39–47.

Thompson, K. (1983). The justification of physical education. *Momentum, 8*(2), 19–23.

Thorburn, M. (1999). "Is it real physical education today?": Knowledge and understanding in standard grade, higher and higher still physical education. *Scottish Journal of Physical Education, 27*(1), 19–29.

Thorburn, M. (2008). Articulating a Merleau-Pontian phenomenology of physical education: The quest for active student engagement and authentic assessment in high-stakes examination awards. *European Physical Education Review, 14*(2), 263–280.

Thorpe, S. (2003). Crisis discourse in physical education and the laugh of Michel Foucault. *Sport, Education and Society, 8*(2), 131–151.

Tinning, R. (2010). *Pedagogy and Human Movement: Theory, Practice, Research.* London and New York: Routledge.

Tinning, R. and Fitzclarence, L. (1992). Postmodern youth culture and the crisis in Australian secondary school physical education. *Quest, 44*(3), 287–303.

Tinning, R. and Glasby, T. (2002). Pedagogical work and the "cult of the body": Considering the role of HPE in the context of the "new public health". *Sport, Education and Society, 7*(2), 109–119.

Tinning, R., Kirk, D., Evans, J. and Glover, S. (1994). School physical education: A crisis of meaning. *Changing Education, 1*(2), 13–15.

Van Dalen, D. and Bennett, B. (1971). *A World History of Physical Education: Cultural, Philosophical, Comparative* (2nd edn). New Jersey, NJ: Prentice Hall.

van Manen, M. (1977). Linking ways of knowing with ways of being practical. *Curriculum Inquiry, 6*(3), 205–228.

van Manen, M. (1997). *Researching Lived Experience: Human Science for an Action Sensitive Pedagogy* (2nd edn). London, Ontario: Althouse Press.

Varela, F., Thompson, E. and Rosch, E. (1993). *The Embodied Mind: Cognitive Science and Human Experience.* Cambridge, MA: The Massachusetts Institute of Technology (MIT) Press.

Victorian Curriculum and Assessment Authority (2010). *Victorian Certificate of Education Study Design: Physical Education.* Retrieved from www.vcaa.vic.edu.au/vce/studies/physicaledu/phyeduindex.html#H2N10069.

Wachter, F. D. (1985). The symbolism of the healthy body: A philosophical analysis of the sportive imagery of health. *Journal of the Philosophy of Sport, XI*, 56–62.

Wandzilak, T. (1985). Values development through physical education and athletics. *Quest, 37*(2), 176–185.

Wandzilak, T., Carroll, T. and Ansorge, C. (1988). Values development through physical activity: Promoting sportsmanlike behaviours, perceptions, and moral reasoning, *Journal of Teaching in Physical Education, 8*(1), 13–22.

Webb, L., Quennerstedt, M. and Öhman, M. (2008). Healthy bodies: Construction of the body and health in physical education. *Sport, Education and Society, 13*(4), 353–372.

Weiss, P. (1979). The challenge of the body. In E. W. Gerber and W. J. Morgan (Eds), *Sport and the Body: A Philosophical Symposium* (2nd edn) (pp. 189–191). Philadelphia, PA: Lea & Febiger.

White, A. (1982). *The Nature of Knowledge*. Totowa, NJ: Rowan & Littlefield.

Whitehead, M. (1990). Meaningful existence, embodiment and physical education. *Journal of Philosophy of Education, 24*(1), 3–13.

Whitehead, M. (2001). The concept of physical literacy. *European Journal of Physical Education, 6*(2), 127–138.

Whitehead, M. (2008). Physical literacy: Philosophical considerations in relation to developing a sense of self, universality and propositional knowledge. *Sport, Ethics and Philosophy, 1*(3), 281–298.

Whitehead, M. (2010). *Physical Literacy: Throughout the Lifecourse*. London: Routledge.

Williams, J. (1930). Education through the physical. *The Journal of Higher Education, 1*(5), 279–282.

Williams, J. (1951). The physical as experience. *The Journal of Higher Education, 22*(9), 464–469.

Williams, K. (1999). Assessment and the challenge of scepticism. In D. Carr (Ed.), *Education, Knowledge and Truth: Beyond the Postmodern Impasse* (pp. 221–237). London and New York: Routledge.

Wilson, M. (2002). Six views of embodied cognition. *Psychonomic Bulleting and Review, 9*(4), 625–636.

Wilson, P. (1967). In defence of bingo. *British Journal of Educational Studies, 15*(1), 5–27.

Winch, C. (2009). Ryle on knowing how and the possibility of vocational education. *Journal of Applied Philosophy, 26*(1), 88–101.

Winch, C. (2010). Vocational education, knowing how and intelligence concepts. *Journal of Philosophy of Education, 44*(4), 551–566.

Wittgenstein, L. (1953/2009). *Philosophical investigations* (G. E. M. Anscombe, P. M. S. Hacker and J. Schulte, Trans.). (Rev. 4th edn). Chichester, UK: Wiley-Blackwell. (Original work published 1953).

Wright, L. (1987). Physical education and moral development. *Journal of Philosophy of Education, 21*(1), 93–102.

Wright, L. (2000). Practical knowledge, performance and physical education. *Quest, 2*(3), 273–283.

Zaner, R. M. (1979). Sport and the moral order. *Journal of the Philosophy of Sport, 6*, 7–18.

Index

Page numbers in **bold** denote figures.